ROUTLEDGE LIBR
HUMAN RESOURCL

M000116717

Volume 24

RECENT DEVELOPMENTS IN JOB ANALYSIS

RECENT DEVELOPMENTS IN JOB ANALYSIS

Edited by
KURT LANDAU AND WALTER ROHMERT

Routledge
Taylor & Francis Group

LONDON AND NEW YORK

First published in 1989 by Taylor & Francis

This edition first published in 2017
by Routledge
2 Park Square, Milton Park, Abingdon, Oxon OX14 4RN

and by Routledge
711 Third Avenue, New York, NY 10017

Routledge is an imprint of the Taylor & Francis Group, an informa business

British Library Cataloguing in Publication Data
A catalogue record for this book is available from the British Library

ISBN: 978-1-138-80870-6 (Set)
ISBN: 978-1-315-18006-9 (Set) (ebk)
ISBN: 978-0-415-78974-5 (Volume 24) (hbk)
ISBN: 978-0-415-78976-9 (Volume 24) (pbk)
ISBN: 978-1-315-21371-2 (Volume 24) (ebk)

Publisher's Note
The publisher has gone to great lengths to ensure the quality of this reprint but points out that some imperfections in the original copies may be apparent.

Disclaimer
The publisher has made every effort to trace copyright holders and would welcome correspondence from those they have been unable to trace.

Recent Developments in Job Analysis

Edited by

Kurt Landau

and **Walter Rohmert**

*Proceedings of the International Symposium on Job Analysis,
University of Hohenheim, March 14-15 1989*

Taylor & Francis
London • New York • Philadelphia
1989

UK	· Taylor & Francis Ltd, 4 John St., London WC1N 2ET
USA	Taylor & Francis Inc., 242 Cherry St., Philadelphia, PA 19106–1906

British Library Cataloguing in Publication Data

Proceedings of the international symposium on
job analysis
1. Job analysis
I. Landau, Kurt II. Rohmert, Walter
658.3'06

ISBN 0-85066-790-9

Library of Congress Cataloguing in Publication Data

is available

Cover design by Russell Beach
Printed in Great Britain by Taylor & Francis Ltd
Basingstoke, Hampshire

CONTENTS

Session VII: Examples for Analysis in Job Design

INTRODUCTION TO THE PROBLEMS OF JOB ANALYSIS – ON THE DEVELOPMENT STATUS OF THE PROCEDURE AND ITS THEORETICAL FOUNDATION*

Kurt Landau
University of Hohenheim
and
Walter Rohmert
Technical University of Darmstadt

Federal Republic of Germany

INTRODUCTION

Human work in the working system

This article discusses human work in the working system. The operational definition of human work includes any activity that an individual undertakes to secure and develop his or her own existence and/or the existence of the society, as far as this activity is accepted and rewarded by the society. This explanation of the work concept outside its social context allows us to distinguish work from play and sports and makes clear that work is more than a purposeful behaviour aimed at the satisfaction of personal needs.

While we reckon play and sports (except for professional sports) among unpurposeful activities, work and learning are purposeful activities. All elements of the active being are interdependent and interrelated.

The defined content of work is - owing to the various technological changes that are taking place with ever increasing speed - subject to continuous variation. While the high physical content of work was highlighted at the beginning of this century, the same applies today to the

---

* This article is a modified translation of the first part of "Aufgabenbezogene Analyse von Arbeitstätig-keiten", published in: Kleinbeck, U; Rutenfranz, J.: Arbeitspsychologie, Göttingen: Verlag für Psychologie Dr. C.J.Hogrefe, 1987

higher mental-emotional components that are implied in the
monitoring or controlling of largely automated production
and management processes. For this reason, an analysis of
work that only relies on the physical elements seems unrealistic and lacks any Human Factors legitimation.

The examination of daily work activities with regard to
their specific work content leads to a number of basic
types. These basic types differ significantly by their
different strain on organs and their use of special abilities. Such differences have led to the formulation of
special terms that are used in the fields of ergonomics
and Human Factors (see Figure 1).

Type of work	Specific work content	Mainly strain of organs and capabilities	Ergonomics term	Examples
mainly physical	producing forces	muscles (in case heart and circulation)	muscular work	handling loads
	coordination of motory and sensory functions	muscles and sense-organs	sensori-motor work	assembling, crane operating
mainly non-physical	converting information into reaction	sense-organs and muscles	mainly non-muscular work	controlling
	transformation from input- to output-information	sense-organs and mental abilities	mainly non-muscular work	programming, air traffic controlling, translating
	producing information	mental abilities	mental work (in the narrow sense of the word)	dictation, designing, problem solving

Figure 1:   Basic types of work tasks (Rohmert, 1972)

Human work is performed in the working system. This
term includes the interaction of individuals and equipment
in the work process at the workplace and in a specific
organisational, chemo-physical and social work environment. The term 'working system' is a synonym of 'man-at-
work system' and is also a generalisation of the term
'man-machine system (MMS)' that is commonly used in industrial psychology.

The working system concept is reflected in national and international standardisation efforts (e.g. German DIN 33 400) and is now commonly used in scientific research and work study.

Working systems are dynamic, socio-technical, open systems. They interrelate with their environment in a material, energetic, and informatory sense. Working systems are generally complex or hyper-complex systems that can be further subdivided on several hierarchical levels but are also parts of higher-level systems. They are both homeostatic, i.e. self-controlled, and externally controlled.

Primarily in the field of work study, the working systems which are present on different hierarchical levels and which are potentially interconnected are designated as micro or macro systems, depending on their extent and complexity. Figure 2 shows the fundamental working system as the basic model of human work, including the two elements 'man' and 'task'.

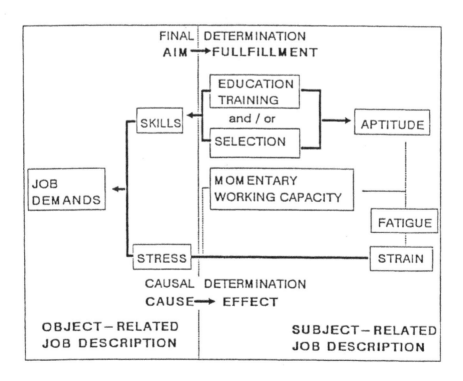

Fig. 2: Working system as the basic model of human work

The model of the working system sees the individual as a system element from a view of work technology. This can be done to such an extent that the system element 'man' is seen and examined as a hyper-complex bio-social structure; however, it becomes immediately obvious that this is a one-sided technical view that is not suitable to cover all aspects of the human nature. This puts a limit to the advantages of the working system view, the most important of which is the possibility to use appropriate mathematical methods to generate system analyses that allow the simulation of work processes (Laurig, 1971).

Objective and applications of task-related job analysis procedures

There are different ways to analyse the structure of the working system and the interaction of its elements. Thus, one cannot speak of the work or job analysis, or of the activity-oriented or the task-related work analysis. How work analyses of working systems are designed and performed depends largely on the underlying theoretical foundation and the related object of the work analysis - i.e. the working system, the job, the individual, etc..

The following criteria, most of which have been developed by Frieling and Graf Hoyos, can be used to evaluate work analysis procedures (Frieling, 1975; Graf Hoyos, 1974):

The procedure should

- be based on a theoretical model that allows a practical interpretation of the results obtained with the work analysis procedure

- offer a complete coverage of all demands that are present on a specific working system

- offer maximum cost-effectiveness with regard to application, data processing, and data evaluation; the application of the procedure should allow standardisation.

- go beyond a merely verbal work description and allow quantitative statements at least at the ordinal scale level.

When applying the procedures, statements should be possible as to

- the reliability with which several raters analyse a working system at the same time (inter-rater reliability), and

- the reliability with which all items of the work analysis procedure can be rated (item reliability).

In addition to these criteria, it is required that the procedure be applicable to all possible physical and non-physical types of work, including work contents that range from the generation of forces to the generation of information (cf. Rohmert, 1972).

Recent task-related work analysis procedures meet above all the last of the above requirements which refers to the applicability of the procedure also to primarily non-physical work. Extensive applications for service and management jobs are now available which go far beyond the executive production jobs with highly partialised activities that have primarily been analysed in the past.

No further taxonomy of work analysis will be made at this point; instead, the interested reader is referred to work by Frieling (1975), Graf Hoyos (1974), von Pupka (1977), Rohmert et al. (1975), and Frei (1981). It is common to many taxonomies that they are particularly eager to meet the test statistical requirements of work analysis procedures, above all their theoretical foundation (Fleishman, 1975; Theologus et al. 1970; Frieling, 1977; Hackman, 1970; McCormick, 1976; Morsh, 1964; Prien and Ronan, 1971; Zerga, 1943).

Obtaining an overview of the different taxonomic strategies in work analysis is made easier when starting the discussion with the fields of application and the objectives of such procedures. Possible applications of work analysis lie in the fields of demand analysis and work design. The evaluation of the work analysis data allows conclusions about the demands that a specific job imposes on the working person. From the work analysis data, the design status of working systems can be analysed, classified, and compared to each other; the analysis also provides information on situations of extreme stress and their possible elimination through corrective design measures. Often work analysis procedures can be used as a forecasting tool, referring to non-existent working systems that are still in the planning phase.

In personnel management, a work analysis that aims at a
demand analysis is a valuable tool when it is combined
with the assessment of required psychical and physical
qualifications (aptitude).

Other possible applications such as job and professional classification, investigations into the cause of
accidents or the deduction of education and training
objectives show the accent on the universal nature of work
analysis procedures.

Fig. 3 summarises some major fields of application and
objectives of work analysis procedures.

Broadband procedures, however, often have the drawback
that results are achieved on a high supercharacter level
so that the relation to practical application is not
always immediately clear. For this reason the enumeration
of applications cannot be left undisputed; also, a broadband approach is not always an advantageous form of work
analysis. With every work analysis procedure that is uni-
versally designed and applicable, information relating to
individuals, organisations, industries, work design, etc.
is lost. Choosing a strain-related interpretation of work
analysis results relies on the fiction that all individuals act in a similar manner within working situations that
are classified as similar (Frei, 1981) - independent of
whether the indidividual faces this work situation for the
first time or handles it in a routine manner. Work analysis procedures that are designed for a universal band-
width, however, are not strictly 'objective', since the
work performance of the individual within the working
system enters the analysis in any case - this is particularly true when the technique of the observation interview
is used to assess the work analysis data.

A desired work analysis procedure with universal band-
width, however, is very important when dealing with problems that apply to more than one company: specific procedures that depend on the situation and the individual fail
in the comparison of working system features beyond the
initial purpose of application. Specific analysis procedures generally do not allow for the implementation of a
job analysis data base which is a prerequisite for a long-
term ergonomic approach that is able to detect ecological
and economic risks.

Field of application	Actual application and possible result
Ergonomic and technical design of working systems	
Documentation and diagnosis of working systems	Description and possibly quantification of system elements and their characteristics, e.g. as to the stresses exerted by them; deduction of design needs; formation and verification of design priorities; prevention of possible impairments by detection of insupportable stresses/strains; purposeful reduction of stress
Product design	Description and possibly quantification of product characteristics as to their human-related impact during their late utilisation by the consumer or investor
Management organisation	
Preparation of reorganisation measures	Analysis of demand profiles of different jobs before and after corporate reorganisation measures or before and after technical/technological changes; forecasting of shifts in demands through technical change
Work process design over working hours	Task and demand sequences

Field of application	Actual application and possible result
Design of shifts and free time	Determination of free times based on stress rankings for working systems; work distribution for specific shifts according to types and extent of demands; prevention of absences through stress-related cause analysis
Personnel administration	
Personnel recruitment	Preparation of personnel ads on the basis of existing job analyses
Selection and positioning	Selection of job applicants according to the degree of congruency bet ween demand and aptitude profiles; determination of aptitude/ fitness criteria
Instruction/training/retraining	Deduction of training needs/training measures according to the task/ demand profile of working systems
Integration of disabled persons and other groups of persons into the organisation	Search for suitable working systems with specific task/demand profiles to ensure tolerability of the work
Qualitatitive personnel planning or personnel appointment planning	Comparison of aptitude and demand features (long-term and short-term view)

Field of application	Actual application and possible result
Personnel representation	Job analyses as discussion basis in talks or disputes between employers and employed
Wage fixing	Review of classifications by comparison of the demand structure of critical working systems with corporate bridge or basic working systems
Diagnosis of payment policy	Comparison of corporate demands and industry-typical demands with regard to the adequacy of a payment policy
Vocational guidance and research	
Job classification	Deduction of a demand- or task-related job classification and comparison with conventional job classifications; health status in different occupational groups; analysis of jobs or occupations as to required psychical and physical aptitude; analysis of seriousness and frequency of accidents according to job/occupational groups; job classification according to socio-demographic factors
Vocational guidance and information	Description of job spectra when providing guidance for school leavers

Figure 3: Selected fields of application of work analysis procedures

JOB ANALYSIS AS TASK ANALYSIS

Job analysis from the engineering point of view

In an attempt to define the second part of the term
'job analysis', 'analysis' in a narrower sense can be
understood as a 'splitting up into elements'. The point is
to subdivide a complex entity - the job - into individual
elements.

This subdivision is possible in the time dimension:
work processes - the interaction in space and time of
indi- viduals and equipment with the work object (REFA,
1978) - are subdivided into partial processes, process
steps, and actions (the 'macro process sections'), into
partial actions, action steps, and action elements (the
'micro process sections').

This classification only allows an estimation of the
time length of process sections and is too inaccurate and
also of little practical use for the purpose of task-
related job analysis.

A second classification is the type encoding of the
process sections. It is made by allocating of process
types. Process types are designations for the interaction
of individuals and equipment with the input (of the working system) within specific process sections.

Possible principles of process type classification:

Preparation of the working system and execution of the work order	Setup/Execution
Possibility for the working person to influence the duration of process sections	Full influence/limited influence/no influence
Type of utilisation of working person and equipment visible	In action/not in action/ work interruption/not
Type of work order execution of execution/no execut-	Execution/interruption ion/work interruption/ not visible

Although such process type classifications are univer-
sally applicable to all forms of work and thus allow a
complete encoding of the process with respect to

- individual work orders
- individual shifts
- individual periods (week, month, quarter, year),

they are primarily oriented at the proceeding of the work,
which limits their usefulness for a human-related job analysis.

Contrary to this time-variant view, the procedure of
task analysis from an engineering point of view also
allows a structural analytical approach. Kirchner and
Rohmert (1973) e.g. subdivide the job into tasks and
functions. In this context, function is used in a purely
technical sense and means the achievement of the purpose
of the working system.

The performance-related job inventories that have been
proven and implemented mainly in the military area fall
into this class of structural analytical task analysis
that is performed under a primarily engineering point of
view.

Research on such job inventories is described e.g. by
Morsh et al. (1961), Morsh (1967), Morsh (1966). Job
inventories are usually designed for a specific workplace
collective (company, plant, department, etc.) and are
subsequently assessed also for a larger collective using
the "auditorium method".

Since the assessment catalogues are formulated exclusively for the job conditions in the examined area, the
expected results are certainly valuable for this area but
cannot (or only to a limited degree) be transferred to
other collectives. Stress comparison and also forecasting
studies, e.g. for the estimation of the consequences of
technological change, are not possible with this procedure.

The work task from the view of organisation theory

While the engineering task analysis discussed above is
oriented at technical performance or technical work functions, the organisation theoretical analysis assumes the
overall task of the enterprise. In this case, it is the
market-oriented production task that, together with 'auxiliary' tasks from the procurement, production, inventory,

and finance areas, that is subdivided into partial tasks according to organisational/formal aspects.

With this approach, the task can be characterised by the following 5 conceptual items or defining elements (Kosiol, 1973, p. 202):

a) Every task comprises a specific performance. This work process is performed either as a (mainly) mental activity or (mostly) as a combination of mental and physical activities.

b) Every task comprises an object on which the required activity is to be performed; the object is either of personal or mental nature.

c) Every task regularly requires the use of physical means (material or work equipment); these serve the implementation of the work process.

d) Every task has its position in space and

e) in time, i.e. it is determined by these two basic conditions of existence.

A task analysis based on organisation theory first yields the task structure – i.e. a taxonomy of partial tasks and subtasks (these are partial tasks that cannot be further subdivided). Next, a task synthesis generates task bundles from the extracted partial or subtasks and allocates these to specific persons/institutions.

The work task from the view of ergonomics and Human Factors

As opposed to the task concepts that have been discussed so far and that see the individual as a system element or production factor, industrial psychology and ergonomics are exclusively interested in the interaction between the individual and the work.

There are four possible approaches to the definition of the task within this interaction (Hackman, 1970; Wheaton, 1968; Graf Hoyos, 1974; Frieling, 1975; Graf Hoyos and Frieling, 1977, etc.):

1. Task as a description of behaviour (Fine, 1967; Rabideau, 1964)
   This purely descriptive task concept is aimed at the description of the obvious and recordable work behaviour of persons by the use of a number of job items. Physio-psychological processes within the individual as well as capacities used are not assessed.

2. Task as aptitude requirement (e.g. Theologus et al., 1970; Fleishman et al, 1970a, b; Fleishman, 1975)
   Tasks are directly described and rated by their characteristic aptitude items - i.e. characteristics, abilities, skills, and knowledge. The aptitude items are allocated to tasks through expert ratings; in this process, factor-analytical approaches for summarising the aptitude items are particularly important. The behaviour of working persons while performing their job - also in a process-dynamical sense - cannot be assessed with this procedure.

3. Task as a behaviour requirement (Miller, 1971)
   This approach describes tasks primarily by the individual information processing functions. A glossary of 24 information processing functions takes account of the fact that work contents of an informative-mental nature are continuing to replace the energetic-effective work contents. The 24 functions are derived from the 6 determinants of the task, 'sequence', 'activity', 'information processing', 'control', 'execution status' and 'tools'. Relationships between the task glossary and the work behaviour of the individual, however, cannot be estalished.

4. Task as a stimulus complex (Hackman, 1969, 1970)
   The task is seen separate from the working person, considering only the stimulus complex associated with it and the required information on the objective and the execution of the task. A task can be assigned to a person or group either by an external person or by himself/itself. Thus, a task consists of a stimulus complex and a number of instructions that specifiy how to respond to the stimuli. The instructions specify which operations have to be carried out by the acting person(s) with regard to the stimuli and/or which objectives are to be met (Hackman, 1970, p. 210 in the translation by Graf Hoyos, 1974).

Elements from these four task definitions are often extracted and combined to form a specific view of the work task. For example, in a scientific explanation of the work task, it is possible to link technological/technical (Handbuch der Tätigkeitsanalyse, 1967), functional (Kirchner and Rohmert, 1973) as well as information theoretical (Miller, 1971) approaches. In this case, the work task is characterised as a scientifically explainable phenomenon by the work process, the work object, the equipment at work and resources — these being the elements of the working system — with regard to the required, typologically determined characteristics, abilities and skills of the working person. A particularly important feature of this approach is that the model of the working system can be utilised for an explanation of the job from its impact on the working person instead of a purely work-technical observation of the individual as a system element.

JOB ANALYSIS AS DEMAND ANALYSIS

In accordance with Hacker (1973) the job demands that are imposed on a working person are defined as the general personal performance requirements that are necessary for the execution of work tasks. Together with environment-related requirements, the job demands determine the totality of demands.

The demands are not expressed in the form of personality variables, i.e. as hypothetical, global 'ability' or 'capability' factors (such as assertiveness, abstractive capacity, etc.), as is done mainly in demand analysis for the purpose of personnel management (cf. e.g. Nutzhorn, 1964) or work evaluation (cf. e.g. Böhrs, 1959; Euler and Stevens, 1952; Hennecke, 1975; Paasche, 1974; REFA, 1977; Wibbe, 1966, etc.). This direct deduction of performance requirements from complex jobs based on approaches of personal psychology has been subject to repeated criticism (e.g. by Hacker, 1978; Graf Hoyos, 1974; v. Pupka, 1977; Volpert, 1973; specifically with regard to work evaluation by Laske, 1975).

To establish an 'activity model of man', the following demand areas can be adopted from Kirchner and Rohmert (1973, p. 24):

(1) Demand area 'information reception': This is the recognition of relevant conditions in order to deduce decisions for activities. Important aspects are the sensory organ and the corresponding perception and

processing of this information that finally lead to the recognition of the condition.

(2) Demand area 'information processing': In this area, the proper, i.e. a meaningful response has to be selected. This decision is based on the knowledge about the objects of the activity, their characteris tics and possible modifications of these, as well as about procedures for activity selection. This know-ledge must be stored in long term memory. In addition, the short term memory is used for temporary storage of information to be combined.

(3) Demand area 'information output/activity': This in cludes not only the performed activity but also its organisation and direct control. In this area, the required skills become evident but may also extend into the decision area.

JOB ANALYSIS AND STRAIN

The stress-strain concept of human work (see e.g. Rohmert et al., 1973; Luczak, 1975), assigns the work task to the 'object area'. In this theoretical model, this object area includes both the work task and the conditions of the work environment, from where job-specific and situation-specific demands result. These characterise the energetic-effective heaviness of work and the informative-mental difficulty of work.

The duration and time distribution of work heaviness and difficulty result in the partial stresses that are related to the work content; these are expressed by fac-tors and quantities describing the exogenous impacts of the working system on the working person that are assessed by an object-related analysis (Luczak, 1975; Rohmert et al., 1985). Together with the situation-specific partial stresses that result from the physical and social working conditions, the work content-specific partial stresses determine the subjective activities or – on the passive side – the response performance of the individual. Activi-ties are in turn influenced by the motivations and dispo-sition of the working person, which can partly be derived from the required skill. The thereby defined relationships for this 'object area' of the enlarged stress-strain con-cept form the starting point of a job analysis such as the Job Analysis Questionnaire (Arbeitswissenschaftliches Er-hebungsverfahren zur Tätigkeitsanalyse, Landau et al.; 1975; Landau, 1978 a, b; Rohmert and Landau, 1979).

Above all, the simultaneous consideration of the categories 'tasks', 'demands', 'environmental conditions', and
'required skill' as determinants of stress can - also in
the sense of a 'work analysis using broadband variables'
(Frieling 1975; McCormick, 1976) - be regarded as a suitable theoretical concept for job analysis in the ergo-
nomic/Human Factors sense.

The causal relationship between the mentioned stress
determinants and partial stresses can be used to prove the
quantitative, functional, and time-related validity of a
cause and effect relationship, at least on an exemplary
basis (cf. Luczak, 1975).

By understanding the task-related job analysis as an
analysis of the stress determinants, it can be assumed
that a quantitative assessment - usually on the ordinal
scale level - of stress sections according to their duration, height, sequence or overlap and to their position in
time within a work shift is possible (cf. Laurig, 1977).

If a task-related job analysis procedure is additionally claimed to allow a strain-relevant description of
stress, this implies:

- the design of the analysis procedure according to strain
  categories (cf. Luczak, 1975), as far as types of strain
  can be analysed in a qualitatively and quantitatively
  repeatable manner (this condition is not met e.g. for
  emotional strain)

- the at least qualitative gradation of the analysis items
  according to the psycho-physical strain described by
  them

- the possibility to assign selected items with characteristic coefficients of psycho-physical strain

- the provision of scaling and rating aids on the basis of
  physiological and psychological strain examinations.

Of course, this form of strain-relevant job analysis
goes beyond a job analysis dealing with the 'object area'
shown in Figure 4.

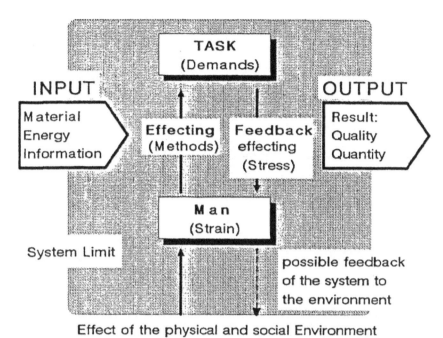

Figure 4. Stress-strain concept

Nevertheless, such tools of job analysis cannot – and should not – assess inter-individual variations in work performance. For example, Hackman (1970) has enlarged the objective side of the work task by the process of 'redefinition'. The working person must initially understand the work task, he/she must be willing to accept it and to cope with the demands imposed by it, and in addition he/she includes his/her experiences and judgements in the work. The influence of previous experiences will also have be considered (Graf Hoyos, 1974).

Subjective task/job analysis procedures deal with the individual differences between working persons, which are reflected both in subjective perception and in the work performance. Since these subjective job analysis tools rely on the condition that one can perceive and describe work processes and since these prerequisites are only met in part, these tools can only cover a limited part of the psychical processes (Gablenz-Kolakovic et al., 1981).

It should, however, be noted that task-related job
analysis procedures that claim universal applicability -
through broadband variables in a job-analytical sense - do
not want to or are not able to cover also this area of
subjective job analysis.

PROCEDURES AND METHODS OF TASK-RELATED JOB ANALYSIS

For the clarity of terms, there should be distinction
between procedures or tools of job analysis on the one
hand and the methods or techniques used to implement the
procedures on the other hand.

While the term 'procedure' covers the entire theoretical concept, including the objectives and possible applications as well as the test-statistical foundation, the
term 'method' or 'technique' only refers to the implementation of the procedure. Therefore, a job analysis procedure can usually be implemented with similar success
through several methods such as interviews, observation
interviews, self-recording, etc..

Moreover, the following discussion should be seen under
the limitation that predominantly demand-oriented job analysis procedures that are based on an engineering approach
are considered as irrelevant in this context and are
therefore not included. For the interested reader, reference is made to the literature (DIN 33 407; Hackstein et
al., 1979; Nutzhorn, 1964; REFA, 1977; Rühl et al., 1980;
etc.). Similarly, procedures for subjective job analysis,
for the analysis of job satisfaction as well as of the
management skills of superiors, etc. are not discussed
(these subjects are discussed in: Bayrisches Staatsministerium, 1976; Benninghaus, 1981; Bowers and Franklin,
1977; Bruggemann, 1976; Celluci and de Vries, 1978; Fischer and Lück, 1972; Fittkau-Garthe and Fittkau, 1971;
Hackman and Oldham, 1974; IG-Metall, 1979; Kern and Schumann, 1970; Lynch, 1974; Mahler, 1974; Martin et al.,
1980; Müller-Böling, 1978; Neuberger and Allerbeck, 1978;
Plath and Richter, 1978; Sims et al., 1976; Smith at al.,
1969; Staehle et al., 1981; Turner and Lawrence, 1965;
Ulich, 1981; Udris, 1977; White, 1975; etc.).

Overviews of job analysis procedures in the broader
sense have been prepared by Frei (1981), Frieling (1975),
Hennecke (1976a), Graf Hoyos and Frieling (1977), Jones et
al. (1953), Karg and Staehle (1982), Kenton (1979), Neunert (1979), Prien and Ronan (1971), Rohmert et al. (1975)
and others.

Several techniques can be employed to implement a job analysis procedure in companies and administration. These techniques can be classified according to their degree of standardisation into non-standardised, semi-standardised and standardised procedures (Frieling, 1975). If a job analysis uses existing job descriptions, information from document analysis, from training reports and from reports by job incumbents, work analysts or managers, this means that a job analysis is performed in a qualitative form according to specific guidelines and is set down in free wording (Graf Hoyos and Frieling, 1977). The discretionary powers of the analyst can be limited by using semi-standardised procedures such as observation and interview guidelines, daily work reports or the 'Critical Incident Technique' developed by Flanagan (1954). If it is desired to minimise the discretionary powers, standardised procedures such as questionnaire, interview, checklist, observation interview, etc. should be used. They allow the qualitative or quantitative assessment of all items of a job, following a fixed scheme. The use of standardised procedures will increase the procedure-related effort, mainly the effort of developing the job analysis procedure. On the other hand, however, implementation and evaluation will become more cost-effective so that the application of a standardised procedure on a long term basis is also recommended for economic reasons. An increasing degree of standardisation should also improve the reliability of a job analysis procedure.

Following this introductory overview, the following papers will document individual job analysis procedures and results.

REFERENCES

Bayerisches Staatsministerium für Arbeit und Sozialordnung, 1976. "Wo drückt uns der Schuh?". Arbeitnehmer in Bayern beurteilen ihre Arbeitswelt. Bayr. Staatsministerium für Arbeit und Sozialordnung. Dokumentation, 1 - 176

Benninghaus, 1981. Zwischenbericht über das Forschungsprojekt "Merkmale und Auswirkungen beruflicher Tätigkeit 1980"; Technische Universität Berlin, Institut für Soziologie, unveröffentlicht

Böhrs, H., 1959. Normalleistung und Erholungszuschlag in der Vorgabezeit. München, Carl Hanser Verlag.

Bowers, D.G.; Franklin, J.L., 1977. Data Based Organizational Change (Survey-Guided Development O7I.) Michigan
1975; La Lolla, Calif.

Bruggemann, 1976. Zur empirischen Untersuchung verschie-
dener Formen der Arbeitszufriedenheit; in: Zeitschrift
für Arbeitswissenschaft, 71 ff., 2.

Celluci, A.J.; Vries, de, D.L., 1978. Measuring Managerial
Satisfaction: A Manual for the MJS: Techn. Report No.
11 des Center for Creative Leadership, Greensboro, N.C.

McCormick, E., 1976, Job and Task Analysis, in: Dunette,
M.D. (Hrsg.): Handbook of Indistrial and Organizational
Psychology. Chicago: Rand McNally College Publishing
Company, 651 - 696.

DIN 33400. Gestalten von Arbeitssystemen nach arbeitswis-
senschaftlichen Erkenntnissen. Berlin/Köln: Beuth-
Vertrieb GmbH

Euler, H.; Stevens, H., 1952. Die analytische Arbeitsbewertung als Hilfsmittel zur Bestimmung der Arbeits-
schwierigkeit (fürHandarbeit) Düsseldorf: Verlag
Stahleisen

Fine, S., 1967. Matching job requeirements and worker
qualifications, in: Fleishman, E.: Studies in personnel
and industrial psychology. Homewood (III.): The Dorsey
Press

Fischer, L.; Lück, H.F., 1972. Entwicklung einer Skala zur
Messung von Arbeitszufriedenheit (SAZ); in: Psychologie
und Praxis. Heft April - Juni, S. 64 ff.

Fittkau-Garthe, H.; Fittkau, B., 1971. Fragebogen zur
Vorgesetzten-Verhaltensbeschreibung (F-V-V-B),
Göttingen

Flanagan, J., 1954. The critical incident theory. Psychological Bulletin, 51, 4, 32 358

Fleishman, E.A.; Teichner, W.H.; Stephenson, R.W., 1970a.
Development of a Taxonomy of Human Performance: A
Review of the secon years progress. Washington, D.C.:
American Institute for Research, Techn. Rep. No. 2

Fleishman, E.A., 1975. Taxonomic problems in human per-
formance research, in: Singleton, W.T.; Spurgeon, P.
(Hrsg.): Measurement of human resources. London: Taylor
& Francis Ltd., 49 - 72

Frei, F., 1981. Psychologische Arbeitsanalyse - Eine
Einführung zum Thema, in: Frei, F. & Ulrich, E.
(Hrsg.): Beiträge zur psychologischen Arbeitsanalyse,
Bern, Huber

Frieling, E., 1975. Psychologische Arbeitsanakyse, Stuttgart: Verlag W. Kohlhammer

Frieling, E., 1977. Occupational analysis; some details of an illustrative German project, in: Int. Rev. App. Psychol., 26, 2, 77 - 85

Frieling, E.; Hoyos, C. Graf, 1978. Fragebogen zur Arbeitsanalyse - FAA. Bern: Hans Huber Verlag

Gablenz-Kolakovic, S.; Krogoll, T.; Oesterreich, R.,; Volpert, W. 1981. Subjektive oder objektive Arbeitsanalyse? Z. Arbeitswissenschaft, 35, 217 - 220

Hacker, W., 1973. Allgemeine Arbeits- und Ingenieurpsychologie. Berlin, VEB Deutscher Verlag der Wissenschaften

Hackmann, J.R., 1969. Toward Understanding the Role of Tasks in Behavioral Research. Acta Psychologica, 31, 97 - 128

Hackmann, J.R., 1970. Tasks and Performance in Research on Stress. In: McGrath, J.E. (Hrsg.): Social and Psychological Factors in Stress. New York: Holt, Rinehart & Winston, 202 - 237

Hackmann, J.R.; Oldham, G.R., 1974. The Job Diagnostic Survey: An Instrument for the Diagnosis of Jobs and Evaluation of Job Redesign Projects, Technical Report No. 4, Department of Administrative Sciences, Yale University, New Haven

Hennecke, A., 1975. Arbeitsanforderungen, Arbeitsbewertung und Arbeigsgestaltung. Mitteilungen des IfaA, 57, 29 - 54

Hennecke, A., 1976a. Neuere Verfahren der Anforderungsvermittlung durch Arbeitsanalyse. Mittelungen des IfaA A, 64, 3 - 19

Hoyos, Graf, 1974. Arbeitspsychologie. Stuttgart: Verlag W. Kohlhammer GmbH

Hoyos, Graf, C.; Frieling, E., 1977. Die Methodik der Arbeits- und Berufsanalyse, in: Seifert, K.H. (Hrsg.): Handbuch der Berufspsychologie, Göttingen: Verlag für Psychologie Dr. C.J. Hogrefe

IG-Metall Bezirksleitung Stuttgart, 1979. Werktage müssen menschlicher werden! Stuttgart

Jones, M.H; Hulbert, S.F.; Haase, R.H., 1953. A survey of the literature of job analysis of technical positions. Personnel Psych., 6, 173 - 194

Karg, P.W.; Staehle, W.H., 1982. Analyse der Arbeitssituation. Freiburg: Haufe

Kenton, E., 1979. Job analysis methodology, National Technical Information Service, Springfield, VA

Kern, H.; Schumann, M., 1970. Industriearbeit und Arbeiterbewußtsein, Europäische Verlagsanstalt.

Kirchner, J.-H.; Rohmert, W., 1973. Problemanalyse zur
    Erarbeitung eines arbeitswissenschaftlichen Instrumen-
    tariums für Tätigkeitsanalysen, in: Bundesinstitut für
    Berufsbildungsforschung (Hrsg.): Arbeitswissenschaft-
    liche Studien zur Berufsbildungsforschung. Hannover:
    Gebr. Jänecke Verlag, 7 - 48
Kosiol, E., 1973. Aufgabenanalyse, in: Grochla, E. (Hrsg.):
    Handwörterbuch der Organisation. Stuttgart: Poeschel
    Verlag
Landau, K., 1978. Das Arbeitswissenschaftliche Erhebungs-
    verfahren zur Tätigkeitsanalyse - AET - Dissertation,
    TH Darmstadt
Landau, K., 1978b. Das Arbeitswissenschaftliche Erhebungs-
    verfahren zur Tätigkeitsanalyse - AET im Vergleich zu
    Verfahren der analytischen Arbeitsbewertung, in: Fort-
    schrittliche Betriebsführung, 27, 1, 33 - 38.
Landau, K.; Luczak, H.; Rohmert, W., 1975. Arbeitswis-
    senschftliche Erhebungsbogen zur Tätigkeitsanalyse. In:
    Rohmert, W.; Rutenfranz, J.: Arbeitswissenschaftliche
    Beurteilung der Belastung und Beanspruchung an unter-
    schiedlichen Arbeitsplätzen. Der Bundesminister für
    Arbeit und Sozialordnung, Bonn.
Laurig, W., 1971. Simulationsmethoden zum Abschätzen des
    Erholzeitbedarfs, Werkstatt und Betrieb, 104, 263 - 267
Laurig, W., 1977. Der Arbeitsinhalt als ergonomische Fra-
    gestellung. Dortmund: Vortrag gehalten auf der Interna-
    tionalen Tagung der Sozialakademie vom 20.-23.06.1977
Laske, St., 1975. Lohnpolitik mit Hilfe von Leerformeln -
    Zum Objektivitätscharakter der Arbeitsbewertung. Wup-
    pertal: Arbeitspapiere des Fachbereichs Wirtschaftswis-
    senschaft der GH Wuppertal
Luczak, H., 1975. Untersuchungen informatorischer Belastung
    und Beanspruchung des Menschen. Fortschritts-Berichte
    der VDI-Zeitschriften, Reihe 10, 2, Düsseldorf, VDI-
    Verlag
Lynch, B.P., 1974. An Empirical Assessment of Perrow's
    Technology Construct; in: Administrative Science Quar-
    terly, 338
Mahler, W.R., 1974. Diagnostic Studies; Reading, Mass.
Martin, W.; Ackermann, E.; Udris, H.; Oegerli, K, 1980.
    Monotonie in der Industrie, Bern, Huber
Miller, R.B., 1971. Development of a taxonomy of human per-
    formance. Washington; American Institutes for Research
Morsh, J.E., 1966. Impact of the Computer on Job Analysis
    in the United States Air Force. Lackland (Texas): Per-
    sonnel Research Laboratory, Aerospace Medical Division,
    Air Force Systems Command, PRL-TR-66-19

Morsh, J.E., 1967. The Analysis of Jobs – Use of the Task
    Inventory Method of Job Analysis, in: Fleishman, E.
    (Hrsg.): Studies in Personnel and Industrial Psychology.
    Homewood (III.); The Dorsey Press.
Morsh, J.E., 1964. Personnel Psychology, 17. Job analysis
    in the United States Air Force.
Morsh, J.E.; Madden, J.M.; Christal, R.E., 1961. Job anal-
    ysis in the United States Air Force. Techn. Report WADD-
    TR-61-113, Lackland Air Force Base, Texas, USA
Müller-Böling, D., 1978. Arbeitszufriedenheit bei automat-
    isierter Datenverarbeitung. München/Wien
Neuberger, O.; Allerbeck, M., 1978. Messung und Analyse
    von Arbeitszufriedenheit; Bern, Stuttgart
Neunert, J., 1979. Der Anfang einer Verständigung? Zusam-
    menfassung der Podiumsdiskussion "Arbeitsanalyse" auf
    dem Frühjahrskongreß der Gesellschaft für Arbeitswis-
    senschaft in Wien, 2.-4. Mai 1979, in: Angewandte
    Arbeitswissenschaft, 82, 57 – 61
Paasche, J., 1974. Die Praxis der Arbeitsbewertung. Köln:
    Müssener-Verlag
Plath, H.E.; Richter, P., 1976. Erfassung von Beeinträch-
    tigung durch Belastungswirkungen, Monotonie und psychi-
    sche Sättigung. Sozialistische Arbeitswissenschaft 20,
    1, 27 – 37
Prien, E.P.; Ronan, W.W., 1971. Job Analysis. A Review of
    Research Findings. Personnel Psychology, 24, 371 – 396
v. Pupka, M., 1977. Anforderungsgerechtes menschliches
    Verhalten bei Transporttätigkeit – Anforderungs- und
    Eignungsprofile. Dortmund: Bundesanstalt für Arbeits-
    schutz und Unfallforschung, Forschungsbericht Nr. 158
Rabideau, G., 1954. Field measurement of human performance
    in man-machine-systems. Human Factos, 6, 663 – 672
REFA (Hrsg.), 1977. 4. Methodenlehre des Arbeitsstudiums,
    Tel 4 – Anforderungsermittlung (Arbeitsbewertung).
    München: Carl Hanser Verlag
REFA (Hrsg.), 1978. Methodenlehre des Arbeitsstudiums,
    Teil 2 – Datenermittlung. München: Carl Hanser Verlag
Rohmert, W., 1972. Aufgaben und Inhalt der Arbeitswissen-
    schaft. Die berufsbildende Schule, 24, 1, 3 – 14
Rohmert, W. und Mitarbeiter, 1985. Arbeitswissenschaft I,
    Umdruck zur Vorlesung, 15. berichtigte und erweiterte
    Auflage, Darmstadt
Rohmert, W.; Landau, K., 1979. Das Arbeitswissenschaft-
    liche Erhebungsverfahren zur Tätigkeitsanalyse (AET).
    Handbuch und Merkmalheft. Bern, Stuttgart, Wien: Hans
    Huber

Rohmert, W.; Luczak, H.; Landau, K., 1975. Arbeitswissenschaftlicher Erhebungsbogen zur Tätigkeitsanalyse - AET,
in: Z. f. Arbeitswissenschaft, 29, 4, 199 - 207

Rohmert, W.; Rutenfranz, J.; Luczak, H.; Landau, K.;
Wucherpfennig, D., 1975. Arbeitswissenschaftliche Beurteilung der Belastung und Beanspruchung an unterschiedlichen industriellen Arbeitsplätzen, in: Rohmert, W.;
Rutenfranz, J.: Arbeitswissenschaftliche Beurteilung der
Belastung und Beanspruchung an unterschiedlichen industriellen Arbeitsplätzen. Der Bundesminister für Arbeit
und Sozialordnung, Bonn , 15 - 250

Sims, H.D.; Szlagyi, A.D; Keller, R.T., 1976. The Measurement of Job Characteristics; In: Academy of Management
Journal. 195

Smith, P.C.; Kendall, L.M; Hulin, C.L., 1969. The Measurement of Satisfaction in Work and Retirement, Chicago.

Staehle, W.H.; Hattke, W.; Sydow, J., 1981. Die Arbeit an
Datensichtgeräten aus der Sicht der Betroffenen. DBW-
Depot-Papier 81-5-1, Stuttgart, Poeschel

Theologus, G.C.; Romashko, T.; Fleishman, E.A., 1970.
Development of a taxonomy of Human Performance: A feasi-
bility study of ability dimensions for classifying human
taks. Pittsburgh: American Institutes for Research, AD
705 672

Turner, A.N.; Lawrence, P.R., 1965. Industrial Jobs and
the Worker, Boston

Udris, I., 1977. Fragebogen zur Arbeitsbeanspruchung;
unveröffentl. Arbeitspapiere. Zürich: Lehrstuhl für
Arbeits- und Betriebspsychologie der ETH

Ulich, E., 1981. Subjektive Tätigkeitsanalyse als Voraus-
setzung autonomieorientierter Arbeitsgestaltung, in:
Frei, F.; Ulich, E. (Hrsg.): Beiträge zur psychologischen Arbeitsanalyse, Bern: Huber

Volpert, W., 1973. Arbeitswissenschaftliche Grundlagen der
Berufsbildungsforschung. Bundesinstitut für Berufsbildungsforschung (Hrsg.): Arbeitswissenschaftliche Studien
zur Berufsbildungsforschung. gebr. Jänecke Verlag, Hannover, 49 - 105

Wheaton, G., 1968. Development of a taxonomy of human performance: A review of classif. American Institutes for
Research Pittsburgh P.A. Washington

White, G.C., 1975. Job Design and Work Organization, Diagnosis and Measurement; Research Unit, Paper No. 4,
Department of Employment, London

Wibbe, J., 1966. Arbeitsbewertung - Entwicklung, Verfahren
und Probleme. München: Carl Hanser Verlag

Zerga, J.E., 1943. Job analysis - a resumé and bibliogra-
phy. Journal of Applied Psychology, 27, 249 - 267.

ON THE APPLICATION OF AET, TBS AND VERA TO DISCRIMINATE BETWEEN WORK DEMANDS AT REPETITIVE SHORT CYCLE TASKS

Seeber, A., Schmidt, K.-H., Kiesswetter, E., Rutenfranz, J.

University of Dortmund
Federal Republic of Germany

INTRODUCTION

The starting point of the present study was the obser-vation by the occupational health service, that the work-ers in a chocolate factory showed many physical com-plaints. Obviously most complaints were connected with performing assembly line tasks. The problem formulated for the psychologist was to point out possibilities for changing the situation.

In view of this aim the first step was to identify those aspects of the tasks responsible for this high rate of work related complaints. This was done by the applica-tion of work analytical procedures.

Most of the psychological procedures in analyzing work focus on the description of the psychic processes by which the working activities are mentally controlled. Typ-ical examples of such kinds of procedures are the "Tätig-keitsbewertungssystem "(TBS, Hacker et al., 1983) and the "Verfahren zur Ermittlung von Regulationserfordernissen in der Arbeit" (VERA, Volpert et al., 1983). These proce-dures provide information about the possibilities and re-quirements of a given work task to build up work related goals and strategies in an individual manner. However, they are not adequate to analyse the physical components of carrying out working activities independent from the level of cognitive control. In contrast to this the focal point of the "Arbeitwissenschaftliches Erhebungsverfahren zur Tätigkeitsanalyse" (AET, Rohmert and Landau, 1979) is to analyse all load components induced by the work tasks including their work and environmental conditions. Because of its wider range of work aspects considered, the AET should be more suited to reflect the physical aspects of the working activities.

Despite these different approaches (Oesterreich and Volpert, 1987; Landau and Rohmert, 1987; Volpert, 1987), the first question arises, whether the analytical methods are sensitive enough to differentiate between the work tasks on assembly lines, which at first glance appear to be very similar in their demands. After that, the second question refers to the possibility of predicting different patterns of complaints on the basis of the analytically classified work tasks.

ANALYTICAL CLASSIFICATION OF THE TASKS

In the chocolate producing factory 5 departments with assembly lines were analysed including nearly 170 work-places in 10 jobs. The job tasks are laying of small parts (for example nuts) on soft chocolates, laying of very thin bars of chocolates or different kinds of chocolates and creams in boxes, wrapping of hollow figures in special paper and polishing the paper surface of the hollow chocolate figures. These types of work tasks are connected with cycle times between 1.5 seconds up to 5 seconds; only wrapping needs nearly 15 seconds. The longest cycle time of about 60 seconds has been observed in a special packing task.

All workplaces investigated were occupied by female workers. The training on the job lasts in the most cases only for some hours up to few days. The similarities between the jobs were
- the highly automated sequence of only a few motor and sensomotor operations,
- the high density of operations per time and the strong time pressure,
- the limited degree of carrying out the operation with individual variations,
- the low level of mental demands.

Differences between the jobs concerned the
- body position and the direction and length of motions,
- minimal degrees of freedom in planning and checking operations,
- complexity of the sensomotor and proprioceptive demands and
- number of elements in the sequences of activity steps.

The application of the three work analytical methods to describe and to distinguish the 10 jobs, however, leads to some problems: Only very few items of the TBS and of the VERA differentiate between the jobs. Comparing the 45 items of the TBS between the 10 jobs, most of the items classify into the same category. Only three items of the TBS could be selected to classify the jobs in two groups (see Table 1 for the number, the verbal description and the corresponding categories). Comparing the 32 items of the VERA, only two items distinguish essentially between the jobs (see Table 1). Following the proposed algorithms to find the correct level of mental operations, all of the jobs are classified into the level 1 R, that means all could be controlled "without thinking operations".

Table 1: Characteristics of subjects and grouping procedures
Definition of groups by the work analytical methods:

Tab. 1: Characteristics of subjects and grouping procedures
Definition of groups by the work analytical methods:

TBS class:		1	2
A 1.3.2	checking and classifying	1	3
A 6.4	planning	0	1/2
D 2.1	orienting and evaluating	1	2/3
Number of subjects		76	21
Age		32 ± 12	35 ± 11
Years in the job		5.4	6.0
VERA class:		1	2
C 11	number of work units	1	2-4
C 12	of that routine units	1	2-4
Number of subjects		61	48
Age		32 ± 12	34 ± 12
Years in the job		5.3	5.7
AET class:		1	2
C 3.2	static holding work	<33	>33
C 3.4	dynamic work, one sided	<67	>67
Number		81	25
Age		32.5 ± 12	31.9 ± 11
Years in the job		4.9	6.2

Classification of the jobs into the groups:	TBS	VERA	AET
Polishing the surfaces of a hollow hare enveloped in special paper	1	1	1
Laying nuts and other small parts on chocolates	1	2	2
Laying very thin bars in the insert of chocolate boxes	1	1	2
Laying chocolates and creams in the insert of chocolate boxes	1	1	1
Wrapping of the hollow hare by special paper	1	1	1
Checking and correcting the content of chocolate boxes	2	2	1
Checking and correcting the weight of chocolate boxes with thin bars	2	2	2
Packing the chocolate boxes in chests	2	2	1
Shoveling the chocolates in large transport boxes	2	2	1

The application of the AET yields some more differentiating aspects between the workplaces and jobs. Especially, those items referring to static and dynamic work.

By this pragmatic way all jobs were classified (see part of Table 1) by those analytical items, presented in Table 1. However, this approach does not result in the same classification aspects. The attempt was made to find

some overlaps of the item contents across all procedures,
but this approach was not successful for a reclassifica-
tion, because of insufficient discrimination by the corresponding items or because of a lack of corresponding
items.

Summarizing the results according to the first question, we have to state that only a few of the items
respectively of the classification procedures of the TBS
and VERA distinguish between the 10 jobs. The reason may
be the work analytical validity of these procedures. They
are based on a model stressing the discrimination in
mental work aspects. On the other side, the AET focuses
on a broader range of load aspects and therefore offers
more possibilities for a grouping of the assembly line
jobs.

In the next step the question arises to which extent
the classifications could be helpful to investigate the
complaints of the workers. Are the complaints caused more
or less by psychic impairments during the working activities? In this case the procedures TBS and VERA stressing
the psychological point of view could be suited to point
out correlations between the groupings of jobs and the
number of complaints. If the complaints are mainly caused
by the physical load components the AET classification
should provide a possibility for a prediction of the physical complaints.

RELATIONS BETWEEN THE WORK ANALYTICAL CLASSIFICATION AND PHYSICAL COMPLAINTS

The questionnaire of complaints

The questionnaire applied to assess the complaints includes a general self-estimation of the strength of complaints on an overall rating scale. Besides that, this
questionnaire shows a body scheme indicating 19 areas of
possible complaints or pains. The subjects have to show or
to cancel if one or more of the areas impair their well-
being. The areas are presented in Table 5. The questionnaire was applied by a short interview at the beginning,
the middle and the end of a shift (t_1, t_2, t_3). The variance analytical results are listed in Table 2, demonstrat-
ing the dependence of the overall ratings to age, job
years and to time course.

Table 2: Intensity of subjective complaints by overall rating in dependence of age, job years and the time course during shift: Variance analyses and means (n = 152 female workers)

	df	F	probab.	x_{t1}	x_{t2}	x_{t3}	$x_{t1...3}$
age ($</> \bar{x}$)	1	0.55	0.45				
job years ($</> \bar{x}$)	1	6.54	0.01				
time	2	87.57	0.00				
age/years	1	1.83	0.18				
young/short				1.5	2.9	5.7	3.4
young/long				4.3	5.6	7.8	5.9
old/short				1.9	3.8	5.5	3.7
old/long				2.0	5.2	6.2	4.6
time/age	2	2.83	0.09				
time/years	2	0.61	0.54				
time/years/age	2	0.86	0.42				

Neglecting the expected variations due to time course, only the length of years in the job influences significantly the intensity of complaints as assessed by the overall rating. As an example for the reliability of answers during 2 following working days the extent of complaints in 3 different body areas is presented in Table 3. It shows a sufficient conformity of the answers.

RESULTS

After the testing procedures of the questionnaire the second question can be treated. Table 4 summarizes the results of variance analyses on the basis of the three job classifications with regard to the overall ratings as dependent measures.

Table 3: Percent of "yes" answers in three body areas during two different working days in the same group of subjects (TBS 1):

		t_1	t_2	t_3
shoulder				
	1. day	23	33	44
	2. day	21	33	44
head				
	1. day	9	9	8
	1. day	9	9	11
middle part				
of abdomen and	1. day	16	28	40
back	2. day	16	34	44

Only the AET classification provides significant differences of the ratings. Higher degrees of static and one-
sided dynamic work are connected with higher ratings during the day. The factor time shows a significant inter-
relation with the AET grouping. In the class of higher
physical load the ratings show a stronger increase than in
the other class. The TBS and VERA groupings do not yield
corresponding relations as assumed before.

Table 4: Intensity of subjective complaints by overall
rating in dependence to work analytical classifications:
Analyses of variance and means

	df	F	probab.	x_{t1}	x_{t2}	x_{t3}	$x_{t1...t3}$
TBS 1/2	1	3.29	0.07				
time 1...3	2	54.22	0.00				
1				3.1	5.1	7.1	5.1
2				1.4	3.2	5.9	3.5
TBS/time	2	0.35	0.70				
VERA 1/2	1	0.31	0.57				
time 1...3	2	77.0	0.00				
1				3.0	4.7	6.5	4.7
2				2.2	4.2	6.7	4.3
VERA/time	1	1.37	0.25				
AET 1/2	1	6.55	0.01				
time 1...3	2	77.13	0.00				
1				2.4	3.9	5.6	4.0
2				3.2	6.2	9.0	6.2
AET/time	2	6.63	0.00				

The analyses of the complaints in the body areas are
summarized in Table 5. It demonstrates firstly, that there
are no relations between the psychological categories of
the TBS grouping and the amount of physical complaints during this type of working activity. Secondly it shows that
there is no consistent pattern of complaints in connection
to the number of work units as the basis of the VERA classification. On the one side, the less work unit per work
cycle the more complaints on the neck/nape and on the
right/left hand. On the other side, the more work units,
the more complaints about the feet are observed. For that,
the confusing factor of body posture while standing could

be the reason. The VERA class 2 contains no standing activities.

Table 5: Number of complaints regarding the items mentioned below (in percent) [1]

	TBS			VERA			AET		
	1	2	probab.	1	2	probab.	1	2	probab.
neck/nape	19.8	3.9	0.58	17.4	5.6	0.01	20.7	1.9	0.06
shoulder	33.7	5.9	.15	22.9	13.7	.32	22.6	14.1	.01
upper arm	12.9	3.9	1.00	10.1	5.5	.59	10.4	4.7	.52
forearm	7.9	1.9	1.00	6.4	2.8	.51	7.6	1.9	1.00
right hand	20.8	4.9	.79	19.3	5.5	.01	24.5	0.0	.01
left hand	15.8	2.9	.55	14.7	2.8	.01	18.9	0.0	.01
chest	6.9	0.0	.35	5.5	0.2	.13	4.7	1.9	.67
abdomen/back									
- upper part	11.9	1.9	.51	7.3	6.4	1.00	6.6	6.6	.02
- middle part	30.7	11.9	.34	20.2	21.2	.24	25.5	14.1	.02
- below part	2.0	0.0	1.00	0.0	1.8	.19	0.0	1.9	.05
right tigh	2.9	1.0	1.00	0.9	2.8	.32	0.0	2.8	.01
left tigh	2.9	1.0	1.00	0.9	2.8	.32	0.0	2.8	.01
right knee	3.9	1.0	1.00	0.9	4.6	.09	1.9	2.8	.08
left knee	3.9	1.0	1.00	0.9	4.6	.09	1.9	2.8	.08
right shank	8.9	2.0	1.00	3.7	6.4	.21	3.8	4.7	.03
left shank	9.9	1.9	.73	4.7	7.3	.13	3.8	4.7	.03
right foot	7.9	3.9	.46	1.8	11.0	.01	3.8	5.7	.01
left foot	7.9	3.9	.46	1.8	11.0	.01	3.8	5.7	.01
head	5.9	1.0	1.00	5.5	0.9	.13	8.5	0.0	.11

[1] This statistics refer to a 2x2 table (Fisher's exact test, two-tailed); for reasons of economy only the first row of the table is presented, describing the occurrence of the mentioned complaint.

As assumed, the AET classification provides the most significant differences in the number of complaints at different body areas, but, as described before, there is also no consistent pattern of complaints. Complaints in the upper part of the body and in the hands are connected with lower degrees of static and dynamic work (class one). Complaints in the lower part of the body are stronger related to the higher degrees of static and dynamic work (class two). An explanation by means of co-variables (standing) is possible only for a part of the subjects included here.

CONCLUSIONS

Obviously there are some difficulties in using the procedures TBS and VERA in the recommended form for analytical purposes in repetitive short cycle tasks with low men-

tal demands. In this range of possible work demands the
TBS does not differentiate in a sufficient way to predict
physical consequences of the one-sided work demands. As
claimed in the manual the method points out many aspects
to change the structures of working activities, but the
typical health problems with this kind of tasks are not
reflected or predictable in sufficient quality.

The algorithm of the VERA method classifying the level
of mental regulation functions does not lead to different
classes in the work tasks observed, but obviously, the
item "number of work units" may serve as a possible pre-
dictor of physical complaints. In this case valid predictions need to take into account possible confusions like
for example body posture.

The AET, directed on both aspects, the physical and
mental load, offers a much better chance to classify the
high repetitive work demands and surrounding conditions.
It is suited to predict different aspects of possible
physical complaints, which are real as well as typical
health problems in this type of working activity.

REFERENCES

Hacker, W., Iwanowa, A. and Richter, P., 1983, Tätigkeits-
    bewertungssystem, (Berlin (Ost): Psychodiagnostisches
    Zentrum)
Landau, K. and Rohmert, W., 1987, Aufgabenbezogene Analyse
    von Arbeitstätigkeiten. In: Kleinbeck, U. and Ruten-
    franz, J. (eds.), Arbeitspsychologie. Enzyklopädie
    der Psychologie, D, III, 1, pp. 74-129, (Göttingen:
    Verlag für Psychologie, Hogrefe)
Oesterreich, R. and Volpert, W., 1987, Handlungstheore-
    tisch orientierte Arbeitsanalyse. In: Kleinbeck, U. and
    Rutenfranz, J. (eds.), Arbeitspsychologie. Enzyklopädie
    der Psychologie, D, III, 1, pp. 43-73, (Göttingen:
    Verlag f.r Psychologie, Hogrefe)
Rohmert, W. and Landau, K. (eds.), 1979, Das Arbeitswis
    senschaftliche Erhebungsverfahren zur Tätigkeitsanalyse
    (AET), (Bern, Stuttgart, Wien: Huber)
Volpert, W., 1987, Psychische Regulation von Arbeitstätig-
    keiten. In: Kleinbeck, U. and Rutenfranz, J. (eds.),
    Arbeitspsychologie. Enzyklopädie der Psychologie, D,
    III, 1, pp. 1-42, (Göttingen: Verlag für Psychologie,
    Hogrefe)
Volpert, W., Oesterreich, R., Gablenz-Kolakovic, S., Kro-
    goll, T. and Resch, M., 1983, Verfahren zur Ermittlung
    von Regulationserfordernissen in der Arbeitstätigkeit
    (VERA), (Köln: Verlag TÜV Rheinland)

STANDARD METHODS USED IN FRENCH-SPEAKING COUNTRIES FOR WORKPLACE ANALYSIS

Dr. Raymond Wagner

ARBED Division de Differdange
Service Médical du Travail
Luxemburg

INTRODUCTION

Over the past twenty years, various methods of analysing workplaces and working conditions have been developed, particularly in France. These developments have been prompted by:
* the need to adopt a global approach to the organization of work, taking greater account of human factors in addition to technical and material factors (Gaussin 1983);
* the need for a common language in the multidisciplinary working parties concerned with the improvement of working conditions in industry (AVISEM 1977);
* the need for tools for analysing working conditions which take account of the holistic nature of human factors and which can easily be used by lay persons (AVISEM 1977);
* the fact that methods used to study working conditions which are based on physiological measurements require specialized staff not generally available within companies (Wagner 1985).
    These methods may be used, for example (IACT 1980), to
* provide pointers for corrective action via a preliminary analysis of working conditions;
* analyse working conditions in workplaces still at the planning stage;
* compare workplaces in terms of the quality of working conditions;
* assess workplace conditions before and after the introduction of new or modified technologies.

The aim of this paper is to present four of these job
analysis methods, as yet little known outside the French-
speaking world -though without passing judgement on their
scientific value or practicability. The methods presented
are:
- the workplace profile method (RNUR 1976)
- the LEST method (Guélaud et al. 1975)
- the AVISEM method (AVISEM 1977)
- the GESIM method (GESIM 1988)

PRESENTATION OF METHODS

The parameters analysed by the various methods are
compared in Tables 1 and 2.

Workplace Profile Method

This method was designed by the Renault company to
analyse working conditions with the following characteristics: repetitive work, short cycle, average precision,
semi-skilled workers. The analysis is performed with the
aid of a handbook. Data are collected by means of observation and interviews. Environmental analyses require measuring instruments. Job analysis is performed by an observer other than the worker. Training is required before
the method can be used. Working conditions are represented
by 27 criteria, subsumed under 8 factors.
Each of these 27 criteria is evaluated in terms of a
five-level scale, ranging from level 1, indicating a
highly satisfactory situation, to level 5, representing a
very poor or highly dangerous situation requiring urgent
improvement.
The results can be represented by two profiles: an
analytical profile containing all 27 criteria, which
enables the critical points in the analysed situation to
be identified, and a global profile of a workplace or
group of workplaces, which summarizes the analytical
profile with a single score for each of the 8 factors.

The LEST Method

Developed at LEST (Laboratoire d'Economie et de Socio-
logie du Travail CNRS, Aix-en-Provence), this method is
intended for analysing the workplaces of unskilled or
semi-skilled industrial workers. The work situation is
analysed with the aid of an observation handbook. Evaluation is based on observation of the workplace and inter-

views with the workers and supervisory staff. The characteristics of the physical environment are evaluated on the
basis of measurements. The method therefore requires an
observer other than the worker.

Workplace analysis is based on 16 criteria. These are
set out in a user guide, preceded by a chapter containing
a description of the task and information on the company
in question.

The criteria are given scores between 0 and 12. Scores
0,1 and 2 represent a normal situation, scores 3,4 and 5 a
slight problem, scores 8 and 9 a significant problem and
score 10 a serious problem to be remedied as a matter of
priority.

Following analysis, these criteria may be set out in
the form of a histogram to provide a rapid overview of the
positive and negative aspects of a work situation.

The AVISEM Method

This evaluation grid is intended to ensure a standard
presentation of the factors used to analyse working
conditions. In addition to the evaluation grid, the manual
also contains a list of standards and procedures, together
with various types of application. The evaluation grid
takes account of ten factors. As it is also based on
observation, interviews and the measurement of physical
environment factors, this method too requires an observer
other than the worker. Internal company training in the
use of the method is provided. It should be noted that the
use of physiological parameter measurements is recommended
as a source of supplementary information.

The ten parameters are rated on a five-level scale,
where 1 signifies a highly satisfactory situation and 5
corresponds to a very poor situation. The results are
presented as a profile of working conditions.

The GESIM Method

GESIM (Groupement des entreprises sidérurgiques et
minières) developed this method as part of a research
project under the Community Ergonomics Action programme.
The essential aim was to develop a method of workplace
analysis based on experience of working conditions as
recorded by a simple evaluation procedure using a questionnaire. Unlike with the other three methods, this analysis is performed by the workers themselves.

The user guide comprises three parts: an introduction
to the method, an evaluation handbook and a set of technical information cards. The evaluation handbook is prefaced
by an outline of the workplace, a description of the work
and possibly a photograph of the workplace as well.

The job analysis uses 7 criteria covering 26 factors. A
total of 91 parameters are evaluated. Each of the parameters is analysed with the aid of the questionnaire. The
questions are of the yes-no type. To the right of the
questions are two columns A and B. If the answer to a
question is in column A, the respondent goes directly to
the next question. On the other hand, if it is in column
B, an evaluation table has to be consulted for the relevant parameter and the appropriate score selected. The
answers are entered in a form at the back of the questionnaire and are assigned a score between 0 and 20 (1 signi-
fying a very poor situation and 20 a highly satisfactory
situation). The scores are used to draw up a profile of
the work situation.

CASE STUDIES

<u>Improving the working conditions of workers involved in
marking hot rolled products</u>

In a Grey beam rolling mill, the beams have to be
marked while traversing the cooling bed when still hot.
Marking used to done manually using chalk, oil or paint or
by stamping or punching. The markers performing this work
were subject to high thermal, postural and noise stresses.
A European Community ergonomics research project (Wagner
et al.,1986) was launched with the aim of improving their
working conditions. The introduction of an automated marking system changed the job of marking into a monitoring
task performed from a control cabin. From the very outset
of the project, it was possible to show that automation
improved working conditions by comparing the existing
situation with the projected situation in an AVISEM
profile (Figure 1).

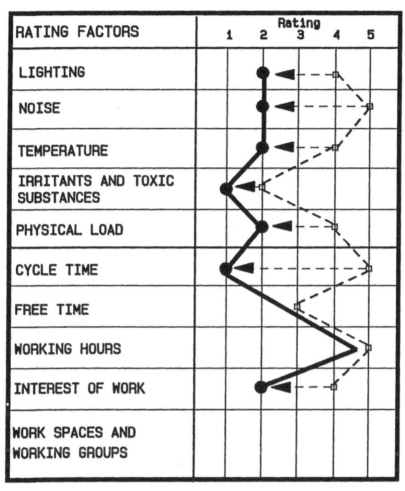

RATING FACTORS	Rating 1 2 3 4 5
LIGHTING	
NOISE	
TEMPERATURE	
IRRITANTS AND TOXIC SUBSTANCES	
PHYSICAL LOAD	
CYCLE TIME	
FREE TIME	
WORKING HOURS	
INTEREST OF WORK	
WORK SPACES AND WORKING GROUPS	

Rating scale : 1 - highly satisfactory   2 - satisfactory
3 - acceptable   4 - poor
5 - very poor

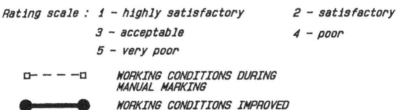

□— — — —□   *WORKING CONDITIONS DURING MANUAL MARKING*

●———————●   *WORKING CONDITIONS IMPROVED BY AUTOMATING MARKING*

Figure 1. This AVISEM profile shows the improvements in working conditions achieved by automating the marking of hot beams.

THE PULLING ALONE

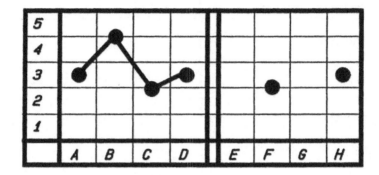

ROTATION BETWEEN THREE JOBS

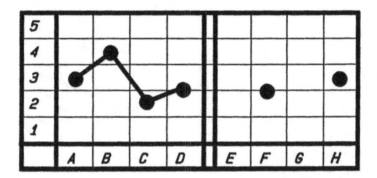

A: SAFETY

B: ENVIRONMENT

C: PHYSICAL LOAD

D: MENTAL LOAD

E: AUTONOMY

F: RELATIONSHIPS

G: REPETITIVENESS

H: JOB CONTENT

Figure 2. This comparison of two "global profiles" prepared using the workplace profile method shows the reduction in work stresses achieved by using a job rotation system. The top profile depicts the initial situation, while the profile below shows that for rotation between three jobs.

Reduction of work stresses at workplace considered to be arduous in a tube works

The activity studied was the job of an operative responsible for manually pulling galvanized tubes from a
zinc bath and placing them in a cleaning installation. For
tubes of small diameter, the work rate is very high (up to
600 tubes an hour), while for tubes of large diameter the
physical load is considerable (metabolism up to 18 kj/
min). In addition, heat and noise stresses are high. The
work cycle is as follows: half an hour of pulling work,
then half an hour of monitoring and adjusting the
installation (the latter taking a few minutes), followed
by a rest break.

As part of the restructuring of the plant, a feasibil-
ity study has been carried out with a view to automating
this arduous job. Pending the result of this study, a job
rotation system has been proposed to secure an immediate
reduction in work stresses. This proposal provides for
rotation between three activities: tube pulling-tube moni-
toring-tube cleaning. The effectiveness of this proposal
in reducing stresses has already been demonstrated by an
analysis using the workplace profile method (Figure 2).

COMMENTS AND CONCLUSIONS

When the various methods are compared, they appear to
be very similar as regards analysis criteria. All were
also designed for repetitive industrial workplaces with
short work cycles and requiring little or no skills. In
addition, their applicability to other workplaces is limited. However, the desired aims can often be achieved in
practice by combining the various methods.

One of the advantages of these methods is that their
use is not restricted to experts in working conditions.
Furthermore, their rating systems permit a rapidcomparison
of work situations, thus enabling companies to evaluate
their plant in terms of working conditions and direct
their efforts to improving these conditions. Their major
advantage, however, lies in the creation of a common
language for specialists in human factors (experts in
occupational medicine, ergonomists, work psychologists,
industrial hygiene specialists) and the two sides of
industry: company managers and worker representatives. All
things considered, we believe that the advantages outweigh
the undoubted flaws. Standardization would nevertheless be
desirable.

With the approach of 1992, it would be desirable for
this standardization to take the form of a European method
for the analysis of working conditions.

ACKNOWLEDGEMENT

The author wishes to thank the Community Ergonomics
Action's Bureau of Information and Coordination for its
help with the English translation of this paper.

REFERENCES

AVISEM, 1977: Techniques d'Amélioration des Conditions de
    Travail dans l'Industrie (Editions Hommes et Tech-
    niques, Suresnes-France).
GESIM (Groupement des Entreprises Sidérurgiques et
    Minières), 1988, Connaissance du poste de travail, II
    conditions de l'activitÇ (GESIM,Metz).
Gaussin, José, 1983: Ergonomie et conditions de travail.
    Notes résumées du cours d'ergonomie et des conditions
    de travail (UnitÇ de Psychologie du Travail et des
    Organisations, Université Catholique de Louvain-La-
    Neuve, Belgium).
Guélaud,F., Beauchesne,M.-N., Gautrat,J.and Roustang,G.,
    1975, Pour une analyse des conditions de travail
    ouvrier dans l'entreprise. Recherche du Laboratoire
    d'Economie et de Sociologie du Travail C.N.R.S. Aix-en-
    Provence, 3rd édition (Librairie Armand Colin, Paris).
Institut pour l'Amélioration des Conditions de Travail
    (IACT), 1980, Les mÇthodes d'analyse des conditions de
    travail (IACT, Lettre d'information 3, Brussels).
Régie Nationale des Usines Renault (RNUR), 1976, Les
    profils de postes. Méthode d'analyse des conditions de
    travail, Collection Hommes et Savoir (Masson, Sirtès,
    Paris).
Wagner, R, 1985, Job analysis at ARBED. Ergonomics, 28, 1,
    255-273.
Wagner, R., et al., 1986, Ergonomic improvement of hot
    working conditions involved in the marking of rolled
    products (Commission of the European Communities,
    Community Ergonomics Action, Luxembourg, research
    project No 7247-11-046).

Table 1A. Comparison of criteria analysed by the various methods for analysing working conditions (workplace analysis, safety, physical environment, physical load).

	RNUR METHOD	LEST METHOD	AVISEM METHOD	GESIM METHOD
I WORKPLACE ANALYSIS	WORKPLACE DESIGN Height-Distance (remoteness) Supply-Removal Dimensions-Accessibility Commands-Signals	WORKPLACE DESCRIPTION		WORK AREA Layout Traffic Postures Commands Signals-Information Safety
II SAFETY	SAFETY Safety			Under I and VIII
III PHYSICAL ENVIRONMENT	PHYSICAL ENVIRONMENT Ambient heat Ambient noise Artificial lighting Vibration Atmospheric pollution Appearance of workplace	PHYSICAL ENVIRONMENT Temperature Lighting Noise Vibration	PHYSICAL ENVIRONMENT Lighting Noise Temperature Irritants and toxic substances	PHYSICAL ENVIRONMENT Appearance of workplace Ambient heat Ambient noise Ambient light Vibration Atmospheric pollution
IV PHYSICAL LOAD	PHYSICAL LOAD Main posture Most unfavourable posture Work effort Work posture Handling effort Handling posture	PHYSICAL LOAD Posture Dynamic load	PHYSICAL LOAD Physical load	PHYSICAL LOAD Handling effort Physical effort other than handling

Table 1B. Comparison of criteria analysed by the various methods for analysing working conditions (psychological/ mental load, psycho-sociological aspects, working time, work space).

	RNUR METHOD	LEST METHOD	AVISEM METHOD	GESIM METHOD
V PSYCHOLOGICAL/ MENTAL LOAD	MENTAL LOAD Mental operations Level of attention	MENTAL LOAD Time constraints Complexity-Speed Attention Meticulousness	SIGNALS, COMMANDS AND MENTAL LOAD Cycle time	MENTAL LOAD Mental fatigue Work rate Complexity of work Precision of gestures Repetitive work
VI PSYCHO-SOCIOLOGICAL ASPECTS	AUTONOMY Individual autonomy Group autonomy RELATIONSHIPS Independent work relationships Dependent work relationships Repetitiveness JOB CONTENT Required skills Responsibility Interest of work	Initiative Social status Communication Cooperation Identification with product	Free time Interest of work	PSYCHO-SOCIOLOGICAL ASPECTS Autonomy Monotony Interest of work Relationships-communication Social environment
VII WORKING TIME		Working time	Working hours	WORKING TIME Work schedule Transport
VIII WORK SPACE			Work spaces and working groups	WORK SPACE Geographical location Safety of work space Material job conditions Manual handling operations

THE CRITICAL EVENT TECHNIQUE IN JOB ANALYSIS

Denny V. Kunak

Industrial and Management Systems
University of South Florida
USA

INTRODUCTION

The notion of certain things in life that must go right in order to survive is as old as human existence. The same can be said about the fact that people have different talents and predispositions to coping with critical situations. While the idea of matching man's talents with critical task requirements dates back to the origins of work division and specialization, it was not until World War I that the first intensive research in this direction took place.

A further major progress in this area is attributable to the Aviation Psychology Program in the U.S. Army Air Forces during World War II. At that time it became evident that a basic prerequisite to effective selection and training of combat personnel and their successful job participation is a clear definition of the critical requirements in terms of both the actual component activities and their relative importance (Flanagan, 1948).

For this purpose, techniques of analytical nature were found to be of greater use than purely descriptive methods known as job description and job classification. Consequently, job analysis became the method of choice. This included both the defining of the activity and the translation of the requirements for success from actual operations into statements of general abilities, aptitudes, and personality traits believed to underlie critical behavior.

The specific method of analyzing successful or unsuccessful behavior of combat personnel to determine critical task requirements was done using the Critical Incident

Technique (CIT) developed and later described by Flanagan
(1954). This technique consists of a set of procedures for
collecting specific incidents or events in such a way as
to facilitate their potential usefulness in solving practical problems.

An incident or event is defined as any observable human
activity that is sufficiently complete in itself to permit
inference and predictions to be made about the person performing the act. To be critical, an incident or event
must occur in a situation where the purpose or intent of
the act seems fairly clear to the observer and where its
consequences are sufficiently definite to leave little
doubt concerning its effects.

"CIT" OR "HAY" APPROACH TO JOB ANALYSIS?

Despite the effectiveness of CIT in getting to the root
of success and failure in all kinds of tasks, this
approach to job analysis has not gained as wide a popular-
ity and acceptance as other techniques. The most popular
of them seem to be questionnaire-based surveys of the "How
Are You?" or HAY-orientation.

The term "HAY" is used in reference to all the questions of generic nature such as "How do you like your job,
supervisor, co-workers, company benefits, late shifts,
office, suppliers, customers, etc.?" which are often used
in analyzing jobs. As discussed later in the text, such
questions are of doubtful value and tend to obscure rather
than clarify the facts about people at work.

The reasons for the seldom use of CIT are not
exactly clear. The relative ease to develop, manipulate,
and evaluate questionnaires with statistics seems to be
one of the reasons. The inherent difficulty and necessary
expertise in analyzing, coding, validating and integrating
critical incidents might be another reason. Other possible
explanations can be derived from the comparison of advantages and disadvantages of different techniques as
given by Mintzberg (1973).

However, some additional comments are in order. It
should be clear that, no matter what technique of scientific inquiry is being used to analyze jobs, the results
and conclusions cannot be better than the data itself.
Using CIT, the data reflects actual events. In case of
HAY- surveys, the data is limited by the knowledge,
experience, and vision of the researcher and his or her
ability to formulate relevant questions for meaningful
interviews or questionnaires.

The situation is further complicated by the fact that HAY-surveys typically lack explanatory immediacy. They put the subject in the position of researcher, tend to replace facts with opinions, and build in subjectivity of those who prove to be poor estimators of their own time and activities (Mintzberg, 1975).

More often than not, such studies reflect general experience, attitudes, judgment values and beliefs rather than critical details regarding a job under investigation. To this extent, validity of HAY-studies is questionable, often untested, and seldom disclosed.

Perhaps the most controversial point in any job analysis of the HAY-type can be illustrated by a subject who has his feet in the refrigerator, his head in the oven, yet on an average he claims to be all right. Apparently, the burden of integrating those two factors and arriving at an overall state of "well-being" remains with the subject. For reasons unknown to the researcher, including no reasons at all, he claims to be all right.

Most employees when being asked HAY-questions will answer in an uncommitted, moody, wishful, temporal, expected, or generic way that is of doubtful value in effective job analysis and job redesign. Many studies try to offset the superficial nature of their HAY-questions by structuring them along interval-like scales. This makes the subjects indicate the degree of their opinion, state of being, or agreement with presented questions.

The point missed here is that HAY-surveys remain what they are, no matter what scale is being utilized to increase the "precision" of obtained information. Typically, they are too superficial, subjective, and non-discriminatory in nature to disclose true details about people at work which could guide further studies.

The picture is different with CIT inquiries. Observing the subject in a kind of oven/refrigerator situation, or having an authentic record of such an event, the HAY-question is inevitably replaced by two specific questions. One question aims at the temperature of the subject's feet, the other at the temperature of his head.

With answers to these questions and possible measurements of the temperature, the researcher can develop a much better understanding of the subject's state of being than in the case of simple HAY-inquiries. Apparently, CIT can provide data that is not only more explicit, but also critical to job design. The following three examples illustrate the wide range of applicability of CIT in analyzing jobs.

"CIT" AND THE MOTIVATION-HYGIENE THEORY

Perhaps one of the most significant transformations of
the CIT-philosophy into our understanding of jobs has been
accomplished through research in the late fifties that
resulted in the formulation of the Motivation-Hygiene
Theory (Herzberg et al., 1959). Based on an original sample of over 200 engineers and accountants, a modified version of CIT disclosed two distinct sets of critical factors. One set of factors, called hygienes, was found to be
primarily responsible for job dissatisfaction. The other
set, called motivators, was predominantly responsible for
job satisfaction.

The point illustrated in the above example of heat and
cold, as two distinct ingredients to overall well-being,
is supported by empirical research and reflected in the
Motivation-Hygiene Theory. This theory suggests that, at
any point of time, man has two parallel needs that require
a certain degree of satisfaction. Accordingly, any effective job analysis must be concerned with two basic
questions, namely, "What makes your employees tick?" and
"What makes them sick?".

The research evidence accumulated from numerous
studies, now totaling over 2,000 critical events, indicates that the three most frequent factors causing
employee dissatisfaction are: company policy and administration, supervision, and interpersonal relationships.
Work conditions, normally being the primary target of
ergonomic interventions, rank fourth among the dissatisfiers.

In contrast, the three most frequent factors that lead
to extreme job satisfaction are: achievement, recognition
for achievement, and fulfilling work content. Responsibility, a factor that many job analysts and designers focus
on first in their approaches, is actually the fourth most
frequent satisfier (Herzberg, 1982).

This potentially dangerous focus is partially due to
the ease with which responsibility can be delegated to
others. The danger becomes obvious with the realization
that "delegated" responsibility is inherently different
from "assumed" responsibility. In most cases, delegated
responsibility is "contaminated" by hygiene factors such
as company policy and administration which are powerful
dissatisfiers.

In contrast, assumed responsibility is a part of
psychological growth and consequence of job enrichment
that relies on the Motivation-Hygiene Theory. Under these

circumstances, responsibility can become a powerful moti-
vator in itself rather than an additional burden to the
employee.

Apparently, due to misunderstanding or misconception of
how critical factors interact, one can actually contribute
to job dissatisfaction while attempting to improve the
basis for job satisfaction. In this respect, CIT was
instrumental in developing a basic understanding of people
at work that translated into the Motivation-Hygiene Theory. This theory, in turn, became the basis to the concept
of job enrichment stressing a well-balanced implementation
of motivators. Finally, job enrichment became a comprehensive philosophy and ongoing effort in the analysis and
improvement of jobs.

"CIT" AT LOW ORGANIZATIONAL LEVELS

To document the effectiveness of CIT in job analysis,
two recent studies conducted by the author are presented
in this section. The first study dealt with industrial
safety programs at an electric company concerned with
associated costs and liabilities. Despite extensive
efforts to improve its safety record, this company ranked
among the worst in the Southeast United States in terms of
its safety performance.

The company engaged in periodic moral surveys,
retrained its field workers, sent supervisors to motivational seminars, stressed teamwork, experimented with
Quality Circles, and implemented new safety procedures.
It emphasized its commitment to safety with slogans such
as "Safety of life shall outweigh all other considerations" and stressed that its corporate mission is to meet
the customers' needs in a safe manner. Yet the number of
work- related injuries and accidents remained above the
industry average.

A situational analysis using CIT indicated several
problems. One of the critical factors that emerged from
that analysis was the management's obsession with ergonomics as the primary foundation to improving its industrial
safety record. Safety per se became an ultimate objective
rather than a consequence of motivating and fulfilling
work.

The company failed to recognize the true causes of its
problem which originated in the organizational structure
and management style which prevented motivators from being
present at work. Instead, the company was fighting the
symptoms of the actual problem utilizing KITA (Kick In The
Ass) techniques.

Herzberg (1968) created this acronym for motivational gimmicks that are often used in the hope of boosting employee morale and productivity. However, the short-term effect of KITA techniques defeats the purpose of genuine motivation and escalates existent problems.

No matter how sincere the electric company was in try-ing to improve its safety record, employees perceived every new change as "another gimmick" to get more work out of them. They were missing a visible commitment to this goal through changes in the organizational structure and managerial practices that were necessary to reach it. Instead, they became demoralized, sarcastic, and careless to the point that their attitudes and behavior increased the chances of injuries and accidents.

The second study refers to a manufacturer of electronic equipment who experienced chronic problems in the areas of product design, technology transfer and manufacturing. Hoping to improve its communication and operation effi-ciencies, the company installed a new management informa-tion system, created teams of design engineers and ordered a manufacturing representative to attend weekly meetings of these teams.

The results were disappointing. While the frequency of interdepartmental communication increased, product quality as the major concern of the company experienced no signi-ficant improvement. Production people claimed that engi-neers designed products that could not be manufactured to meet required specifications; engineers felt that manufac-turing interfered too much with the functional purpose of their design.

A sample of critical events first suggested that orga-nizational communication was indeed the key factor to quality improvements. However, a closer analysis of the data revealed that this factor was not directly responsi-ble for the existing problems. Much more, it was a symptom of certain organizational inadequacies and misconceptions that made the communication efforts fail to produce expected quality and productivity improvements.

For example, the company failed to clarify and imple-ment the client relationship among its individual depart-ments and employees. It also provided no opportunities for unique expertise and new learning. Design engineers never saw their products being assembled and had no expertise in manufacturing. The presence of a manufacturing representa-tive at engineering meetings could not offset the lack of direct learning opportunities. Similarly, manufacturing personnel had no idea about design work and associated difficulties. Both groups then failed to provide each other with critical information.

Furthermore, imposing on the employees regular meetings with selected representatives from other departments introduces a serious hygiene factor that, at some point of time, will cause job dissatisfaction. The reasons can be found in the previous discussion of delegated vs. assumed responsibility. Last but not least, decisions of this kind are directly counterproductive in respect to the proven elements of good jobs: direct feedback, direct communication authority, personal accountability, and self scheduling.

Considering some other critical factors identified by CIT, coupled with the fact that management information systems leverage efficiencies just as inefficiencies while tending to generate information overload, it became evident that intensifying organizational communication alone could not produce the desired effects.

On the contrary, due to the hygiene-loaded environment, employees were trapped into a series of rules and procedures including those of formal communication. Without realizing the potential consequences, the company insisted on the usage of the new information system. Yet, prior to its implementation, none of the decision makers had ever asked the employees what their needs for such a system might be.

Obviously, the name of the game was communicating rather than engaging in a responsive, direct, and efficient dissemination of critical information. Flooded with mostly irrelevant information, the employees stopped reading messages altogether. They occasionally missed some critical information and, consequently, became injured due to their ignorance of current changes in their environment.

"CIT" AT HIGH ORGANIZATIONAL LEVELS

Similar to the previous examples, CIT proved to be effective in analyzing jobs of top managers, especially in regard to strategic decision making. Based on a sample of 200 critical events associated with exceptional business growth or survival, over 40 factors were identified as inputs to strategic decisions (Kunak, 1987).

Of course, the actual number of factors considered in a particular decision was much smaller and differed from case to case. On average, top managers considered seven factors when making decisions on how to induce the growth of their companies. Interestingly enough, they considered only five factors when deciding on how to stay in business. The three most frequent factors in business survival were firing, cash drain, and effective leadership. In business growth, these factors were organizational structure, timing of actions, and efficient management.

The findings that some factors were mainly associated with business growth, while others with business survival, were statistically significant, suggesting a dual focus in strategic decisions. One focus was on surviving and protection, the other on growing and risk taking. According to the critical events, most managers had no difficulty understanding that survival is a necessary prerequisite to business growth. Obviously, one has to survive before one can grow.

However, it was not as obvious to many of them, that survival alone does not induce business growth. For whatever reason, too many "protectors" among the top decision-makers focused on survival factors and defensive measures, only to see their competitors surpassing them. Apparently, successful protectors do not necessarily make good growers. Thus, it must be emphasized that survival is a necessary yet insufficient prerequisite for business growth.

In contrast, there were "risk takers" among the subjects, too. Their concern was growing their organizations under all and any circumstances, as if business growth would guarantee perpetual survival and existence. They excluded any consideration of critical survival factors from their decisions and, by pursuing an exceptional growth rate, they virtually grew their companies into bankruptcy. Opposite to the previous notion, successful growers do not necessarily make good protectors. It must be also recognized that growth alone is no indicator of the company's survival strength.

The dynamics of these two states of business existence are inherently different. Each of them requires special considerations, decisions and actions. It is one thing to save a company from bankruptcy (business survival) and another thing to bring it to new, exceptional heights of existence (business growth). Yet there is also the whole thing which requires a well-balanced consideration of both states of existence and corresponding factors at all times.

There were a few factors appearing equally often in growth and survival events. The three most frequent factors were communication, planning, and new contracts. However, only the factor "communication" was frequent enough to be considered among the most critical factors. This factor ranked third in both types of events, thus preceding effective leadership and efficient management as next most frequent factors in business survival and growth, respectively.

In regard to the previous comments on organizational communication, it should be noted that survival events were typically associated with extensive, ineffective or failing communication. On the other hand, growth events were mostly associated with the simple, direct, timely and efficient dissemination of critical information.

Unfortunately, this type of study does not permit for a conclusion whether ineffective communication was one of the causes of failing businesses or merely a consequence of it. Similarly, it is not clear whether efficient information dissemination was one of the causes or just a result of exceptional business growth.

As indicated before, critical factors do not act in isolation. Consequently, good communication is likely to be part of a good organizational structure and management; bad communication is always going to be part of a bad structure and management. As long as critical factors will be identified and used in conjunction, the causal relationship among them should be of no critical importance.

CONCLUSIONS

The studies presented in this paper only add to the long record of successful applications of CIT. This technique is powerful in analyzing jobs and separating facts from opinions. It offers a unique opportunity to develop a good understanding of organizations and differentiate between forces that stimulate success and those that impede it.

CIT has a wide range of application and should be the technique of choice in exploratory and descriptive studies serving as a basis to causal studies. Since it relies on actual incidents, it has a clear advantage over questionnaires and surveys that are based on library research, other studies of a similar nature, generalized opinions, or pure armchair speculations.

The typical claim of expertise bias in analyzing critical events and validity of derived factors does not hold. Every set of factors can be validated and put under the scrutiny of statistical testing. It is the task of the researcher to do so rather than to perfect a questionnaire that is based on unrealistic assumptions and wishful thinking.

The position taken in this paper is that no matter how much we know about particular jobs, there are always idiosyncrasies that cannot be derived from other studies nor assumed based on one's experience. In order to be certain of these idiosyncrasies, job analysis and job redesign must become ongoing efforts in every organization concerned with the direction of its development.

The only reliable way to find out the truth about people at work is the objective way of fact-oriented inquiries. CIT is a means to creating a sound and reliable basis for further causal studies, better understanding of jobs and significant improvements in the quality of worklife.

REFERENCES

Flanagan, J. C., 1948, The Aviation Psychology Program in the Army Air Forces (Report No. 1). In: <u>Army Air Forces Aviation Psychology Program Research Reports</u> (Washington, D.C.: U.S. Government Printing Office), pp. 3-310.

Flanagan, J. C., 1954, The Critical Incident Technique. <u>Psychological Bulletin</u>, 51, 327-358.

Herzberg, F., 1968, One More Time: How Do You Motivate Employees? <u>Harvard Business Review</u>, January-February.

Herzberg, F., 1982, <u>The Managerial Choice</u>, 2nd ed. Salt Lake City: Olympus.

Herzberg, F. et al., 1959, <u>The Motivation to Work</u>. New York: Wiley.

Kunak, D. V., 1987, Strategic Decisions in Times of Critical Business Growth and Survival. In: <u>Proceedings of the Eight Annual Meeting</u>, St. Louis, edited by the American Society for Engineering Management, 147-151.

Mintzberg, H., 1973, <u>The Nature of Managerial Work</u>. New York: Harper & Row.

Mintzberg, H., 1975, The Manager's Job: Folklore and Fact. <u>Harvard Business Review</u>, July-August, 49-61.

ASSESSMENT OF JOB STRESS: THE RHIA INSTRUMENT

Birgit Greiner and Konrad Leitner

University of Technology Berlin
Federal Republic of Germany

GENERAL DESCRIPTION OF THE INSTRUMENT

The "Instrument to Identify Regulation Hindrances in Industrial Work" is a psychological work analysis procedure (Leitner et al., 1987). The instrument was developed over a period of four years and tested on approximately four hundred jobs from twelve branches of industry. RHIA can be used to identify, describe and quantify task-related mental stress of various work tasks in all industrial branches.

The stress investigation is an abstraction from personal evaluation of different workers. If it is necessary to move to the other end of the machine to read an important dial, one operator may consider this a disturbance and another may not. These different (subjective) evaluations do not affect the (objective) fact of an inappropriately placed dial which causes additional effort for every operator. With RHIA work conditions are assessed, therefore its approach is focused on conditions rather than individual appraisal (see Oesterreich and Volpert, 1987). The assessment method used is known as theory-aided assessment technique. Before using the RHIA instrument, the investigator must be familiar with the theoretical basis, definitions and procedures in the manual. The manual questions are formulated in technical language and are directed only towards the investigator. The information necessary for answering the questions is collected through informal talks with the operators during observation of their worktask. The instrument is standardized with exact instructions for the observation and with specified item-categories. The definitions derived from the theory of

action regulation provide the investigators with a precise
assessment of psychological aspects of their observed
phenomena. Such a procedure for the assessment of mental
stress avoids the disadvantages of rating scales, which
may give distorted results when the investigators use
different standards of judgement, or change them over
time.

The work must be fully trained in the task in order for
the stress to be accurately determined. Otherwise con-
fusion may arise between lack of training and stress-
inducing work conditions.

The final stress analysis is completed only after the
work task has been fully described. The stress factors so
identified are then specified in their content, classified
and summarized quantitatively.

STRESS CONCEPT

The basic stress concept of RHIA is derived from the
Theory of Action Regulation developed by Hacker (1980),
Oesterreich (1981) and Volpert (1975, 1987). The approach
attempts to represent the psychic structures of human
actions (generation of action plans, performance, feedback
about goal attainment), and assumes an active, goal-
oriented regulation of actions.

The principles of action regulation also apply to regulation processes of working activities. But considering
the conditions of industrial work in our society we must
state certain restrictions, which can be (referring to
Volpert, 1979) summarized by the term "partialization of
action". These restrictions are expressed for instance as
limited reqirements for planning and decision processes or
reduced work-related communication.

But above all, when a conflict between specified work
results and conditions of a work task exists, partialization can be a source of mental stress. This contradiction
is instantiated for a concrete work task in more or less
obvious regulation hindrances.

Regulation hindrances are understood as working conditions which hinder the achievement of results without the
possibility of effective worker response. The most effective response could lie in a fundamental technological or
organizational solution which removes the hindrances after
it first appears. A less effective reaction (because it
affects only the actual situation) would be temporarily to
reduce standards for quality and quantity of the work
product. The least effective, and most stress-inducing,

response requires the worker to overcome the hindrance through an increased expenditure of energy.

This stress concept differs from cognitive stress theory considerations as well as from the stress-strain concept. Cognitive-oriented stress theories emphasize the role of individual appraisals and are therefore more applicable a a basis for analysis instruments focused on persons.

In the stress-strain concept, stress is conceived as external conditions which produce strain through interaction with the person's individual characteristics. This differentiation between external causes and the resulting effects on the worker is helpful, but does not supply a complete approach to psychological stress. When any demand produced by work is classified as stress, as Kirchner (1986) stated, work itself must be stress, because work without demand of human effort is not imaginable. When two, until now, little differentiated aspects of work are separately considered, the implied equation of work and stress can be avoided:

- job reqirements, for which a person uses work capacity in order to attain a certain goal (for the area of mental requirements the "Instruments for the Assessment of Regulation Requirements in Industrial Work" (VERA) can be applied, see Volpert et al., 1983);

- job stress, (Regulation Hindrances) which increases the difficulty of reaching the defined goal causing (unnecessarily) an additional expenditure of energy.

The object of our stress analysis is not to investigate all external conditions which have demanding effects on the person, rather to search for those conditions which hinder the achievement of the goal and therefore demand additional expenditure.

TYPES OF REGULATION HINDRANCES

Regulation hindrances exist in two main forms, regulation barriers (RB) and hindrance through capacity overtaxing (CO).

Regulation barriers influence the action regulation directly and require short-term reactions from the worker. Capacity overtaxing exists when certain continous conditions reduce the mental and physical achievement capacity of the worker over the course of the workday. Both of

these main types of regulation hindrances will be
differentiated further (see Figure 1).

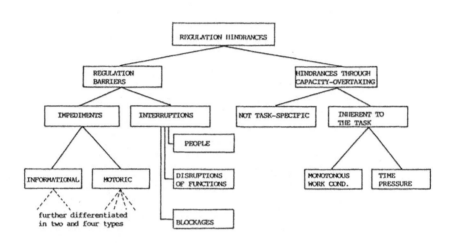

Figure 1. Types of Regulation Hindrances

Regulation Barriers

Regulation barriers can first be classified as to
whether they impede a specific work operation or if they
interrupt the continuity of operations (see Figure 1).
When an impediment exists a specific operation is more
difficult to perform but still possible to complete.
Informational and motor components of an operation can be
affected.

An example of an informational impediment could be when
certain information is not available, digits on a gauge
are poorly displayed or confusing. Impediments to motor
processes occur for example when operational elements are
not dependable, handwheels or levers are poorly placed or
difficult to move, or inappropriate tools must be used.

As opposed to impediments, which can be differentiated according to the impeded operation, interruptions are dif- ferentiated according to specific disturbances. They can occur at any time and therefore interrupt any operation. Interruptions can be caused by persons (e. g. telephone calls), malfunctioning equipment (e. g. material jam-up in a machine) or blockage (e. g. lack of materials).

Independent of the type of barrier, all RB can be quan- tified using a common scale. Missing information must be found, objects restricting the body movement removed, a work piece reprocessed, in order to achieve the quality and quantity of production standards. The common dimension used is the length of additional time required to respond to the barriers.

A high value of this measure due to RB, does not neces- sarily indicate strong psychological stress. The stress can be minor when the task has no stringent time con- straint, allowing workers to distribute the additional time expenditure according to their own schedule. "Time- binding", measured on an ordinal scale, varies from a max- imum, at which every movement is time-constrained, to a minimum, where workers completely control the scheduling of their work. Given a specific amount of additional time expenditure in response to RB, the mental stress is higher the stronger the time-binding of a task.

Hindrances through Capacity Overtaxing

Capacity overtaxing (CO) is the second main type of regulation hindrance. This is broken down into factors which are inherent to the task and those which are not task-specific (Figure 1). "Monotonous working conditions" and "time pressure" are related to specific tasks; whereas environmental factors (for example: noise, heat, dust) "affect" the performance of all tasks within the immediate area without being connected to the specific content of a certain task.

Monotonous Working Conditions: "Monotony" is often referred to as a type of qualitative underload (see Gubser, 1968; Martin et al., 1980; Udris, 1982; Ulrich, 1960), although many authors emphasize the high level of focused mental concentration during performance of monoto- nous work (see Bartenwerfer, 1957; Hacker and Richter, 1984). Our stress definition includes the concept of mono- tonous working conditions, but not the subjective state often described as "monotony". Monotonous working condi- tions exist when a repetitive task allows the worker no opportunity for planning and decision making concerning

the content, yet at the same time cannot be performed
automatically. This is the case when visual information
must be constantly processed during task performance. This
form of concentration is - along with lack of planning and
decision making - a necessary criterion for the identification of monotonous working conditions and distinguishes
these from "boring" tasks. The combination of required
concentration on task execution and repetition of identical task operations overtaxes the human regulation capacity. According to this concept of monotonous working conditions, they either exist or they do not (for more
details see Hennes, 1986). When monotonous conditions
exist they ae measured according to duration.

Time pressure: Time pressure is the second type of
overtaxing inherent to a task (see Figure 1). A common
definition states that time pressure exists when a job
must be completed within a time that forces a worker to
work faster than he normally would (Nachreiner and
Wucherpfennig, 1975). Although this seems plausible, its
operationalisation is impossible within a stress concept
focused on work conditions. Distinctive criteria for
defining a state of time pressure are neither formulated
by Nachreiner and Wucherpfennig nor by other authors.
A possible approach to this problem is to consider time
pressure not as a nominal variable (with the alternatives
"existent/non-existent"), but as a continuous characteristic of work tasks. The degree of time pressure is indicated by the speed of work necessary for achieving the
work results. If a high rate of work is continously
required, the action regulation capacity of the worker is
overtaxed; the worker cannot adjust his performance to
normal fluctuations of capacity.

Time pressure is increasingly higher, the less the
worker can afford to let the task rest. Under conditions
of high time pressure he cannot compensate for any delay.
In order to determine time pressure, the investigator must
answer the question of how long the worker can completely
suspend performance of his task without falling short of
output standards or causing other specific consequences
such as increase in errors, breaking of safety rules, etc.
The ratio between the suspension phase and the total working time gives a quantitative estimate of time pressure
expressed in percent.

Non-Task-Specific Hindrances: This category includes
all environmental conditions, exept those already identified as RB, which can influence the regulation capacity of
the worker (for example: noise, heat, cold, moisture,

etc.). Because these are less important for understanding the present stress concept, they will not be mentioned further.

"DOUBLE-ANALYSIS" AS A METHOD FOR RELIABILITY ESTIMATION

Before reporting the test-theoretical criteria of the RHIA instrument, the method used for reliability estimation will be presented (to our knowledge it has only been used twice: in the VERA-Project by Volpert et al., 1983; and for parts of the sample in the project "Mental stress at Workplaces", Greif et al., 1983).

Objectivity and reliability are recognized (along with validity) as the most important test-theoretical criteria. Often both of these criteria are examined separately. Using the so-called double-analysis method obviates the necessity of separate estimation.

In classical test theory, reliability is defined as the ratio of true variance to total variance. Total variance is the sum of true variance and error variance. The total variance expresses the total variation in measurement of a variable and is the only known term.

If a work task (and not a person) is the object of analysis, only the differences between the work tasks create true variance, all other influences have to be considered as measurement errors. This holds for RHIA as well as for any other work analysis instrument designed to measure characteristics of a task rather than of an individual. This means that in addition to the inaccuracy of the instrument, differences between investigators as well as those between workers must also be included as sources of error variance in the reliability estimation.

The method of double-analysis meets these requirements (see Figure 2).

Each work task is assigned to a randomly chosen pair of investigators. The investigators analyse the same work task independently, with investigator A observing worker X (in the early shift, for example), and investigator B observing worker Y (in the late shift). As a consequence, judgement errors of the investigators as well as individual differences between workers (such as inter-individual differences in work style, perception, etc.) are taken into account. Analysis of the agreement of the results obtained using this method provides a measure for both objectivityand reliability in one step.

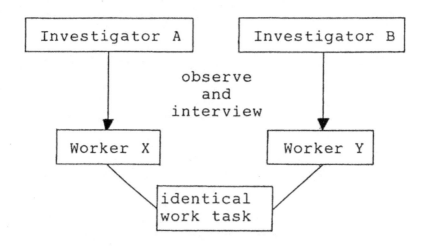

Figure 2: Double-Analysis Scheme

    Attempts to estimate objectivity of the results
obtained using observations of the same worker by different investigators are inadequate because it is not possible to separate work task variance from individual performance variance. Performance differences between workers,
thus taken as (true) task variance, produce an artificially inflated value for the estimation of objectivity.
    Performing a separate estimation of reliability would
also be questionable. In this case an investigator would
have to judge the same work task with (at least) two different workers. Having already established a description
of the work task in the first analysis, the "good" investigator could only refine this further in subsequent analyses, thus producing artificially consistent results. This
effect diminishes the longer the interval between assessments are, yet cannot be totally avoided. Retesting by the
same investigator definitely leads to an over-estimation
of reliability.
    The method of double-analysis completely avoids the
over-estimation discussed für the procedures above, and
is, therefore, a more stringent testing procedure than the
following common approaches: the same worker being observed by multiple independent observers (as in AET, FAA,
TBS); or the same person observed twice by the same observer after an interval of several months (also in TBS).

RESULTS OF RELIABILITY ESTIMATION

In the central survey, twenty investigators were employed. They completed 75 double-analyses of shift-work places.

Considering the wide scope of branches RHIA can be applied to (which present an unlimited set of hindrances) it is impossible to provide the investigator with a catalogue of potential regulation barriers. Thus the manual can only contain rules about how to identify regulation barriers.

A regulation barrier was coded as concordant when both investigators described its content identically and classified it as the same type (see Figure 1). None of the common statistics (such as contingency coefficient) could be used as a measure of concordance, because the total number of objects to be judged must be known for these calculations. For this reason, the percent of concordance (PC) was used as an easily understood indicator. With 218 agreements from a total of 351 RB this quotient yields a value of 62.1 percent. A test of significance for this indicator is not possible but also not necessary: If a list of RB with item categories "exists/does not exist" had been used, the probability of guess would have been 50 percent. Without such a list the probability that two investigators would coincidentally identify an identical RB is nearly zero.

In addition to the description of the content of the RB and its classification in one of the nine types (two informational and four motor impediments plus three interruptions), each one was given a value for the dimension "additional expenditure". For a given work task, the sum of additional expenditure for all RB is a measure of the amount of direct hindrance present.The reliability for this and the following variables was calculated as a Pearson correlation (for our purposes weighted kappa is identical). The reliability for the variable "total additional expenditure" was $r=0.56$ and is significant at the level of $p<.001$. When interpreting this correlation, note that a comparison of this value with reliability values obtained using rating-scales is misleading. This is illustrated in the following example: Calculating the correlation for only the 218 concordant RB, this would then approximate the method used for rating scales, yielding a value of $r=0.79$ ($p<.001$).

The level of "time binding" ($r=0.83$, $p<.001$) and the "duration of monotonous work conditions" ($r-0.74$, $p<.001$) show similar considerable agreement.

Less satisfying is the reliability of the variable
"time pressure" (r=0.62, p<.001). An inquiry into the
reasons for this low value revealed that the applied operationalisation of this variable led to misunderstandings
for some investigators. The formulations in the published
manual have been improved so that in future investigations
a more stable assessment of "time pressure" can be
expected.

Considering the stringent method used for reliability
testing, coefficients are high in comparison to other
instruments.

TESTING THE VALIDITY OF THE INSTRUMENT

Criterion validity is recognized to be the most important type of validity (see for instance Bortz, 1984). It
is calculated as a correlation between the results of an
instrument and external criteria for which a theoretical
connection is expected.

We chose two dindicators successfully testsd in the
project of Greif et al., (1983). The "Freiburger Beschwerdeliste (FBL)" from Fahrenberg (1975) revised by Mohr
(1986) is used for assessing psychosomatic complaints
which can be seen as long-term effects of stress inducing
working conditions. The second scale, also developed by
Mohr (1986) assesses "Irritation" (I), a shorter term
effect. Like Greif et al. (1983) we achieved good internal
consistency results (usinge Cronbach's alpha) for both
scales (FBL: alpha = .84; I: alpha = .81). Table 1 shows
the results of the validity test.

Table 1: Criterion Validity of RHIA-Results

Validity Criteria		
RHIA-Results	FBL	I
Time binding	-.07 n. s	.19*
Additional expenditure	.19*	.23*
Monotonous working conditions	.30**	.07 n. s
Time pressure	.20*	.27**
Multiple correlation	.33**	.28*

For each of the four RHIA results at least one significant (alpha-adjusted) correlation exists with one of the
two validity criteria. The correlations have the expected
direction (the negative correlation is beyond the 20 percent significance level and therefore has to be considered
as a zero correlation). The multiple correlation show the
explained variance of FBL and I accounted for by the RHIA
results. The size of the correlation coefficients found in
the validity tests should be judged against the background
of the assessment methods applied: Correlations between
variables obtained by using an identical procedure (questionnaires) tend to be higher ("method variance") than
those reported above, between questionnaire results and
(objective) RHIA-indicators. Correlations of the latter
kind are generally smaller (Greif et al., 1983, p. 398 ff.
had similar findings). Considering the absence of common
method variance in our case, the validity coefficients
obtained are remarkable.

By no means all of the stress-relevant characteristics
of work are assessed with the RHIA instrument. Insecurity
of employment, bad shop morale, or low promotion prospects
are examples of potentially important sources of stress
which are not covered by the RHIA analysis. Rather the
emphasis in RHIA is task-related mental stress measured by
the four indicators previously described. The fact that
these show direct (disregarding the wide variety of imaginable moderating effects) significant relationships to
psychosomatic complaints supports the validity of the RHIA
instrument.

FIELD OF APPLICATION FOR THE RHIA INSTRUMENT

RHIA provides a classification of task-related stress
factors applicable to all tasks in all industrial
branches. Because the emphasis in the analysis is on the
psychic structure of the task and is, therefore, not
linked to any specific tools or machinery, it can be used
for jobs with all levels of technical complexity.

One general field of application for the RHIA instrument is scientific research, e. g. studies concerning the
impact of task-related stress on the physical and mental
health of workers. In this case results of the work analysis would be used in conjunction with workers' health
inDicators obtained through other methods.

A more specific application is in impact assessment
studies of technical/organizational changes (automation,
new machinery, etc.). Affected tasks would be analysed

before and after implementation of the modifications. The
RHIA-stress indicators would show increases or decreases
in each of the specified stress categories. Comparison of
these stress profiles, showing, for instance, a decrease
in one factor (e. g. reduction of impediment of motor
processes through more comfortable jigs) but an increase
in another (e. g. impediment of informational processes
through poorly arranged dials) gives a more complete
picture of the total impact due to the new environment.

RHIA also has application when comparing similar tasks
under different technical systems or organizational
concepts. This evaluation would allow identification of
the "best" solution; the one that produces the least
stress.

As Moldaschl and Weber (1986) have shown, RHIA analysis
can contribute to work task design at a time when task
description are still subject to definition.

The detailed description of the RB and their causes
together with the level of time binding, the characterization of monotonous conditions, and the estimation of the
degree ot time pressure, which are the main results of the
RHIA analysis, give work designers specific information
enabling design of a reduced-stress environment.

ACKNOWLEDGEMENT

We are grateful to Mark Weitzel for his assistance in
translation of this paper.

REFERENCES

Bartenwerfer, H., 1957, Über die Auswirkungen einförmiger
Arbeitsvorgänge. Untersuchungen zum Monotonieproblem.
    (Marburg: Elwert).
Bortz, J.,1984, Lehrbuch der empirischen Forschung.
    (Berlin: Springer).
Fahrenberg, J., 1975, Die Freiburger Beschwerdeliste FBL.
    Zeitschrift für klinische Psychologie, 4 79-100.
Greif, S., Bamberg, E., Dunckel, H., Mohr, G., Rückert,D.,
    Rummel, M., Semmer, N. and Zapf, D., 1983, Psychischer
    Streß am Arbeitsplatz - Hemmende und fördernde Bedin-
    gungen für humanere Arbeitsplätze. Abschlußbericht an
    den Projektträger HdA, (Berlin, West): Institut für
    Psychologie der Freien Universität Berlin (Photodruck)
    2 Bände.
Gubser, A., 1968, Monotonie im Industriebetrieb. Schriften
    zur Arbeitspsychologie, (Bern: Huber), Band 11.

Hacker, W., 1980, Allgemeine Arbeits- und Ingenieurpsychologie. Psychische Struktur und Regulation von Arbeitstätigkeiten. In: Schriften zur Arbeitspsychologie,
   edited by E. Ulich (Bern: Huber Verlag), Band 20.
Hacker, W. and Richter, P., 1984, Psychische Fehlbeanspru-
   chung. (Berlin: Springer).
Hennes, K., 1986, Theoretische Überlegungen und experimen-
   telle Untersuchungen zum Problem monotoner Arbeits-
   bedingungen. Sind Frauen monotonieresistent? (Berlin:
   Freie Universität Berlin) (unpublished diploma thesis).
Kirchner, H.-J., 1986, Belastungen und Beanspruchungen .
   Zeitschrift für Arbeitswissenschaft, 2,40,69-74.
Leitner, K., Volpert, W., Greiner, B., Weber, W., and
   Hennes, K., 1987, Analyse psychischer Belastung in der
   Arbeit. Das RHIA-Verfahren. Handbuch und Manual. (Köln:
   Verlag TÜV Rheinland).
Martin, E., Ackermann, U., Udris, I., and Oegerli, K.,
   1980, Monotonie in der Industrie. Schriften zur
   Arbeitspsychologie, Band 29, (Bern: Huber).
Mohr,G., 19816, Die Erfassung psychischer Befindensbeein
   trächtigungen bei Industriearbeitern. (Frankfurt a. M.:
   Peter Lang).
Moldaschl, M. and Weber, W.-G., 1986, Prospektive Arbeits-
   platzbewertung an flexiblen Fertigungssystemen. Psy-
   chologische Analyse von Arbeitsorganisationen, Qualifi-
   kation und Belastung. In: Forschungen zum Handeln in
   Arbeit und Alltag, edited by W. Volpert and R. Oester-
   reich (Berlin: Technische Universität), Band 1.
Nachreiner,F. and Wucherpfennig, D., 1975, Arbeits- und
   sozialpsychologische Aspekte der Arbeit unter Zeit
   druck. Betriebsärztliches, 2, 22-36.
Oesterreich, R., 1981, Handlungsregulation und Kontrolle.
   (München: Urban & Schwarzenberg).
Oesterreich, R. and Volpert, W., 1987, Handlungs-
   theoretisch orientierte Arbeitsanalyse. Arbeits-
   psychologie. Enzyklopädie der Psychologie, edited by J.
   Rutenfranz and U. Kleinbeck, Themenbereich D, Serie
   III, Band 1, (Göttingen: Hogrefe).
Udris, I., 1982, Psychische Belastung und Beanspruchung.
   In: Belastung und Streß am Arbeitsplatz. Humane Arbeit
   - Leitfaden dür Arbeitnehmer, edited by L. Zimmermann
   (Reinbek: Rowohlt), Band 5, pp. 110 121.
Ulich, E., 1960, Unterforderung als arbeitspsychologisches
   Problem. Psychologie und Praxis, 4, 156 - 161

Volpert, W., 1975, Die Lohnarbeitswissenschaft und die
    Psychologie der Arbeitstätigkeit. In: Lohnarbeits-
    psychologie. Berufliche Sozialisation – Emanzipation
    zur Anpassung, edited by P. Groskurth and W. Volpert
    (Frankfurt a. M.: Fischer), 11–196.
Volpert, W., 1979, Der Zusammenhang von Arbeit und
    Persönlichkeit aus handlungspsychologischer Sicht.
    In: Arbeit und Persönlichkeit – Berufliche Sozialisa-
    tion in der arbeitsteiligen Gesellschaft, edited by P.
    Groskurth (Reinbeck: Rowohlt Taschenbuch), p. 21–46.
Volpert, W., 1987, Psychische Regulation von Arbeits-
    tätigkeiten. In: Arbeitspsychologie. Enzyklopädie der
    Psychologie, edited by J. Rutenfranz and U. Kleinbeck
    (Göttingen: Hofgrefe), Themenbereich D, Serie III,
    Band 1.
Volpert, W., Oesterreich, R., Gablenz-Kolakovic, S.,
    Krogoll, T. and Resch, M., 1983, Verfahren zur
    Ermittlung von Regulationserfordernissen in der
    Arbeitstätigkeit (VERA). Handbuch und Manual. (Köln:
    Verlag TÜV Rheinland).

VALIDITY OF VARIOUS METHODS OF MEASUREMENT IN JOB ANALYSIS

N. Semmer
University of Bern,
Switzerland

D. Zapf
University of Munich
Federal Republic of Germany

INTRODUCTION

An important aim in work related stress research is to investigate relations between work stressors and stress reactions like somatic complaints or psychological dys-functioning. From a methodological point of view, much of this research is often criticized for the following reasons:

(1) In many studies both work stress and stress reactions are measured by incumbents' ratings only. Relationships between the two are often suspected to be method artifacts because of a lack of discriminant validity between independent and dependent variables which are both measured by self-report (Kasl, 1978, 1986). However, we could show in our own research (Greif et al., 1983; Greif et al. 1989) that this critique is only partly true. Using different measures of work stressors, we could show that the common variance between stressors and psychosomatic complaints could in part be explained by method variance. However, a substantial part of common variance was due to true variance (Zapf, 1989a,b).

(2) Those studies which used other methods of measurement like observers' ratings often show rather low relations between independent and dependent variables. Therefore, the relevance of these relationships could be called into question. However, one has to consider first that relationships between stressors and stress reactions are usually underestimated for methodological reasons when stressors are measured by observer data and stress reactions by questionnaires (Zapf, 1989a), and second, there

67

are a lot of theoretical reasons that relationships between work stressors and stress reactions may not be very
high but nevertheless very important (Frese, 1985; Frese &
Zapf, 1988; Semmer et al., 1988).

The analyses presented here are intended to carry our
analyses of the validity of job analysis data somewhat
further. They concentrate on convergent and discriminant
validity between stressors. As already mentioned, we could
show discriminant validity between stressors and stress
reactions. But is there also discriminant validity between
several stressors? Can they be empirically differentiated?
Furthermore: Which method of measurement shows best validity for which stressor? In particular, observers' ratings
show strong halo-effects (e.g. Algera, 1983; Greif et al.,
1983; Jenkins et al., 1975; Semmer, 1984. C.f. Zapf,
1989a, for further literature). So, how many stressors can
external observers differentiate?

Usually, work related stress studies investigate
whether stress at work in general relates to indicators of
health and well-being in general. The more specific question of which stressors are related to what kind of stress
reaction is investigated rather seldom (for an exception,
see Broadbent, 1985). Studies on the discriminant validity
of stressor measurement are an important prerequisite for
this kind of specific study.

METHODOLOGICAL CONSIDERATIONS

In the following part we concentrate on the question of
discriminant and convergent validity of work stressors.
Convergent and discriminant validity can best be investigated within the multitrait-multimethod matrix first
introduced by Campbell and Fiske (1959). Complete analyses
can be done if there are at least three traits and three
methods.

Multitrait-multimethod data (MTMM data) are best analyzed with linear structural equations, in particular con-
firmatory factor analyses (CFA) (for details see Dwyer,
1983, Kalleberg & Kluegel, 1975; Kenny, 1979; Schmitt,
1978; Schmitt & Stults, 1986; Schwarzer, 1982; Widaman,
1985), e.g. using the computer program LISREL˅V (Jîreskog
& Sîrbom, 1981). LISREL offers many advantages: First, it
is possible to compare different theoretical models with
given empirical data. Second, LISREL combines a **measurement model** which describes the relationship between
(empirical) indicators and the (theoretical) latent variables which are to be estimated and a **structural model**

which describes relationships between the theoretical constructs. The measurement models follow the logic of factor analysis, the structural models follow the logic of path analysis (c.f. Dwyer, 1983).

The worst assumption with regard to validity leads to the specification of a so-called **"Method Model"**. It implies no correlation between different measures of a latent stressor because the indicators are exclusively determined by the method used, e.g questionnaire or observer ratings. This would indicate a complete lack of convergent validity, and if there is no convergent valid- ity there is also no discriminant validity between stres- sors.

The simple counterpart to this Method Model is the **Trait Model**. It assumes that all indicators of a stressor measure exactly what they ought to. Thus, indicators of time pressure measure time pressure, indicators of uncer- tainty measure uncertainty etc. This would imply high con- vergent as well as discriminant validity.

A more sophisticated alternative to these naïve assump- tions of the Trait Model would be a **Multitrait-Multi- method-Model** (MTMM-model I). It implies that each empiri- cal indicator is influenced both by the trait it should measure and the measurement method used (for a detailed description of this research strategy see Zapf, 1989a). Provided that there is some convergent validity, **discrimi- nant** validity can be demonstrated if (1) indicators do not load on a "wrong" latent stressor, that is, a stressor they are not intended to measure (MTMM model II), and (2) correlations between (at least two) latent stressors are equal to 1 (MTMM model III, that is, the stressors cannot be distinguished (c.f. Widaman, 1985). To the extent that there is discriminant validity, models that make these assumptions should not fit the data well.

Widaman (1985) has criticized the fact that in a lot of studies a rationale for the analysis of MTMM – data is lacking. As a consequence, the results are often inciden- tal. He presents a general scheme which allows a decision whether any models are hierarchically nested. Two models are hierarchically nested if a model with more free param- eters includes all free and fixed parameters of the more restricted model using the same set of observed variables (Jîreskog & Sîrbom, 1981). As a strategy for analyzing MTMM – data, Widaman (1985) suggests a systematic intro- duction of method and trait factors. One can consider a trait model as a special MTMM model without method factors and the method model as a special MTMM model without trait factors. Both models are hierarchically nested in the MTMM model. For reasons of parsimony we confine ourselves to the presented models, although a lot of other models could be tested (c.f. Zapf, 1989a, Semmer et al., 1988).

SAMPLE

This chapter is based on a study of stress at work in nine different steel and automobile companies in the Federal Republic of Germany. All subjects were male blue-collar workers whose mother tongue was German and who had worked for at least one year at their respective work places. A wide range of blue collar workers was included. Subjects were selected by multiple random drawings. In the first step the names of blue-collar workers were drawn from the company pay register. Once a worker was in this random sample, three or more persons who were doing the same kind of work were randomly selected. All in all, 842 workers were interviewed and 406 workers were observed (for details, c.f. Frese, 1985, Greif et al., 1983, Udris, Dunckel & Mohr, 1989).

In general, the measures used in this study were first developed after a qualitative interview study with open ended exploratory questions. They were then tested in several pilot studies in which care was taken to ascertain that the items were understandable and that the scales were reliable (a detailed description of all measures, item characteristics, internal consistency of scales etc. can be found in Zapf et al., 1983).

For the measurement of stressors at work, Semmer (1982, 1984) has developed an Instrument for **ST**ress-oriented **A**nalysis of work (ISTA, see also Dunckel & Semmer, 1987, Semmer & Dunckel, 1989). The instrument is standardized and objective in the sense that general work characteristics are measured independently of individual performance. Since we wanted to measure job characteristics by various methods, the instrument includes a **questionnaire** version for the incumbents themselves, and a **rating version** for trained observers. Items which were aggregated to scales were estimated by trained observers after an observation period of one and a half to two hours. (More information on the observation and the inter-rater reliabilities are given in Semmer, 1982, 1984 and Greif et al., 1983.) As far as possible the workers had to answer the same items. As already mentioned, several workers with the same jobs were interviewed. For each job where three or more persons performing the same task (but not necessarily working

together in the same group) filled out the questionnaire,
the median of their scores for each job dimension was used
as a **group estimate**. This group estimate was used as a
third indicator of job characteristics, in addition to
self-report and observer data. Since there were some jobs
with fewer than 3 workers, the number of cases for which
we attained group measures is smaller than the overall
number of subjects. Altogether, there were 274 cases where
individual, group, and observers' estimates could be calculated.

RESULTS AND DISCUSSION

The results for each of the models, analyzed with
LISREL˘V of Jîreskog & Sîrbom (1981) are presented in
Table˘1. (For an illustration of how to specify MTMM data
with LISREL, see Dwyer, 1983, Schmitt & Stults, 1986).

Table 1: LISREL – parameters for stressors

	df	chi	p	GFI	AFI	RMR	rho	delta
Null-model	105	1740.50	0	.41	.33	.30	0	0
Method-model	87	608.99	0	.73	63	.09	.61	.65
Trait-model	80	643.34	0	.70	.55	.11	.55	.63
MTMM-model I methods orthog.	65	105.28	.00	.93	.88	.05	.96	.9
MTMM-model II	64	85.41	.04	.95	.90	.04	.98	.95
MTMM-model III	65	119.88	0	.93	.87	.04	.95	.93
MTMM-model IV methods correlated	62	99.69	.00	.93	.87	.05	.96	.94

Table 1 is to be read as follows: LISREL V calculates
chi^2 estimates for each˘model. For the degrees of freedom
(df) given, the probability is calculated that the empirical data could stem from the theoretical model. (Note that
this is in opposition to the usual application of chi^2,
where one is interested in high chi^2 values. In LISREL
small chi^2 values stand for high similarity of the theoretical model and the empirical data.) Since the chi^2 test
is dependent on sample size, some more parameters for the
fit of the whole model are necessary: the Goodness of fit
index (GFI) and the Adjusted goodness of fit (AFI), which
should be above .90, and the root mean squares residuals

(RMR), which should be less than .05 (Jöreskog & Sörbom, 1981). Bentler & Bonett suggest two more indices: rho is a relative index of the degree of off-diagonal covariance among the observed variables. Delta is the absolute measure. Both measures should be above .90, otherwise the models could easily be improved (Bentler & Bonett, 1980; Widaman, 1985). The so called null model is necessary to compute rho and delta. Finally, Schmitt (1978) suggests that a chi^2/df ratio larger than 10 indicates an inadequate fit, while a chi^2/df ratio less than 1.00 indicates the model fits too well. Such a model would be unlikely to remain stable in future samples.

The results are to be interpreted as follows: (1) The assumption of a complete lack of convergent validity which is modelled by the **method model** does not fit the empirical data. (2) However, simple models of convergent validity like the **Trait Model** also cannot explain the empirical data, the parameters do not satisfy the criteria for an acceptable model, as Table 1 shows. (3) The **MTMM** models which assume that all indicators are influenced both by the latent traits and by the methods are much better than the trait and the method model. (3.1) The parameters of the MTMM-model with **uncorrelated method factors** already explain the empirical data quite well (MTMM-model I). (3.2) The model with correlated method factors is not significantly better (MTMM model IV). This means that the methods used in this study are sufficiently independent. (3.3) However, the maximum modification index (Jöreskog & Sörbom, 1981) of MTMM-model I shows a mis-specification for the observer indicator of danger. An additional free parameter of this indicator on the latent stressor time pressure leads to a considerable improvement of the model (MTMM-model II). All parameters of this model achieve the criteria for an acceptable model mentioned above. Obviously, the observers were not able to estimate the risk of accidents at work independently of the time pressure they observed. Rather, they inferred this risk from the time pressure given. (3.4) A further test for discriminant validity is modelled in the MTMM model III where the highest latent correlation between two stressors is fixed to 1. It is the correlation between time pressure and uncertainty (cf. Table 2). This would imply that one cannot differentiate between these two stressors. However, this model is worse than the model without fixed latent correlations. Thus, the best model is the MTMM model II which is shown in Figure 1.

loadings on the
method factors

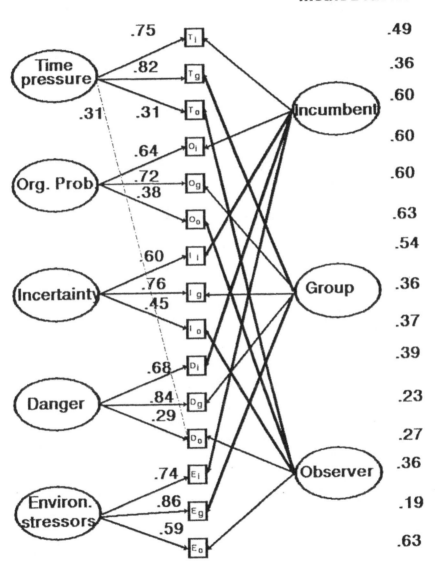

Figure 1. LISREL estimates of the MTMM model II

Figure 1 shows in the middle all indicators used in
this study. They all have loadings both on a **trait** factor
(five stressors on the left side of Figure 1) and a **method
factor** (three method factors on the right side of Figure
1). There is a more or less strong method bias for all
used measurement methods, as shown by the loadings on the
method factors. The high loadings of the observer data on
their respective method factor show the halo-effect which
has often been found for such data. Observers seem to have
more difficulties in differentiating between stressors
than job incumbents themselves. The loadings on the trait
factors can be interpreted as validity coefficients. They
are sufficient, albeit not very high, for the observer
data.

The MTMM Model contains correlations of the latent
stressors. They are not shown in Figure 1 because of clarity but are summarized in Table 2. In some cases, they are
rather high. But, as demonstrated by the rejection of the
MTMM model III, they are significantly different from 1.

Table 2: correlations between latent stressors

	Org. Prob.	uncert.	danger	environmental stressors
time pressure	.53	.77	.39	.51
Org problems		.56	.28	.41
uncertainty			.41	.58
danger				.65

In sum, the data show the following:
(1) In line with many other analyses we have conducted,
these analyses show that results **are** influenced by method
variance but they cannot be simply reduced to measurement
artifacts. Rather, all indicators are influenced **both** by
method variance **and** by true variance.
(2) Going beyond this general statement, the analyses
we presented specifically show that it is possible to
distinguish various stressors. Their correlation is not
equal to 1, that is, there is discriminant validity.
(3) There are problems of validity, however, with one
of the latent variables, that is "Danger" when measured by
observation. This is reflected by the factor loading of

the observer indicator of danger in the latent factor time pressure (MTMM-model II). Obviously, the observers partly inferred the existence of accident risks from the existence of time pressure.

This also implies that questions like" are questionnaire data valid?" or "are observer data valid?" do not make much sense. One has to ask much more specifically: Do questionnaire (observer etc.) data yield valid measures of a specific variable? No method can **a priori** be assumed superior, and strength as well as weaknesses may be very specific.

(4) In general, the best single measure seema to be our group data, as shown by the high loadings on the latent stressors. They do not have the bias of individual incumbents'rating and are not afflicted with the observation problems of external observers.

Self reports are sometimes regarded as useless and invalid, while other measures, such as observer data, are seen more favourably. Our results show a) that self reports are not without distortions but that these do not render them completely invalid, and b) that choosing other methods of assessment such as observation is no general remedy, as these also have their problems.

Supplementing self report data by observation data is, therefore, no cure. Rather, **multiple methods of assessment** should be used, and their **combined information** promises to yield more valid data.

(5) While it seems a promising strategy to complement self-report data by observation data or the so-called "observation-interview" (Morsh, 1964; Frieling, 1975; Hacker et al., 1983; Leitner et al., 1987; Semmer, 1984; Volpert et al., 1983), the introduction of new technologies sets limits to this strategy. New technologies lead to an increase of mental work. Mental processes cannot be observed, and even an observation interview depends very much on the incumbents' statements (c.f. Rîdiger, 1988). At the same time, the increasing possibilites of individualized work design (Ulich, 1978, 1983) associated with new technologies sets limits to our method of group data, as there might be less and less cases where several people are performing the same tasks.

Therefore, additional methods of assessment have to be used and developed, such as experimental methods (cf. Matern, 1984), analyses of errors (cf. Moll & Ulich, 1987), etc. Using the information from these methods of assessment and applying them in analyses which allow to combine them by statistical models like linear structural equations, is a promising way of dealing with the problems of validity in psychological job analysis.

REFERENCES

Algera, J.A. (1983). "Objective" and perceived task characteristics as a determinant of reactions by task performers. Journal of Occupational Psychology, 56, 95-107.

Campbell, D.T., Fiske, D.W. (1959). Convergent and discriminant validation by the multitrait-multimethod matrix. Psychological Bulletin, 56, 81-105.

Bentler, P.M., Bonett, D.G. (1980). Significance tests and goodness-of-fit in the analysis of covariance structures. Psychological Bulletin, 88, 588-606.

Broadbent, D.E. (1985). The clinical impact of job design. British Journal of Clinical Psychology, 24, 33-44.

Dunckel, H., Semmer, N. (1987). Streßbezogene Arbeitsanalyse: Ein Instrument zur AbschÑtzung von Belastungsschwerpunkten in Industriebetrieben. In Kh. Sonntag (Ed.), Arbeitsanalyse und Technikentwicklung (pp. 163-177). Köln: Wirtschaftsverlag Bachem.

Dwyer, J.E. (1983). Statistical Models for the Social and Behavioral Sciences. New York: Oxford University Press.

Frese, M. (1985). Stress at work and psychosomatic complaints: a causal interpretation. Journal of Applied Psychology, 70, 314-328.

Frese, M., Zapf, D. (1988). Methodological Issues in the Study of Work Stress: Objective vs. Subjective Measurement and the Question of Longitudinal Studies. In C.L. Cooper & R. Payne (Eds.), Causes, Coping, and Consequences of Stress at Work. Chichester: Wiley.

Frieling, E. (1975). Psychologische Arbeitsanalyse. Stuttgart: Kohlhammer.

Greif, S., Bamberg, E., Dunckel, H., Frese, M., Mohr, G., Rückert, D., Rummel, M., Semmer, N., Zapf, D. (1983): Psychischer Streß am Arbeitsplatz - hemmende und fördernde Bedingungen für humane Arbeitsplätze. Unpublished research report: Osnabrück.

Greif, S., Semmer, N., Bamberg, E. (1989). Psychischer Streß am Arbeitsplatz. Göttingen: Hogrefe, in press.

Hacker, W., Iwanowa, A., Richter, P. (1983). Tätigkeits-Bewertungssystem. Berlin (DDR): Diagnostisches Zentrum.

Jöreskog, K.G., Sörbom, D. (1981). LISREL V: Analysis of linear structural relationships by maximum likelyhood and least squares methods. Uppsala, Sweden: University of Uppsala.

Kalleberg, A.L., Kluegel, J.R. (1975). Analysis of the
   multitrait-multimethod matrix: Some limitations and an
   alternative. Journal of Applied Psychology, 60, 1-9.
Kasl, S.V. (1978). Epidemiological Contributions to the
   Study of Work Stress. In C.L. Cooper & R. Payne (Eds.),
   Stress at Work (pp. 3-48). Chichester: Wiley.
Kasl, S.V. (1986). Stress and Disease in the Workplace: A
   Methodological Commentary on the Accumulated Evidence.
   In M.F. Cataldo & Th.J. Coates (Eds.), Health and
   Industry. A Behavioral Medicine Perspective. New York:
   Wiley.
Kenny, D.A. (1979). Correlation and Causality.
   New York: Wiley.
Leitner, K., Volpert, W., Greiner, B., Weber, W.G.,
   Hennes, K. (1987). Analyse psychischer Belastung in der
Arbeit. Das RHIA-Verfahren. Köln: Verlag TÜV Rheinland.
Moll, T., Ulich, E. (1988). Einige methodische Fragen in
   der Analyse von Mensch-Computer-Interaktionen.
   Zeitschrift für Arbeitswissenschaft, 42, 70-76.
Morsh, J.E. (1964). Job analysis in the United States Air
   Force. Personnel Psychology, 17, 7-17.
Rödiger, K.H. (1988). Das Arbeitsanalyseverfahren VERA/B
   in der Softwareentwicklung. In E. Nullmeier & K.-H.
Rödiger (Eds.), Dialogsysteme in der Arbeitswelt (pp. 185-
   205). Mannheim: Wissenschaftsverlag.
Schmitt, N. (1978). Path analysis of multitrait
   multimethod matrices. Applied Psychological Measure
   ment, 2, 157-178.
Schmitt, N, Stults, D.M. (1986). Methodological Review:
   Analysis of Multitrait-Multimethod Matrices. Applied
   Psychological Measurement, 10, 1-22.
Schwarzer, R. (1982). Convergent and discriminant valida-
   tion in personality assessment: Techniques for
   distinguishing trait and method variance. Paper
   presented at the meeting of the American Educational
   Research Association. New York.
Semmer, N. (1982). Stress at Work, Stress in Private Life,
   and Psychological Well-Being. In W. Bachmann &
   I. Udris (Eds.), Mental Load and Stress in Activity.
   Amsterdam: North Holland.
Semmer, N. (1984). Streßbezogene Tätigkeitsanalyse.
   Weinheim: Beltz.
Semmer, N., Dunckel, H. (1989). Tätigkeitsanalyse. In
   S. Greif, N. Semmer & E. Bamberg (Eds.), Psychischer
   Streß am Arbeitsplatz. Göttingen: Hogrefe, in press.

Semmer, N. Zapf, D. Greif, S. (1988). Stressbezogene
  Arbeitsanalyse und arbeitsplatzbezogenes Befinden.
  Vortrag auf dem 36. Kongreß der Deutschen Gesellschaft
  für Psychogie. Bern, München, Osnabrück: Manuscript.
Udris, I. (1981). Redefinition als Problem der Arbeits-
  analyse. In F. Frei & E. Ulich (Eds.), Beiträge zur
  psychologischen Arbeitsanalyse (pp. 283-302).
  Bern: Huber.
Udris, I., Dunckel, H., Mohr, G. (1989). Das Projekt
  "Psychischer Streß am Arbeitsplatz": Methodischer
  Ansatz, Stichproben, Untersuchungsphasen. In S. Greif,
  N. Semmer & E. Bamberg (Eds.), Psychischer Streß am
  Arbeitsplatz. Göttingen: Hogrefe, in press.
Ulich, E. (1978). Über das Prinzip der differentiellen
  Arbeitsgestaltung. Industrielle Organisation, 47,
  566-568.
Ulich, E. (1983). Differentielle Arbeitsgestaltung – ein
  Diskussionsbeitrag. Zeitschrift für Arbeitswissen-
  schaft, 37, 12-15.
Volpert, W., Oesterreich, R., Gablenz-Kolakovic, S.,
  Krogoll, T., Resch., M. (1983). Verfahren zur Ermitt-
  lung von Regulationserfordernissen in der Arbeitstätig
  keit (VERA). Köln: TÜV Rheinland.
Widaman, K.F. (1985). Hierarchically nested covariance
  structure models for multitrait-multimethod data.
  Applied Psychological Measurement, 9, 1-26.
Zapf, D. (1989a). Selbst- und Fremdbeobachtung in der
  psychologischen Arbeitsanalyse. Methodische Probleme
  bei der Erfassung von Streß am Arbeitsplatz.
  Göttingen: Hogrefe.
Zapf, D. (1989b). Streß und Gesundheit: Realer Zusammen-
  hang oder Methodenartefakt. In S. Greif, N. Semmer & E.
Bamberg (Eds.), Psychischer Streß am Arbeitsplatz.
  Göttingen: Hogrefe, in press.
Zapf, D., Bamberg, E., Dunckel, H., Frese, M., Greif, S.,
  Mohr, G., Rückert, D., Semmer, N. (1983). Dokumentation
  der Skalen des Forschungsprojekts "Psychischer Streß am
  Arbeitsplatz – hemmende und fördernde Bedingungen für
  humane Arbeitsplätze. OsnabrÅck: Unpublished research
  report.

SITUATIONAL DIAGNOSIS VS. SOCIAL CONSTRUCTION OF JOBS
META ANALYSIS OF THE QUESTIONNAIRE "SUBJECTIVE JOB ANALYSIS"

Udris, I. / Nibel, H.

Work and Organizational Psychology Unit
Swiss Federal Institute of Technology, Zurich
Switzerland

(This paper was not available at the time of print.
A summary of its contents will be given below.)

Questionnaires for job and task analysis are primarily developed to measure aspects or "dimensions" of specific work situations. Job holders are asked to describe their job by using the dimensions of the questionnaire. The studies can be taken as a quasi-objective diagnosis of the work situation under study. This interpretation is questioned by authors of the "social information processing approach", SIP (e.g. Salanik & Pfeffer, 1978; Thomas & Griffin, 1983). According to the SIP approach, the descriptions of jobs are subject to social and reference group norms: They do not reflect the "objective" situation but are the result of a socially constructed "world of work".

The objective of the paper is twofold:
(1) to present the questionnaire "Sujective Job Analysis" (SAA) by Udris & Alioth (1980) which was developed as a diagnostic instrument for group surveys,
(2) to shed more light upon the validity of this instrument by examining the "situation diagnosis" vs. the "social construction" hypothesis.

The (German language) questionnaire SAA consists of 50 items grouped in six categories ("dimensions") and 14 subcategories which reflect Blauner's (1964) psychological theory of alienation. Additionally, the SAA measures aspects of work overload and underload. It is to some extent comparable to the "Job Description Survey" (JDS) by Hackman & Oldham (1975).

In order to study the validity of the SAA, a meta
analysis of the categories, sub-categories and items was
carried out on the basis of 22 different samples with a
total of 2300 subjects. The samples were grouped by type
of work (jobs in industry/production and in administration) and by education level of the subjects (semi-
skilled, skilled and college/university). Analysis of
variance were run to test the differences between the
groups.

The paper presents those results of the meta analysis
which are relevant to the question whether such job analysis questionnaires can be used as instruments of "situational diagnosis" to differentiate between types of jobs
or whether they do reflect social norms, attitudes, cognitive "schemes" or emotional reactions which are not an
effect of the "objective" quality of the job, but of its
"social construction". Improvements of the questionnaire
are recommended which consider the consequences for job
design and organizational development.

REFERENCES

Blauner, R., 1964, Alienation and Freedom. The Factory
    Worker and his Industry. Chicago, University Press

Hackman, J.R. and Oldham, G.R., 1975, Development of the
    Job Diagnostic Survey. Journal of Applied Psychology,
    60, pp. 159-170

Salanik, G. and Pfeffer, J., 1978, A social Information
    Processing Approach to Job Attitudes and Task Design.
    Administrative Science Quarterly, 23, pp. 224-253

Thomas, J. and Griffin, R., 1983, The social Information
    Processing Model of Task Design: A Review of the liter-
    ature. Academy of Management Review, 8, pp. 672-682

Udris, I. and Alioth, A., 1980, "Fragebogen zur Subjek-
    tiven Arbeitsanalyse" (SAA). In: Monotonie in der
    Industrie, edited by E. Martin, I. Udris, U. Ackermann
    and K. Oergeli (Bern: Huber) pp. 61-68 and 204-207.

METHOD FOR MONITORING PSYCHIC STRESS FACTORS BY OCCUPATIONAL HEALTH PERSONNEL

Anna-Liisa Elo

Institute of Occupational Health
SF-00250 Helsinki
Finland

INTRODUCTION

The concept 'job' comprises several tasks, but on the operational level (in job analysis methods), a job is often considered as one task. Human tasks can be classified in several ways. Fleishman and Quaintance (1984) identified five approaches to describing human tasks:
1. The criterion measures approach
2. Information theoretic approach
3. Task strategies approach
4. Ability requirement approach
5. Task characteristics approach

The first approach describes tasks on the basis of the criteria which should be reached, the second and third on the basis of those specific functions in which the person is involved when executing the task, and the fourth on the basis of the required resources. The last approach describes the task on the basis of its objective characteristics. In psychology, schemes relying on objective task descriptors are scarce, possibly because of psychologists' greater interest in human responses and processes than in situational variables (Fleishman and Quaintance 1984). However, the importance of situational variables has been emphasized in many psychology theories.

In stress research, the importance of the objective situation has been accentuated e.g. by Magnusson and Ekehammar (1975). They have measured the situation via the persons' own perception of it. This kind of approach has been criticized as measuring only the subjective environment (Roberts and Glick 1981). The person-environment fit theory of adaptation has postulated the objective environ-

ment as an essential aspect in contrast to the subjective
environment (French et al. 1981). However, the pragmatic
and philosophical problems in the measurement of the
objective environment are considered to be notable (Caplan
1987).

Job analysis methods describe jobs (work tasks) on the
basis of their objective characteristics. Some attempts
have been made to assess the objective stressfulness of
jobs, and methods have been developed to this end. Ergonomic checklists are one example of this. In psychology,
expert assessment methods have been developed in research
projects, but they are seldom used repeatedly (Hackman and
Lawler 1971, Gardell 1971, Semmer 1984). The main dimensions covered by these kinds of methods are responsibility, decision-making, precision, maintenance of attentiveness, variety, autonomy vs. pressure on performance, and
social contacts.

The roots of these methods can be found in the classical job satisfaction study of Turner and Lawrence (1965),
in which the "Requisite task attribute index" was developed. The index comprised the dimensions of variety,
autonomy, interaction, skill and knowledge, and responsibility. The dimension of autonomy or related concepts
(degrees of freedom, job decision latitude, control) has
later been emphasized as a modifier between the stressful
environment and the individual response (Karasek 1979), or
as the main job characteristic (Gardell 1971, Hackman and
Oldham 1976).

In recent years, the preventive approach has been
emphasized in occupational health care. Work conditions
should be monitored and designed to support workers' well-
being. Psycho-social factors have gained special attention
and methods for measuring them have been urged repeatedly
(Psychosocial factors at work 1986). An observation method
was developed for the assessment of psychic stress factors
to be included in the more traditional methods for screening health hazards (Elo 1982, Swedish and English translations 1986). The method was meant to be used by occupational health personnel. In Finland these people are
responsible for the health monitoring of work conditions.

The stress factor was defined as a deviation from an
optimal situation. This can be presented by the model of
underload and overload (Kahn 1973, Frankenhauser and
Gardell 1976, Figure 1). In the model underload and
overload are further divided into qualitative and quantitative load. In work stress research, underload and overload are usually measured by the workers' subjective

evaluation (e.g., questionnaires), which has been interpreted to measure the subjective person-environment fit
(Coburn 1976).

	UNDERLOAD	OVERLOAD
QUANTITATIVE	"TOO LITTLE"	"TOO MUCH"
QUALITATIVE	"TOO EASY"	"TOO DIFFICULT"

Figure 1. Underload and overload

The observation method was developed on the basis of
the central dimensions of the previous job analysis
methods and on the results of job stress research. Job
stress research has investigated the meaning of various
job characteristics on strain. The aim was to develop a
method to cover the most common underload and overload
situations in industrial jobs. Twelve stress factors are
defined in the method (Table 1). Other potential stress
factors, such as noise, chemicals, and physical load, must
also be taken into consideration when the overall assessment of psychic stress is made.

The objective of the study was to investigate the
applicability (reliability and validity) of the observation method for psychic stress factors at work.

The problems studied were:

1. Do different observers agree on the psychic stress
    factors of industrial jobs (reliability)?
2. Can they use the given concepts in the same way, and
    can they distinguish the concepts from one another
    (convergent and discriminant validity)?
3. Does the observation method cover the dimensions of
    qualitative and quantitative underload and overload
    and of control (content validity)?
4. Do the workers' opinions coincide with the observers'
    opinions?

MATERIAL AND METHODS

The reliability and validity of the method was investigated in two studies: in the first phase, in the paper,
electronics, and metal industries; and in the second
phase, in the rubber industry. One hundred jobs were
assessed (observation combined with an interview of the
supervisor) in five plants. For every job, the observations were made by five people. The observers were an
occupational health nurse, a safety delegate, a supervisor, and two psychologists. Four-point Likert-type
rating scales were used in this study. 211 workers from
55 jobs filled in a questionnaire about their perceptions
of the stress factors in their jobs.

The reliability of the observation method was studied
by interrater agreement. Validity was studied from different aspects. Construct validity was investigated with a
modification of the multitrait-multimethod matrix (multi-
trait-multirater) and with factor analysis (principal
axis). The connection of the possibility of controlling
one's situation at work to the different stress factors
was also investigated. The third aspect was the agreement
between the observers' and the workers' perceptions of the
stress factors.

The validity results were based on the sum scales which
were formed additively of the two psychologists' ratings.

The possibility of controlling one's situation at work
was measured by both observation and questionnaire:
1. Observed control, task level (2 items from AET):
   structural restraints and type of instruction given to
   the incumbent (AET, Rohmert and Landau 1979)
2. Perceived control, task and role level (4 items, questionnaire): planning of tasks, learning and development, skill and knowledge, and autonomy (Work stress
   questionnaire, Institute of Occupational Health, Helsinki).

RESULTS

The agreement on the psychic stress factors was satisfactory between the two psychologists, with a few excep-
tions (Table 1). Factors connected to human relations,
such as responsibility for other people, and burdensome
contacts, proved to be difficult to assess. The agreement
between the other assessors was somewhat lower but statistically significant.

Table 1. Reliability of the method (n=100)

Stress factor	Kendall coefficient of concordance[a]	Spearman-Brown index of reliability[b]
Responsibility for safety	0.51	0.84
Responsibility for other people	0.37	0.39
Responsibility for material values	0.55	0.79
Solitary work	0.62	0.79
Burdensome contacts	0.32	0.90
Repetitiveness	0.68	0.81
Forced pace	0.63	0.81
Structural restraints	0.59	0.71
Demands for attentiveness/combined with few stimuli	0.56	0.76
Demands for precise discriminations	0.40	0.70
Haste	0.51	0.89
Demands for complex decision-making	0.43	0.86
Overall assessment of psychic stress	0.54	0.81

[a] between all assessors, [b] between the two psychologists

The agreement between different assessors can also be interpreted as convergent validity, which was satisfactory. Discriminant validit was unsatisfactory in some cases. In one case the correlation between different stress factors was higher than between the same factors observed by different assessors. Repetitiveness and structural restraints correlated between different assessors r=.75 (reliability of repetitiveness was r=.69 and structural restraints r=.56)

Construct validity was investigated further by factor analysis. It partly revealed the dimensions of qualitative and quantitative underload and overload (Table 2). The factors were combinations of the basic concepts of underload and overload, as can be expected in real work situations.

Table 2. Factor analysis of the observed stress
factors (the highest loadings)

Factor	Loading
I Qualitative (under)load	
Structural restraints	0.78
Repetitiveness	0.73
Responsibility for material values	−0.71
Complex decision-making	−0.62
Overall assessment of psychic stress	0.37
II Quantitative overload	
Haste	0.80
Overall assessment of psychic stress	0.79
Forced pace	0.73
Repetitiveness	0.52
Structural restraints	0.40
III Qualitative overload	
Responsibility for safety	0.64
Attentiveness/few stimuli	0.58
Solitary work	0.46
(Overall assessment of psychic stress	0.21)

Variance explained: 53.3%.

The first factor described qualitative load, underload
and overload forming one dimension. The second factor
described quantitative overload combined with qualitative
underload. This kind of situation is typical in industrial
work, i.e. haste combined with repetitiveness. The overall
assessment of psychic stress had the strongest connection
with this factor. The third factor described a work situation where responsibility for safety is combined with high
demands for attentiveness in a low stimuli situation and
solitude. Qualitative overload and quantitative underload
are the basic dimensions in this kind of situation. The
factor of quantitative underload did not appear, probably
because it is exceptionally rare in working life.

The observed stress factors correlated highly both with
observed control and with the workers' self-assessment of
control (Table 3).

Table 3. Correlation between observed stress factors and control (observed control n=100 tasks, perceived control n=211 workers) and the workers' assessment of stress factors

Observed psychic stress factor	Observed control	Perceived control[a]	Perceived stress factor[a]
Responsibility for safety	.25	.24	.50
Responsibility for material values	.52	.32	.27
Solitary work	-.22	-.11	.60
Repetitiveness	-.84	-.44	.50
Forced pace	-.31	-.26	.59
Structural restraints	-.87	-.45	.43
Attentiveness/few stimuli	.32	.19	.34
Precise discriminations	-.28	-.24	.24
Haste	-.46	-.32	.48
Complex decision-making	.61	.38	.36
Overall assessment of psychic stress	-.68	-.46	–

n=211, r ≥ .22, p < .001   [a] questionnaire

The workers' self-assessment of the stress factors (sum scales of two items) correlated with the corresponding observed ones statistically significantly but not very highly.

DISCUSSION

The reliability of the observation method was satisfactory in the psychologists' use. The agreement in the assessment between the other people was lower, but statistically significant. Difficulty in the assessment of responsibility for other people and burdensome contacts may have been due to their low occurrence in industrial tasks, which also makes the statistical indices unreliable. The reliabilities could be heightened by detailed anchoring of

each category in the scales, but this might cause stereo-
typed assessment and reduction of validity. The reliability results can be interpreted also as an indication of
convergent validity.

The validity results were partly in accordance with
the theoretical basis of the method. The discriminant
validity of the separate stress factors was not satisfactory, but the basic dimensions of underload and overload
could be identified. However, quantitative underload was
not reprensented. The high correlations between different
stress factors may have been caused by their simultaneous
occurrence rather than by conceptual contamination. By
definition, only the concepts of repetitiveness and structural restraints are dependent on each other.

The results indicate, on one hand, that control is an
important variable in the psychic stressfulness of work
and, on the other hand, that the observation method
measures the possibilities of controlling one's situation
in work. In industrial tasks responsibility and complex
decision-making are often positive rather than negative
factors.

The correspondence between the observers' and the workers' assessments of the stress factors was only partly
satisfactory. Quantitative stress factors were assessed in
better agreement than qualitative ones. The reasons for
the problems are found on every level of the measurement.
Weaknesses can be found in the reliability and validity of
the measures. Problems relating to workers' self-assessment of the characteristics of their work have earlier
been discussed under the concepts of redefinition of the
task, social information processing, and the cognitive
model. Similar problems are involved in the observation of
environment, altough they are usually discussed under the
concept of bias. The problems in the measurement of environment have not been overcome.

According to the results, the observation method is
feasibly valid and reliable for the preliminary monitoring
of work conditions. The method is widely used in Finland.
The experiences from the occupational health care centres
on workplaces have indicated that team work improves the
reliability and validity of the assessment of psychic
stress factors with this method. However, the changes in
work carried out on the basis of psychic stress factors,
should be based on more detailed information and planned
in cooperation with psychologists.

REFERENCES

Caplan, R.D., 1987, Person-environment fit theory and organizations: Commensurate dimensions, time perspectives, and mechanisms. Journal of Vocational Behaviour, 31, 248-267.

Coburn, D., 1975, Job-worker incongruence: consequences for health. Journal of Health and Social Behavior, 2, 198-212.

Elo, A-L., 1982, Psyykkisten kuormitustekijöiden arviointi työssä. Työterveyshuolto 7. (Helsinki: Työterveyslai tos).

Elo, A-L., 1986, Assessment of Psychic Stress Factors at Work. Occupational Health Care 7. (Helsinki: Institute of Occupational Health).

Fleishman, E.A. and Quaintance, M.K., 1984, Taxonomies of Human Performance. (Orlando, Florida: Academic Press, Inc.).

Frankenhauser, M. and Gardell, B., 1976, Underload and overload om working life: outline of a multidisciplinary approach. Journal of Human Stress, 3, 35-46.

French, J.R.P Jr., Rogers, W. and Cobb, S., 1981, A model of person-environment fit. In Society, Stress and Disease, Working life, vol 4, edited by L. Levi (Oxford: Oxford University Press).

Gardell, B., 1971, Produktionsteknik och arbetsglädje. (Stockholm: Personal Administrative Rådet).

Hackman, J.R. and Lawler III, E.E., 1971, Employee reactions to job characteristics. Journal of applied psychology monograph, 3, 259-286.

Hackman, J.R. and Oldham, G.R., 1976, Motivation through the design of work: Test of theory. Organizational Behavior and Human Performance, 16, 250-279.

Kahn, R.A., 1979, Job demands, job decision latitude and mental strain: Implications for job redesign. Administrative Science Quarterly, 24, 285-308.

Magnusson, D. and Ekehammar, B., 1975, Perceptions of reactions to stressful situations. Journal of Personality and Social Psychology, 6, 1147-1154.

Psychosocial Factors at work: Recognition and Control, 1986, Occupational Safety and Health Series No. 56. (Geneva: International Labour Office)

Roberts, K.H. and Glick, W., 1981, The job characteristics approach to task design: A critical review. Journal of Applied Psychology, 2, 193-217.

Rohmert, W. and Landau, K., 1979, <u>Das Arbeitswissenschaft-liche Erhebungsverfahren zur Tätigkeitsanalyse</u>. (Bern: Verlag Hans Huber)

Semmer, N., 1984, <u>Stressbezogene Tätigkeitsanalyse</u>. <u>Psychologische Untersuchungen zur Analyse von Stress am Arbeitsplatz</u>. (Weinheim und Basel: Beltz Verlag).

Turner, A.N. ad Lawrence, P.R., 1965, <u>Industrial Jobs and the Worker</u>. (Boston: Harvard University Press).

VERA MICROANALYSIS:
APPLIED TO A FLEXIBLE MANUFACTURING SYSTEM

Wolfgang-Georg Weber and Rainer Oesterreich

University of Technology Berlin
Federal Republic of Germany

INTRODUCTION

With VERA ("Verfahren zur Ermittlung von Regulationserfordernissen in der Arbeitstätigkeit", "Instrument to
Identify Regulation Requirements in Industrial Work"; Volpert, et al., 1983) the extent of a worker's planning-,
thought- and decision-processes required by the industrial
work task can be assessed. The analysis of these cognitive
processes is based on a general psychological ten-step-
model. Different industrial work tasks can be compared
regarding their mental requirements by using this empirically approved method.

In the case of a conventional application of VERA the
steps of regulation requirements for a whole work task are
identified. By VERA microanalysis a whole work task is
subdivided into a sequence of sub-tasks of which each is
analysed separately. Thus those parts of a work task which
are especially demanding (as to the human criterion of
regulation requirements) can be identified. At present
VERA microanalysis is applied within a research project*
that compares CNC work structures.

---

*"Arbeitspsychologische Typisierung und Bewertung ver-
schiedener Einsatzformen der CNC-Technologie unter
Gesichtspunkten humaner Arbeit" ("Industrial psychological typology and evaluation of different forms of
application of CNC technology considering aspects of
humane working conditions"), sponsored by the Federal
Ministry of Science and Technology (sign: 01HG 0278).

THE THEORETICAL MODEL

VERA is based on the action regulation theory which is a general psychological and industrial psychological theory (Volpert, 1982, 1987; Oesterreich, 1981; Hacker, 1973). The theory attempts to represent the regulation of human action and particularly of work action. Every kind of concrete human activity can be represented by a general psychological process structure consisting of interconnected single actions and movements with different complexity (see Volpert, 1982).

Among other things a specific model of regulation requirements for work activity has been developed which is based on general characteristics of human action organisation (Oesterreich, 1981). Depending on his position within the framework of industrial division of labour a working person faces certain goals and working conditions: these are his "action demands". The working person fulfils these action demands by an appropriate regulation of his/her work actions. From the psychological point of view action demands represent regulation requirements as well as regulation chances. The concept of regulation requirements is a theoretical generalisation of usual concepts in industrial psychology like "complexity", "scope of action" or "degrees of freedom" (see Volpert et al., 1983).

Through application of VERA it is investigated during the job analysis whether all actions a working person executes are directed exactly towards one single goal, i. e. whether they are directed to the work result. If so these work actions constitute exactly one work task, otherwise there will be several work tasks.

The instrument focus is the "ten-step-model of regulation requirements". With this model the level of regulation requirements of any industrial work task can be identified. A brief description of the model only can be given there (see Table 1).

Five "levels" of regulation requirements are subdivided into two "steps". If working tasks are included under a "restrictive step" (marked with an "R") it means that they do not demand active planning from the worker at the respective level, but only the carrying out of plans that already exist.

The lower the level of a particular work task, the stronger the "partialization" of the worker (see Volpert, 1975; Oesterreich and Volpert, 1986). He is denied complex planning processes and possibilities for learning; negative consequences for his psychic well-being and the condition of his physical health are possible.

Table 1: Ten-Step-Model of Regulation Requirements
(Synoptic Definition)

Level 5	Establishing new working processes
Step 5:	New interactive working processes, their coordination and material conditions are to be planned.
Step 5R:	As for Step 5; the new working processes are complements to processes already in operation, to which as few changes as possible should be made.
Level 4	Coordinating several working processes
Step 4:	Several sub-goal plans (in the sense of Step 3) for inter-acting parts of the working process are to be coordinated with one another.
Step 4R:	Although only sub-goal planning is required, conditions for other sub-goal plans (not to be formulated by the worker himself) must be considered here.
Level 3	Sub-goal planning
Step 3:	Only a roughly determined sequence of sub-activities can be planned in advance. Each of them requires the worker to make plans of his own (in the sense of Step 2). After the completion of a sub-activity, further action must be thought through.
Step 3R: in advance.	A sequence of sub-activities is determinded Each sub-activity requires the worker to make plans of his own.
Level 2	Action planning
Step 2:	The sequence of work steps must be planned in advance; the planning, however, only extends to the result of the work.
Step 2R:	The sequence of work steps is pre-ordained. However, it varies repeatedly to such an extent that it has to be mentally processed in advance.
Level 1	Sensory-motor regulation
Step 1:	No conscious planning is required for the projection of the sequence of work movements to be regulated, although a different tool occasionally has to be used.
Step 1R:	As for Step 1, but only the same tools are required in each case.

The method of investigation is an "observation interview" in the sense of a theory-aided assessment technique.
The strictly theory-related questions and instructions of
the VERA Manual are directed to a practically trained
investigator. By means of observation and interview of a
working person during his work performance the task can be
described as a sequence of actions and/or sub-actions.
Based on these sequences of work units regulation requirements can be identified, so the investigator relates concrete thought processes and movements of the working person with the
general model of mental structure and regulation of work
activities.

The analysis of regulation requirements is focused on
working conditions; individual characteristics of the single working person will not be taken into account. Moreover those action demands are registered which result from
goals and conditions for any sufficiently experienced
worker performing this task.

VERA has been tested on 260 industrial work tasks of
different branches and has been proved empirically. In the
meantime it has been applied to some hundred work places;
Swedish (Institutet för Arbets-Miljöforskning, Solna) and
Finnish (Helsinki University of Technology) translations
are available. Adaptations for the domain of mental labour
are in preparation (see Resch, M., 1988).

VERA MICROANALYSIS

A conventional VERA analysis identifies regulation
requirements for the work task as a whole. A whole work
task can be broken down analytically into "sub tasks" or
so-called work units. The object of VERA microanalysis
(Moldaschl and Weber, 1986) is the evaluation of these
work units. The assessment of regulation requirements of
single work units in addition to the conventional analysis
is a useful enlargement of VERA.

Depending on the goal of the work task, each work unit
has an "intermediate goal" which can be realized by means
of a "sub program". According to the complexity of the
whole work task, sub-programs can be related to simple
motor sequences or sensor performance (e. g. to set-up a
blank) as well as to more sophisticated parts of actions
(e. g. NC-programming; machine-setting).

The intermediate goal of a work unit can either be
material or cognitive (e. g. to understand the drawing of
a work piece). More detailed than in conventional VERA
application, the VERA microanalysis specifies for each

work unit the documents, tools, materials and machines used. If relevant to a work unit, parallel technical processes will be identified, too. The following case study shows the advantages of VERA microanalysis for the design of work tasks.

CASE STUDY: OPERATOR'S TASKS IN A FLEXIBLE MANUFACTURING SYSTEM

The case study (results are presented in Figure 1) is based on an observation for several days. Activities of operating on a flexible manufacturing system (FMS) were analysed during the testing period in the manufacturer's plant (see Moldaschl and Weber, 1986).

WORK UNITS OF THE SYSTEM OPERATOR	REGULATION REQUIREMENTS OF THE WORK UNIT (VERA-STEP)	WORK ORGANIZATION			
		TESTING PERIOD (CASE 1)	MANAGEMENT's CONCEPTION (CASE 2)	JOB-ENRICHMENT (CASE 3)	WORKING GROUP (CASE 4)
1 COORDINATION OF TASKS	4				■
2 SETTING THE ORDER OF BATCHES	2	■			■
3 PROGRAMMING AND OPTIMIZATION	3			○	○
4 TOOL PRE-SETTING AND STORAGE	1	■			
5 PREPARING THE HOLDING FIXTURE	2R		○	○	○
6 CLAMPING DOWN WORK-PIECES	1		○	○	○
7 WORK-PIECE SUPPLY AND REMOVAL	1R				
8 CONTROL OF THE ACCURACY IN SIZE	1				
9 CORRECTION OF WORK RESULTS	2R				
10 MONITORING	1	○			
11 SUPPORT OF MAINTENANCE	3R				
VERA-STEP OF THE TASK		2	2R	3	4

■ = work units carried out by the system operator
○ = work unit requires more than 15% of the total time

Figure 1: Regulation Requirements for the Operator's Work Task in an FMS with different Forms of Work Organization

The study was focused on the identification of regulation requirements (besides this, analysis of mental load
and communication requirements were performed, no further
mentioned here). Having conducted our analysis during the
testing period the FMS-manufacturer's conception for normal production conditons was evaluated in a prospective
way (see Ulich, 1980) and alternatives were drawn up.

Figure 1 shows a comparison of regulation requirements
of the work task "operation and monitoring of the machinery" with varying forms of work organization. Work units
that have been evaluated by microanalysis are represented
by synoptic terms. The FMS that has been analysed consists
of two CNC (4 axis-)machining centres, a handling system
for system loading with tools and work pieces (which are
clamped on work-holding fixtures) and an instrument for
tool presetting. An intergrated centralized tool magazine
and pallet-buffers minimize non-cutting times. Control of
the system is aided by an "organization computer" which is
superior to both machine computers. The FMS is designed
for the production of small and medium series of prismatic
work-pieces (drilling and milling). During the testing
period it was handled by two skilled workers working on
the shift. For full time running 1 - 1 1/2 operators
working on two shifts (in addition: night shift without
operator) are scheduled.

Case 1: Status Quo Analysis of the FMS Testing Period

The regulation requirements of the operator's whole
task during the testing period were evaluated as "Step 2"
(action planning). This results mainly from the fact that
the two operators have to set the order of the batches of
production parts (work unit 2). Therefore they receive
batches for 1 - 2 days ahead which they dispose in a way
to reduce changeover times (e. g. for installing holding
fixtures). Thus they obtain a temporal scope for carrying
out other work units. Two more work units (5 and 9) have
to be mentally processed in advance (step 2R): the assem-
blage of work holding fixtures using clamping elements
according to a given CAD drawing and the correction of
occurring weakness in the cutting process
(e. g. caused by tool wear or material weakness). However
most of the time is spent on routine activities of which
system monitoring (work unit 10) is predominant. These
operations do not require any planning- and decision processes. Work tasks on a higher level of regulation (1, 3,
11) have not been integrated into the FMS operation but
are separated organizationally.

Case 2: Prospective Evaluation of the Management-Concept for Normal Production

Interviews with managers of the manufacturer allow predictions of the concept proposed and recommended by the
manufacturer as to how the FMS shall run under conditions
of normal production: As setting the order of batches is
supposed to be withdrawn from the operator, regulation
requirements of the operator's task will decrease to step
2R (restrictive form of action planning). The "organization computer" which is connected with the department of
central production control will emit a list of priorities
including fixed times for the production of each lot;
appropriate part programmes will be transmitted by a DNC
system. Thus temporal scope will be reduced considerably.
The restrictive form of action planning will be left only
as for re-setting of piece-holding fixtures. If the correction of the system-software is completed and an integrated sensor system monitors the entire cutting operation, the majority of human activities will be loading
activities (work units 5 to 7). Most of the corrective
interventions will become unnecessary, and monitoring by
the working person will decrease sharply.

An FMS concept like this would be unfavourable because
in comparison with the tasks of skilled metal workers
(regulation requirements: level 3) it would cause a significant reduction of the FMS operator's qualifications.
From discussions with engineers who had been involved in
the development of the FMS, two alternative conceptions of
work design were proposed. For this purpose we had to take
into consideration the results of VERA microanalysis of
comparable (sub-)tasks such as "NC programming", "manufacturing control" and "preventive and corrective maintenance". These include higher regulation requirements and
could be used for job enrichment.

Case 3: Prospective Design: "Job Enrichment"

Programmes for new parts should be composed and opti-
mized by the system operator himself, aided by a decentralized programming system. Moreover he should be left to
set the order of the batches; thus a decrease of time
binding will give opportunity to coordinate programming
and other work units. Regulation requirements of the work
task that has been enriched in such a manner will reach
the level of sub-goal planning (level 3; work tasks for
conventional skilled metal workers usually include this

level). This is due to the fact that composition of part
programmes (work unit 3) requires sub-goals to be planned
by stages and to realize them step by step through appropriate action programmes (e. g. disposition of set-up and
machining sequences; translation of geometric and technological data into programme language, programme optimization and correction). However, this proposal can only be
realized for a spectrum of parts with extensive lot sizes
and relatively long operating times per work-piece. Otherwise, too little time for programming would be left to the
system operator.

Case 4: Prospective Design: "Semi-Autonomous Work Group"

Even the manufacturer noticed that a second system
operator (especially a "loader") would be needed for lot
sizes below average and if new programmes frequently
occurred. For this reason we are recommending a "two-
person-operation" of the FMS if job enrichment as
described in case 3 cannot be implement. In addition to
the work units mentioned in case 3, two highly skilled
system operators should perform work units as "coordination of tasks" (work unit 1) and "support of maintenance".
Depending on the manufacturer's structure, this can be
effected also by integrating the FMS into a decentralized
production island. This form of FMS operation would
include high regulation requirements (level 4: coordinat-
ing several working processes), because the workers would
have to coordinate their action fields in common. In this
arrangement they could optimize distribution of work,
through-put and trouble-shooting.

PRESENT APPLICATION OF VERA MICROANALYSIS

At present VERA microanalysis is applied within an
industrial psychological research project which aims to
investigate CNC technology in different firms. The analysis is based on a research manual, which includes the conventional VERA and instructions for carrying microanalysis. Organizationally connected work tasks of several NC-/
CNC- work structures (e. g. NC-programming, manufacturing
control, machine setter's activities, machine tool operation, quality assurance and maintenance) are compared
regarding the regulations requirements, mental load (see
Leitner et al., 1987) and task-related communication (see
Oesterreich and Resch, 1985). These work structures show
differences in work organization, level of automation,

degree of integration in an information technique network and economic conditions. Concerning regulation requirements different work task-structures will be typified and evaluated comparatively considering the following aspects:

- How do regulation requirements differ according to vary ing tasks (and work units) within respective types of work structures?

- Which differences do regulation requirements show if a comparable work task is performed in different working structures?

- What forms of CNC-work structures with relatively homogenous versus inhomogenous distributions of regulation requirements among all work task do exist?

In order to create an industrial and organizational psychology typology, it can be referred to the typologies of CNC-work organization already proposed by industrial engineers (e. g. Rempp et al., 1981, Nitzsche and Pfennig, 1988).

Based on results of the comparative investigation of work structures, a collection of examples will be developed including type-related recommendations suitable for work designers in the field of practice. It is a specific purpose of VERA microanalysis to identify those work units which are relevant for an "anthropocentric" reintegration of dispositive work tasks into skilled CNC labour (see Brödner, 1985; Erbe, 1986).

REFERENCES

Brödner, P., 1985, Fabrik 2000: Alernative Entwicklungspfade in die Zukunft der Fabrik. (Berlin: Edition Sigma Bohn).

Erbe, H.H., 1986, Die Werkstatt als Mittelpunkt des Fertigungsprozesses. In: Rechnergestützte Facharbeit, edited by M. Hoppe and H.-H. Erbe. (Wetzlar: Jungarbeiterinitiative), Band 7, 33–48.

Hacker, W., 1973, Allgemeine Arbeits- und Ingenieurpsychologie. Psychische Struktur und Regulation von Arbeitstätigkeiten. (Berlin DDR: Deutscher Verlag der Wissenschaften).

Leitner, K., Volpert, W., Greiner, B., Weber, W.-G. and Hennes, K., 1987, Analyse psychischer Belastung in der Arbeit. Das RHIA-Verfahren. Handbuch and Manual. (Köln: Verlag TÜV Rheinland).

Moldaschl, M., and Weber, W.-G., 1986, Prospektive
   Arbeitsplatzbewertung an flexiblen Fertigungssystemen.
   Psychologische Analyse von Arbeitsorganisation, Quali-
   fikation und Belastung. In: Forschungen zum Handeln in
   Arbeit und Alltag, edited by W. Volpert and R. Oester-
   reich (Berlin: Technische Universität), Band 1.
Nitzsche, M. and Pfennig, V., 1988, Einsatz von CNC-
   Werkzeugmaschinen. Organisation, Arbeitsteilung, Quali-
   fikation. (Köln: TÜV Rheinland).
Oesterreich, R., 1981, Handlungsregulation und Kontrolle.
   (München: Urban and Schwarzenberg).
Oesterreich, R. and Resch, M.-G., 1985, Zur Analyse
   arbeitsbezogener Kommunikation. Zeitschrift für Sozia-
   lisationsforschung und Erziehungssoziologie, 2, 271-
   290.
Oesterreich, R. and Volpert, W., 1986, Task analysis for
   work design on the basis of action regulation theory.
   Economic and Industrial Democracy,7, 503-527.
Rempp, H., Boffo, M. and Lay, G., 1981, Wirtschaftliche
   und soziale Auswirkungen des CNC-Werkzeugmaschinen-
   einsatzes. (Karlsruhe: Fraunhofer-Institut für System-
   technik und Innovationsforschung).
Resch, M., 1988, Die Handlungsregulation geistiger Arbeit
   (Bern: Huber).
Ulich, E., 1980, Psychologische Aspekte der Arbeit mit
   elektronischen Datenverarbeitungssystemen. Schweize-
   rische Technische Zeitschrift, 75, 66-68.
Volpert, W., 1975, Die Lohnarbeitswissenschaft und die
   Psychologie der Arbeitstätigkeit. In: Lohnarbeits-
   psychologie. Berufliche Sozialisation: Emanzipation zur
   Anpassung, edited by P. Groskurth and W. Volpert
   (Frankfurt a. M.: Fischer), pp. 11-196.
Volpert, W., 1982, The model of the hierarchical-
   sequential organization of action. In: Cognitive and
   motivational aspects of action, edited by W. Hacker, W.
   Volpert and M. v. Cranach (Amsterdam: North Holland
   Publishing Company), pp. 35-51.
Volpert, W., 1987, Psychische Regulation von Arbeits-
   tätigkeiten. In: Arbeitspsychologie. Enzyklopädie der
   Psychologie, edited by J. Rutenfranz and U. Kleinbeck
   (Göttingen: Hogrefe), Themenbereich D, Serie III,
   Band 1. pp. 1-42.
Volpert, W., Oesterreich, R., Gablenz-Kolakovic, S.,
   Krogoll, T. and Resch, M., 1983, Verfahren zur
   Ermittlung von Regulationserfordernissen in der
   Arbeitstätigkeit (VERA). Handbuch und Manual. (Köln:
   TÜV Rheinland).

ANALYSING THE SOCIAL IMPACT OF NEW TECHNOLOGIES IN THE ENGINEERING OFFICE

Martin Resch

University of Hannover
Federal Republic of Germany

INTRODUCTION

Computer Aided Design (CAD) is one of the more recent computer applications in domains which seem to be dominated by skilled human labour. It has increasingly attracted social science research (see e.g. Rader et al., 1988, Frieling and Klein, 1988). Our research project, however, is concerned with a branch hardly explored. In addition, there is a lack of psychological job analysis tools for this type of mental labour. We are testing a newly developed job analysis instrument for mental labour, the VERA-G, in a rather unknown research field, the building and construction trade.

THE RESEARCH PROJECT

Our research project analyses the "introduction of computer aided design in civil engineering offices". It is sponsored by the German Federal Ministry of Research and Technology within the programme "humanization of working life". We are a team of sociologists, psychologists and engineers.

The situation in the civil engineering branch can in short be described as follows: Many independent partners are usually involved in building projects: the client commissions an architect, who himself commissions engineering offices and construction firms. One of the main tasks of engineering offices is to carry out the stress calculations for the building and to produce the building plans.

The average engineering office has about nine or ten employees, but there exist one-person-offices as well as

firms with about 300 employees. In the last few years a
lot of these firms have introduced interactive computers
for designing and drawing (Abel and Brede, 1989). We start
our research with the hypothesis that the introduction of
CAD will be accompanied by changes in work organization,
work content and work load. In order to prove our hypothesis we carried out a lot of interviews and job analyses.
In this paper the method and some of the first results of
these job analyses will be reported.

A METHOD TO ANALYSE MENTAL LABOUR: VERA-G

The social science research concerned with CAD has usually been carried out without using standardized job analysis intruments. There are two reasons for that: On one
hand, some research teams prefer to use qualitative interviews instead of more standardized instruments. On the
other hand, some researchers complain that a psychological
job analysis is not feasible in this domain (e.g. Wingert,
1985). In fact, although many job analysis instruments
(e.g. AET, Rohmert and Landau, 1979, TAI, Frieling et al.,
1984) claim to be applicable to all branches, applications
of these instruments to the work of designers and draftspeople are rare. The TAI was applied in the design office
recently and the empirical findings are partly published
(Derisavi-Fard et al., 1988). We suppose that one reason
for the rarity of applications in this field lies in the
nature of design work - special features of mental labour
seem to require an adaptation of work analysis methods.
Indeed, supplements are recently available to some task
analysis instruments which have originally been developed
for blue collar work (TBS-GA, Rudolph et al., 1987, VERA-
G, Resch 1988b). Within our research project we are applying the VERA-G (Verfahren zur Ermittlung von Regulationserfordernissen in der geistigen Arbeit, i.e. Instrument to
Identify Regulation Requirements in Mental Labour), a task
analysis instrument which is developed to analyse mental
labour in industrial production. It is based on the VERA
(Volpert et al., 1983), an instrument which was successfully used for more than 300 task analyses on the shop
floor (for a short review in English see Oesterreich and
Volpert, 1986). The VERA measures the regulation requirements of a work task. Regulation requirements are closely
related to notions like "job decision latitude" or "scope
of action" (Ulich, 1972). They can be described as task-
related objective qualification demands.

The main problem in developing a supplement for the analysis of mental labour is to define what is the difference between the two types of work. Although there exists a rather clear idea of what mental labour is, notions like "blue collar worker" and "white collar worker" are not sufficient for deeper analysis. Some authors define mental labour by saying it is not manual. However, there is no human work activity which does not comprise any manual parts. It is trivial to say that all work comprises mental and manual components. But on the other hand, the division of labour has led to a distinction between manual and mental labour. Therefore additional characteristics are required to distinguish between both types of labour (see Resch, 1988a).

Our definition of mental labour refers to the historical process in which manual and mental labour was divided. In the early days of mankind, the necessity arose of using distinct means of planning. As soon as it becomes the special task of a person to produce these means of planning, he conducts mental labour. He produces a symbolic object, which contains the results of human planning processes. The plan will be realized by other people, so, in a way, mental labour is the task to do the planning for other people.

The distinction between mental and manual labour can be described in the terms of Leont'ev's theory of activity (Leont'ev, 1978). Each activity is directed towards the changing of circumstances. Activity, therefore, is related to a concrete object. This relation is obvious as far as manual labour is regarded. The relation is mediated in mental labour. This type of activity is not directed towards the immediate change of reality, but produces a symbolic object which guides other workers to execute the changing of circumstances (Resch, 1988b). This characteristic of mental labour can be further described within the framework of the theory of action regulation (see e.g. Volpert, 1982). Human action is conscious and goal-oriented. It is performed within an action-sphere (Handlungsfeld, see Oesterreich, 1981). The action-sphere describes all possibilities of action a person has at the moment. These possibilities are determined by his abilities, the objective circumstances, and the time. The mental worker, indeed, has to act within two action-spheres: the reference-sphere (Referenz-Handlungsfeld) is the area the designing process refers to. The real action-sphere (faktisches Handlungsfeld) is the area within the worker produces the symbolic object. Both action-spheres require

mental processes, i.e. planning and thinking, but only
one, the real action-sphere, requires observable performance. Activities concerning the reference-sphere are not
observable, even though they are of great significance.

    The VERA-G is based on the theoretical assumptions
described above. The procedure leads to a measurement of
regulation requirements in both action-spheres. The steps
of regulation requirements are defined differently for
each action-sphere. We defined five steps for the real
action-sphere. These steps are similar to the originate
VERA levels (see Volpert et al., 1983). The reference-
sphere is the area of planning, wherein activities are not
observable. Therefore we had to redefine the original VERA
levels. Because of the higher regulation requirements in
design work we form seven steps of regulation requirements
in the reference-sphere. The two scales of regulation
requirements are shown in Table 1.

    The steps - although they are defined differently -
refer to the same theoretical framework (see Oesterreich,
1981). What is called "several working processes" in the
real action-sphere (step 4 and 5), is - because there do
not yet exist real working processes - called "areas" in
the reference-sphere. Step 4 and 5 had been subdivided for
the reference-sphere, so we have a seven-step-model in
this sphere.

Table 1. Steps of regulation requirements

Real action-sphere		Reference-sphere	
1	Sensory-motor regulation	1	Determinations
2	Action planning	2	Single decisions
3	Sub-goal planning	3	Strategic decisions
4	Coordinating several working processes	4	Decisions in fixed areas
		5	Decisions about areas
5	Establishing new working processes	6	Supplying areas
		7	Exploring new areas

The lower the level of a particular work task, the stronger the "partialization" of the worker in this sphere (see Volpert, 1975). He is cut off complex planning processes and possibilities for learning; negative consequences for his mental and physical health are possible.

The procedure VERA-G was published in a shortened form in Resch (1988b). We developed an elaborated form, which was used in our project for the first time and is not yet published. Meanwhile the procedure has as well been used in other projects analysing production planners and office work.

Before we report our first findings, we will in short discuss some of the problems in analysing complex mental work activities.

- Amount of time is increasing.

Our experience shows that task analyses with VERA-G in the engineering office take more time. This is due to the fact that the most important activities are not observable but have to be inquired by dialogue. Therefore the designer has to interrupt his work several times. Task analyses in the design office are more disturbing than in the shop floor. So, another difficulty occurs: we had problems in finding offices wherein we could carry out our task analyses.

- Professional knowledge is demanded.

Many of the work tasks we analysed with the normal VERA are easily to understand by observing the movements of the worker. Only a few special details have to be explained additionally. In the analysis of mental labour matters are quite different. Especially if one wants to conduct a VERA-G analysis in engineering tasks, a lot of professional knowledge is demanded, which cannot be deduced from observation. So we held lessons for our researchers, who are social science students, and taught them some basic knowledge of the construction and building trade. We have found this way satisfactory although it takes a lot of time.

DOES CAD CHANGE THE REGULATION REQUIREMENTS OF THE ENGINEER'S AND DRAFTSMAN'S TASK?

We conducted VERA-G-analyses on 13 work places of engineers and draftspeople and will conduct further task analyses. Our preliminary results are reported below.

First of all we found that CAD influences only regulation requirements in the real action-sphere. Regulation requirements in the reference-sphere are not at all influenced by CAD, but are determined by work organization and the complexity of the construction. This is due to the fact that at the present stage CAD was used as a sort of an "electronic pencil". In the construction and building trade, organizational changes as reported e.g. by Manske and Wolf (1986) for the engineering industry, cannot be observed yet.

If CAD mainly was used as another instrument to draw building plans, a change of regulation requirements in the real action-sphere can be expected. We were disappointed that we did not find yet any overall differences in the step of regulation requirements, but this result is similar to results reported by others (see e.g. Wingert et al., 1984).

However, a deeper analysis revealed that the work activities which are deciding for the step of regulation requirements had altered in an important manner.

To draw a building plan at a drawing-board requires planning processes as
- Placing the drawing at the plan.

The draftsman has to consider the total size of the drawing, he has to chose the appropriate scale, has to use the space within the plan economically, so that he can insert some of the detail drawings, and so on.
- Considering simplifications and savings.

Manual drawing is tiring. The draftsman considers several ways to simplify the drawing, for example he can illustrate several parts with one drawing which has varia-ble measurements. Or he can consider which views and meas-urements are really necessary for the building workers and omit the rest, and so on.

To draw a building plan with a CAD-system makes the considerations, desribed above, rather unnecessary. Dif-ferent planning processes are required as:
- Planning ahead to use the facilities of CAD.

If the draftsman wants to benefit from CAD, he has to use facilities like predefined cells, reflection transfor-mations, copying, and so on. To use these facilities he had to plan ahead the sequence of his work activities.
- Chosing old drawings.

In some cases it could be useful to edit an old drawing instead of making a complete new drawing. The drafts-man has to consider which of the stored drawings can be edited with little expense.

Both activities – drawing in a conventional manner or with CAD – have regulation requirements on step 2, but the deciding activities are – as shown above – rather different. Additional, we found significant differences in mental and physical load. Space precludes a detailed description of methods and results, but it should be mentioned that nearly everybody working on CAD complained on troubles with eyes, neck, and headache.

CONSEQUENCES FOR WORK DESIGN

The introduction of CAD in the building and construction trade has just begun. Therefore possible organizational change cannot be seen yet. This renders possible a prospective work design (Ulich, 1983), i.e. the design and evaluation of a future working situation. On the other hand, there are several factors influencing the further development, which can hardly be predicted (see Abel, 1988).

At the present stage, there exist a need for work design in order to reduce mental and physical load. Criteria concerning hardware and software ergonomics should be given more attention.

If CAD is used as an "electronic pencil", there is no danger that regulation requirements will decrease. But we have our doubts that this usage of CAD can ever be productive.

If organizational change will occur in future, work design should be influenced by the following criteria:
- Every draftsman should have his "own" screen. Any form of a pool-organization will support the tendency towards a new division of labour and new forms of shiftwork.
- Any specialization should be prevented. CAD should be used by all employees in the engineering office. This requires an elaborated CAD-training, which has a key function for design of work (see e.g. Gottschalch, 1986).
- The user should be able to make his own application programming. This is necessary, if one wants to use all facilities of CAD for a given task. "The user best knows the design problems he has to solve and can best estimate when it would be useful and helpful to his work to have additional CAD routines and programmes available ..." (Manske and Wolf, 1986, p.44). By the way this subtask would enhance the step of regulation requirements in the real action-sphere.

REFERENCES

Abel, J., 1988, CAE in Ingenieurbüros der Bauwirtschaft. Überlegungen zur weiteren Forschungsarbeit (Hannover: unpublished paper).

Abel, J. and Brede, M., 1988, CAD in Ingenieurbüros der Bauwirtschaft - Erste Ergebnisse einer Fragebogenaktion. Beratende Ingenieure (in press).

Derisavi-Fard, F., Hilbig, I. and Frieling, E., 1988, Belastung und Beanspruchung beim computerunterstützten Konstruieren - Erste Ergebnisse einer Felduntersuchung. In: Rechnerunterstützte Konstruktion. Bedingungen und Auswirkungen von CAD, edited by E. Frieling and H. Klein, (= Ulich, E. (Ed.) Schriften zur Arbeitspsychologie, Nr.46), (Bern: Huber), pp. 288-306.

Frieling, E. and Klein, H. (Eds.), Rechnerunterstützte Konstruktion. Bedingungen und Auswirkungen von CAD (= Ulich, E. (Ed.) Schriften zur Arbeitspsychologie, Nr.46) (Bern: Huber).

Frieling, E., Kannheiser, W., Facaoaru, C., Wöcherl, H. and Dürholt, E., 1984, Entwicklung eines theoriegeleiteten, standardisierten, verhaltenswissenschaftlichen Verfahrens zur Tätigkeitsanalyse (München: Universität München).

Gottschalch, H., 1986, The key function of CAD training for scope and contents. In: Skilled based automated manufacturing, IFAC workshop, preprints, edited by P. Brödner, (Düsseldorf: VDI/VDE-Gesellschaft Mess- und Automatisierungstechnik), pp. 35-40.

Leont'ev, A. N., 1978, Activity, consciousness, and personality (Englewood Cliffs (NJ): Prentice-Hall).

Manske, F. and Wolf, H., 1986, Organisation forms and work sequences in CAD usage. In: Skilled based automated manufacturing, IFAC workshop, preprints, edited by P. Brödner, (Düsseldorf: VDI/VDE-Gesellschaft Mess- und Automatisierungstechnik), pp. 41-47.

Oesterreich, R., 1981, Handlungsregulation und Kontrolle (München: Urban & Schwarzenberg).

Oesterreich, R. and Volpert, W., 1986, Task analysis for work design on the basis of action regulation theory. Economic and Industrial Democracy, 7, 503-527.

Rader, M., Wingert, B. & Riehm, U. (Eds.), 1988, Social science research on CAD/CAM. Results of a first european workshop (Heidelberg: Physica-Verlag).

Resch, M., 1988a, CAD as mental labour. A theoretical
    approach and some practical consequences. In: Social
    science research on CAD/CAM. Results of a first
    european workshop, edited by M. Rader, B. Wingert and
    U. Riehm, (Heidelberg: Physica-Verlag), pp. 91-103.
Resch, M., 1988b, Die Handlungsregulation geistiger
    Arbeit. Bestimmung und Analyse geistiger Arbeitstätig-
    keiten in der industriellen Produktion (= Ulich, E.
    (Ed.) Schriftenreihe zur Arbeitspsychologie, Nr.45)
    (Bern: Huber).
Rohmert, W. and Landau, K., 1979, Das Arbeitswissenschaft-
    liche Erhebungsverfahren zur Tätigkeitsanalyse (AET),
    (Bern: Huber).
Rudolph, E., Schönfelder, E. and Hacker, W., 1987, Tätig-
    keitsbewertungssystem - Geistige Arbeit (TBS-GA),
    Verfahren zur objektiven Analyse, Bewertung und Gestal-
    tung Rechnerunterstützung, (Berlin: Psychodiagnostisches
    Zentrum der Humboldt-Universität).
Ulich, E., 1972, Arbeitswechsel und Aufgabenerweiterung.
    REFA-Nachrichten, 25, 265-275.
Ulich, E., 1983, Differentielle Arbeitsgestaltung - ein
    Diskussionsbeitrag. Zeitschrift für Arbeitswissen-
    schaft, 37, 12-15.
Volpert, W., 1975, Die Lohnarbeitswissenschaft und die
    Psychologie der Arbeitstätigkeit. In: Lohnarbeits-
    psychologie. Berufliche Sozialisation: Emanzipation zur
    Anpassung, edited by P. Groskurth and W. Volpert,
    (Frankfurt am Main: Fischer), pp. 11-196.
Volpert, W., 1982, The model of the hierarchical-sequen-
    tial organization of action. In: Cognitive and moti-
    vational aspects of action, edited by W. Hacker, W.
    Volpert and M. von Cranach, (Amsterdam: North-Holland
    Publishing Company), pp. 35-51.
Volpert, W., Oesterreich, R., Gablenz-Kolakovic, S.,
    Krogoll, T. and Resch, M., 1983, Verfahren zur Ermitt-
    lung von Regulationserfordernissen in der Arbeits-
    tätigkeit (VERA). Handbuch und Manual, (Köln: TÜV
    Rheinland).
Wingert, B., 1985, Ist Konstruieren ein eigener psycholo-
    gischer Handlungstyp? In: Internationale Konferenz
    über Konstruktion. Tagungsband, edited by V. Hubka,
    (Zürich: Heurista), pp. 884-892.
Wingert, B., Duus, W., Rader, M. and Riehm, U., 1984, CAD
    im Maschinenbau. Wirkungen, Chancen, Risiken
    (Berlin/West: Springer).

CONTROVERSIAL OR LOGICAL RESULTS ?
COMPARISONS WITH DIFFERENT METHODS

Matti Vartiainen

Laboratory of Industrial Psychology
University of Helsinki
Finland

INTRODUCTION

The challenge: flexibility

Technological change in working life has been easily
noticed by everybody. Microcomputers and computer terminals are proliferating in the office environment, and the
increasing number of robots and flexible manufacturing
systems are making the change perceptible on the shop
floor. The change in production philosophy and the new
ideas on how work should be organized are even more important than the technological change itself, because they
have created the need to implement new technologies. The
era of traditional mass production and bureaucratic services is gone forever in industrialized countries. This is
the time of individual products and diverse services.
Enterprises and organizations are competing with each
other both in domestic and foreign markets to supply goods
on the basis of quality, product range and delivery time.
The new key factor is multi-skilled and motivated personnel with the ability to think and solve problems independently. At the same time, the above-mentioned changes provide a new opportunity to alter essentially the demands of
jobs in terms of content and learning. In summary, to
achieve high productivity and flexible production, an
enterprise should have a good work environment and work
content, highly qualified and internally motivated personnel, and a new style of leadership.

The problem: the partialized nature of work

There are, however, two barriers which prevent enterprises from achieving the above-mentioned flexibility. The first barrier is an organizational one, and the other is its psychological consequences.

The present problems of working life are primarily a consequence of the Tayloristic division of labour. The goals of flexibility cannot be achieved by increasing the division of labour, i.e. by separating organizationally the planning of the work from its execution. This kind of division of labour causes several problems in work. The most important of these is the absence of thinking demands. The present structure of an organization can be described with a simplified organizational diagram (Figure 1).

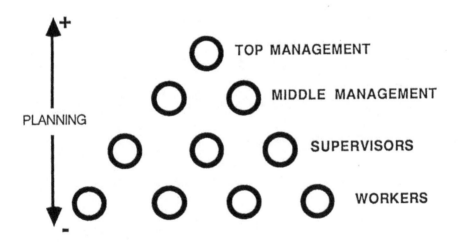

Figure 1. The simplified hierarchical organization of enterprises and of administration.

The planning of activities takes place at the higher levels of the hierarchy. The degree of freedom allowed with regard to time, goal setting and procedures decreases progressively with each downward step through the hierarchy. Various trials have been carried out over an extended period time with the objective of rebuilding the hierachy.

Most private enterprises and organs of state administration, however, still have hierarchical organizations with an excessive number of levels. The main barrier to the growth of personality in work and the crucial contradiction in the development of work is not determined by the intrinsic nature of new technology. The reason is that the present division of labour stands in opposition to the very nature of basic human qualities. A person is an intelligent being who plans, sets goals, selects, checks, controls and is able to organize his/her activities. Because of errors in the division of labour, these human qualities often cannot be realized in work.

The hierarchical (heterarchical) structure of mental regulation (Hacker, 1973) gives the psychological bases to change the traditional organization of work, which divides work into planning and executing jobs (Figure 2). The concepts of complete and incomplete, i.e. partialized actions (Volpert, 1974), are crucial. The reason for the partialized task structure is the residual allocation of tasks between persons. The partialized task structure shrinks the developmental possibilities of the intellectual level of regulation. According to Volpert a partialized action is, on one hand, isolated and, on the other hand, restricted. The isolation means that it is not possible to participate in planning and organizing of work at the level of an organization, i.e. under the traditional division of labour. Thus, it is impossible to use the intellectual level of regulation. The work is restricted when a person regulates his/her individual work actions at the lower levels of mental regulation. There is nothing left to learn in work, and it is monotonous. Summarizing: partialized work is neither sequentially nor hierarchically complete (Hacker, 1986a). The sequentially complete work structure includes preparation (goal-setting, designing action programs, autonomous decision-making), executing, checking and organizing. In addition, the work should be hierarchically complete, i.e. the execution of work is regulated at the different levels of mental regulation. There should be demands on various levels of regulation, i.e. real information processing including non-algorithmic intellectual demands.

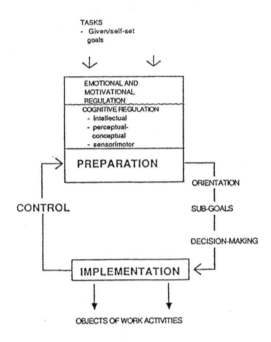

Figure 2. The cyclic unit of an action, and the hierarchical levels of mental regulation (Vartiainen, 1987).

The function of work analysis is to help to evaluate the "goodness" of work and to be a tool of a change used by the personnel. In this paper, good work is defined as complete work as opposed to partialized work. Two well-known methods concentrate especially on this aspect of the work: the VERA-method analyzes the thinking and planning requirements in industrial production (Volpert et al., 1983), and the TBS-method (Hacker et al., 1983) analyzes the completeness vs. partialized nature of work activities. There are also other methods used in this study. First, a case will be presented in which different methods were used. Then, the following problems will be discussed: (1) Not all persons respond positively to the complete tasks structures; the work is sometimes perceived as monotonous and dissatisfying. Conversely, a partialized job may be perceived as satisfying and motivating. Is it possible to find global job characteristics and criteria for "humane work"? How can different results of work analysis be combined?

(2) What is the role of work analysis as a tool of the change in work? Is work analysis a tool for a researcher to manage and activate development and/or a tool for the personnel to become subjects who theoretically master the change?

A CASE

Introduction

Many enterprises are applying the Just-In-Time philosophy of production and implementing small production units to achieve the flexibility necessary to meet the needs of their customers. The aim of this case study was to investigate the work content in a new "home-like" work environment and how the work was perceived by the personnel. The study is a part of the project "Analysis and Development of Work", which was financed by the Finnish Environment Fund.

Material and methods

The personnel of the new factory consisted of a manager, three skilled male employees (a repairer, a quality controller and a stock keeper), 17 female "ordinary" employees and a part-time cleaner. The study concentrated especially on the 17 employees doing assembly work. The employees rotated their jobs: they were loading and unloading (two days) Pater Noster, i.e. a stock-system, assembling terminals (13 days), and packing ready-made products (two days). The employees had been selected from among one hundred candidates with the help of psychological performance tests. No former work education was required. The employees received two weeks on-the-job training. The factory was situated in the countryside about fifty kilometers from Helsinki. The standard products were computer terminals. Production had started three months before the investigation.

Tasks and work flows were analyzed and described as a lay-out by observing and interviewing the personnel.

The sequential and hierarchical completeness of the assembly work was evaluated by the Task Diagnostic Survey (TBS, Hacker et al., 1983). The planning requirements of tasks were evaluated by the VERA-method (Volpert et al., 1983).

Job characteristics, experienced psychological states, affective outcomes of the work, context satisfaction, and

the strength of an individual growth need were studied
using the Job Diagnostic Survey (JDS, Hackman and Oldham,
1980).

Short-term mental load was studied using structured
scales which measure mental well-being at a certain
moment: BMS-scale (Plath and Richter, 1978) and EZ-scale
(Nitsch, 1976).

Results

The job of the assembly workers consisted of three
separate tasks, i.e. loading and unloading Pater Noster,
assemblying terminals and packing. The most demanding
tasks had been separated from their jobs. There were three
specialized skilled workers doing repairing, quality controlling and stock-keeping of incoming material and parts.

Most of the scores in TBS were in the critical area.
The job, however, included some preparing, a lot of executing, very little checking and some organizing, although
the job rotation was predetermined. The job was sequentially complete, albeit at a low level. The job was hierarchically partialized. The task mainly required information processing and classifying, sporadic instances of
algorithmic thinking with incomplete rules, and rare
instances of algorithmic thinking with complete rules. The
results of VERA showed low thinking requirements: the regulation requirements of the job were assigned to level 2R.

The employees considered their work characteristics as
good: the averaged motivation potential score (MPS) was
117. Only feedback from agents was scored low (x = 3.4,
sd = 1.2, rtt = .77). Critical psychological states,
affective outcomes, and context satisfactions - with the
exception of pay-satisfaction - were rated with scores
over 5.0. Individual growth need strength was 4.4.

The employees' mental state was good both at the
beginning and at the end of a working day:
- EZ-scale: motivation (6.0 vs 6.1) and mental strain
  (6.8 vs 7.7)
- BMS-scale: mental fatigue (55.8 vs 54.1), monotony
  (56.0 vs 56.6) and mental satiation (54.8 vs 56.7).

Discussion

The findings are somewhat controversial; the objectively simple work is perceived and self-rated as good and
satisfactory. It is easy to find reasons for the findings:

(1) The time of the investigation. The study was carried out only three months after the implementation of the new factory. There was certainly something left to learn in the tasks, i.e. the learning potential of the job was still high.

(2) Individual characteristics of the employees and their subcultural predispositions as intervening variables may account for the findings. For example, many employees were ex-housewives and mothers of small children coming from the surrounding countryside. For them the job gives opportunities to satisfy basic social needs.

DISCUSSION

<u>The benefits and problems of different methods</u>

Turner and Lawrence (1965) had a basic hypothesis that every job contained certain technologically determined task attributes which would influence employees' responses. The attributes or characteristics of each job studied, and expressed in the RTA index, were taken as independent variables. On the other hand, the employees' responses, e.g. job satisfaction, high or low motivation and absenteeism, were the dependent variables. What was the most important thing in their approach? - The independent and dependent variables were assessed independently from each other! The job attributes were studied by one or more members of the three-man field research group. They observed the performance of the job and interviewed the immediate supervisor of the job and some of the workers. Job satisfaction and other dependent variables were investigated by means of a questionnaire which was given to small groups of workers.

It must be noted that Turner and Lawrence did not find a significant relationship between task attribute scores and job satisfaction scores for the total population. They did, however, find that perceived task attribute scores were positively related to requisite task attribute scores and to job satisfaction scores. This may be the reason that Hackman and Oldham (1975) tried to collect data on the independent, dependent and even intervening variables using only one employee questionnaire. This was a fatal error. There is often an incongruence between objective task characteristics and how they are perceived. It is the redefined task rather than the objective task that the individual tries to perform. Schnake and Dumler (1985) noted that "It is the objective task that managers manipulate in order to make the individual perform it". Aldag et

al. (1981) discussed alternative ways of measuring task
characteristics and suggested a radical departure from the
Turner and Lawrence paradigm. They underlined the need for
more objective measures, like the critical incident technique and job inventories, to evaluate job characteristic.
In their critical review, Roberts and Glick (1981) also
noted that the job characteristics approach and the JDS as
a unidimensional measure of tasks had failed to distinguish situational attributes of tasks and incumbent cognitions about these attributes. They proposed a complete
theory that would simultaneously model situational (taxonomic), within-person (cognitive consistency), and person-
situation (task-incumbent response and environment-incum-
bent response) relations.

    Hacker (1973, 1986b) utilized some ideas of the Turner
and Lawrence original design on a qualitatively new level.
In the TBS, work was again conceptualized as an independent variable and a dependent variable. Characteristics of
work as an independent variable are directly and indirectly designable ones. Directly designable characteristics are, for example, the number of subtasks and autonomy
concerning procedures (part A "Technological and organizational requirements" of the TBS). Indirectly designable
characteristics are, for example, the amount of cooperation and responsibility for results (part B "Cooperation
and communication" and part C "Responsibility" of the
TBS). The independent variable determines the mental
demands (part D "Mental (cognitive) processes" of the TBS)
and the learning potential (part E "Qualification demands"
of the TBS) of the work. The sequential completeness of
work is evaluated through the kind of subtasks the job
includes, i.e. only task execution or also preparation,
checking of quality and organization. The hierarchical
completeness is evaluated through the level of mental regulation.

The necessity of multi-leveled analysis

    It is necessary to analyze work both in the case of an
individual employee and in the case of a group as independent and dependent variables (Table 1). In addition, there
is a need to determine possible intervening variables. The
analysis and evaluation of work should be done at the following levels:
1. overt, executive actions, i.e. "what seems to be
happening". Job descriptions are often obtained by using
methods of traditional work studies, such as method and

time studies. Part A of the TBS and parts A and B of the VERA help in analysing technical and organizational requirements of work which are regarded as independent variables.

2. cognitions, i.e. what a person "perceives and says he/she is doing". The cognitive analysis and evaluation reveal:

(a) How a person perceives task characteristics. The core dimensions of the JDS may be used to analyze the perceived task characteristics.

(b) What is the level of mental regulation. Part D of the TBS and part C of the VERA prescribe the level of thinking requirements in a job. In-depth interviews, verbal protocols and other means of diagnosing mental models may be used to analyze the person's present state, what he/she regards as the goals and sub-goals of his/her work and the means of achieving them.

3. affective aspect of the work, i.e. "how it feels". Measurement of mental load and job satisfaction is a typical approach. The measurement shows the mental strain during a change process as well as the effects of job design and training after the change. BMS- and EZ-scales are used for this purpose.

Developmental strategies

The crucial phases in the development of work, in which the sequential and hierarchical completeness vs. incompleteness are determined, are work design and work implementation. The participation of personnel in work design is a part of work education. Work analysis by the personnel is the key factor in real participation and learning. The intellectual level of mental regulation by increasing learning requirements should be the psychological aim of work design.

Table 1. The measurement of work as independent and dependent variables, and some examples of methods.

RESEARCH OBJECT

	individual	group
F independent **O** variable **R** **M** objective requirements **O** visible **F** formal **A**	PERFORMANCE, TIME, PROCEDURES, LAYOUT Time and method studies TBS - part A, VERA - parts A, B	PRODUCTION PROCESS, TIME, LAYOUT, DIVISION OF WORK Time and method studies Costs/benefits, task analysis
C dependent **T** variable **I** **V** subjective **I** consequences **T** **Y** hidden informal	MENTAL REGULATION (a) cognitive (b) emotional and motivational Level of mental regul- ation: TBS - part D, VERA - part C Perceived task charac- teristics: JDS Mental load: EZ, BMS	GROUP "REGULATION" (a) communication, cooperation, qualifi- cations (b) norms, values, athmosphere TBS - parts B, C, E Sociograms

In work design the man-machine task division and the
allocation of tasks between persons are decided. The
objects of change are products, tools (programs), organization, procedures and the whole work environment. New
information technology has many possible applications in
the replacement of human routinized work tasks. In flexible production and office systems many routines are accomplished by machines. Information technology also creates
demanding new tasks, e.g. programming tasks, the allocation of which depends on the traditional division of
labour. Artificial intelligence is to replace algorithmic
thinking routines that demand higher education.

Technology is not, however, crucial from the standpoint of work content. Of more importance is the implementation strategy and the resultant division of labour. In fact, participative work design and implementation are the same as learning to manage the change and tasks. To learn, it is necessary to be able to analyze work. Therefore, the participation of personnel and the use of work analysis are needed from the very beginning.

A traditional approach to the realization of sociotechnical change is unidirectional. The technological and/or economic aims are set without consulting the personnel. A group of experts analyses the requirements and designs the technology and the completing human side, including the division of labour. In an alternative sociotechnical approach based on the participation of a worker, both the technological/economic aims and the social aims are handled simultaneously. The goals are set in general and joint discussions are held as early as possible after the necessity for the change has been realized. The exact direction, means and goals are still unclear. Not until the goals are unanimously set can the required technology and organization be discussed. When necessary, the original goals of the change can be evaluated and changed. Preparations take longer compared with the traditional approach, but the functionality and the level of know-how of personnel is at a higher level.

The benefits of participation result from the possibility of the personnel thinking for themselves. The forms of participation can naturally be different. The participation may be:

(a) Consultative participation, i.e. a designer/project manager does the whole analysis and design work. He/she collects data concerning the organization and analyzes the requirements of work by interviewing selected members of the personnel.

(b) Representative participation, i.e. a project group is composed of selected/elected representatives of the personnel.

(c) Participation of all, i.e. all the personnel participate in the analysis and design of their own task structures. Developmental groups may be established.

(d) Nonparticipative participation, i.e. the changes to come are announced to the personnel.

Problems of developmental strategies

There are several possible developmental strategies. Traditional rationalization concentrated on the technological and organizational requirements as independent variables. The dependent variable was an employee as a passive subject. The researcher was an outside observer or a specialist making work studies. In action research, work analysis is done by a researcher. He/she activates development through his/her theoretical mastery of work and by training the personnel. The personnel is, however, considered a subject capable of developing its own work. Developmental work research (Toikka, 1984; Engestrîm and Engestrîm, 1986) was born as a criticism of traditional confirmative work research. At the same time, developmental work research aims at developing further the approach of action research. Action research is, however, criticised because of its untheoretical naature, i.e. the methodological cycle of research, training and developing is based on the everyday experience and consciousness of the individual.

The crucial new element in developmental work research is the theoretical mastery of work achieved through learning. Engestrîm (1987) uses the term 'learning activity' to refer to activity that combines work, learning and research in a new way. The goal of learning activity is increased mastery of practical work, and the tools are the analyses and models describing the work. The subject is the team of researchers, planners and workers. The work process is regarded as the developing activity system instead of the bipartite combining of the given framework and workers. The development of work may be consciously influenced by knowing its own developmental logic and internal contradictions. Workers should become the subjects of their work.

In developmental work research, the research of work as well as the learning activity and the participation of personnel are all tightly combined. The approach presupposes close and long-lasting cooperation organized as a project involving researchers, planners and performers of the work.

There are also some theoretical problems in developmental work research (Vartiainen, 1989). One unsolved problem is the empirical context of the methodological cycle of the approach. The theoretical arguments have been extensively developed and refined, but they seem to be based more on logical analysis than on empirical results.

Another unanswered problem is the extent and depth of personnel participation in the developmental process; how to
guarantee the theoretical mastery of work through personal
growth of all the personnel?

The learning challenges can be permanently included in
work contents by the participative work design. The learning contents made by other persons are, however, not
enough. Participative implementation strategies in organizational change, career advancement possibilities, and
different forms of group work, make possible the independent use of the intellectual level of mental regulation in
work. The essence of complete work structures is the
degree of freedom allowed in one's own work. The inflexi-
ble tradition of dividing labour into planning and executing tasks can be changed by participative work analysis,
design and training.

REFERENCES

Aldag, R.J., Barr, S.H. and Brief, A.P., 1981, Measurement
    of Perceived Task Characteristics. Psychological
    Bulletin, 90, 415-431.
Engeström, Y., 1987, Learning by expanding. (Helsinki:
    Orienta-Konsultit Oy).
Engeström, Y. and Engeström, R., 1986, Developmental work
    research: the approach and an application in cleaning
    work. Nordisk Pedagogik, 6, 2-15.
Hacker, W.,1973, Allgemeine Arbeits- und Ingenieur-
    psychologie. Berlin: VEB Deutscher Verlag der Wissen-
    schaften.
Hacker, W., 1986a, Arbeitspsychologie - psychische
    Regulation von Arbeitstätigkeiten. (Berlin: VEB
    Deutscher Verlag der Wissenschaften).
Hacker, W.,1986b, Towards the design of working tasks for
    the future. In: Psychological aspects of the technolo-
    gical and organizational change in work, edited by L.
    Norros and M. Vartiainen, (Helsinki: Yliopistopaino),
    pp. 115-142.
Hacker, W., Iwanowa, A. and Richter, P., 1983, Tätigkeits-
    Bewertungs-System, TBS. Berlin: Psychodiagnostisches
    Zentrum.
Hackman, J.R. and Oldham, G.R., 1975, Development of the
    Job Diagnostic Survey. Journal of Applied Psychology,
    60, 159-170.
Hackman, J.R. and Oldham, G.R., 1980, Work redesign.
    (London: Addison-Wesley).

Nitsch, J.R., 1976, Die Eigenzustandskala (EZ-Skala) Ein
    Verfahren zur hierarchisch-mehrdimensionalen
    Befindlichkeitsskalierung. In: Beanspruchung im Sport,
    Beiträge zur psychologischen Analyse sportlicher
    Leistungssituation, edited by J.R. Nitsch and I. Udris.
    (Wiesbaden: Schriftenreihe Training und Beanspruchung).
Plath, H-E. and Richter, P., 1978, Ermüdung-Monotonie-
    Sättigung-Stress (BMS). Verfahren zur skalierten
    Erfassung erlebter Beanspruchungsfolgen. Handanweisung.
    Berlin: Psychodiagnostisches Zentrum.
Roberts, K.H. and Glick, W., 1981, The job characteristics
    approach to task design: A critical review. Journal of
    Applied Psychology, 2, 193-217
Schnake, M.E. and Dumler, M.P., 1985, Affective response
    bias in the Measurement of Perceived Task Characteris-
    tics. Journal of Occupational Psychology, 58, 159-166.
Toikka, K., 1984, Toteava ja kehittävä työntutkimus eli
    voiko ja kannattaako ihmistä tutkia työssä ihmisenä?
    Psykologia, 19, 259-265. (In Finnish).
Turner, A.N. and Lawrence, P.R., 1965, Industrial Jobs and
    the Worker. (Boston: Harvard University).
Vartiainen, M. (1987) The hierarchical development of
    mental regulation, and training methods. Helsinki Uni-
    versity of Technology, Industrial Economics and Indus-
    trial Psychology, report 100. Otaniemi: TKK Offset.
Vartiainen, M., 1989, The Psychological Requirements of
    Qualifications (in press). Proceedings of "Kvalifika-
    tions forskningens teorie och användning"-konferensen
    29.8.-1.9.1988 Hanasaari, Finland.
Volpert, W., 1974, Handlungsstrukturanalyse als Beitrag
    zur Qualifikationsforschung. (Köln: Pahl Rugenstein).
Volpert, W., Oesterreich, R., Gablenz-Kolakovic, S.,
    Krogoll, T. and Resch, M., 1983, Verfahren zur Ermitt-
    lung von Regulationserfordernissen in der Arbeitstätig-
    keit (VERA). Köln: Verlag TÜV Rheinland.

CONTRASTIVE TASK ANALYSIS

Heiner Dunckel

University of Technology, Berlin
Institute for Human Sciences in Work and Education
Federal Republic of Germany

INTRODUCTION

This paper presents a guideline for analyzing and designing work tasks involving computer systems on the basis of industrial psychology. The guideline is being developed at the Institute for Human Sciences in Work and Education at the Technical University of Berlin as part of the research project "Development of a Guideline for Contrastive Task Analysis in Clerical and Administrative Work" (KABA). This project is funded by the German Federal Ministry for Research and Technology under their research programme on the "Humanization of Working Life".

The following sections look briefly (as required by the scope of the paper) at the problems addressed by the project and what it sets out to achieve. The theoretical background is touched upon, and details are given of the methodical approach adopted and the instrument used for task analysis.

PROBLEMS ADDRESSED BY THE PROJECT

The increasing use of information and communication technologies and networks for clerical and administrative work has confronted organizers, system and software designers and other management experts with the task of evaluating and designing work systems not only in accordance with technical and/or managerial criteria, but also to include social and human considerations. For the industrial psychologist, the analysis and design of work tasks is of paramount importance here, the work task playing a key role with respect to effectiveness, stress and personality

development (cf. Hacker (1987), Oesterreich & Volpert
(1987).

   The problem is that, so far, no suitable and practi-
cally-oriented methods or instruments have been available
which might enable organizers and software designers to
evaluate existing or projected work systems, and more especially work tasks, along psychological lines, in accordance with so-called "human criteria". In software ergonomics and design, there have been discussions calling for
software design to include, and indeed be primarily concerned with, work (task) design. However, the methods and
instruments developed so far have been confined basically
to the analysis, design and evaluation of interactive computer systems (cf. Bullinger et al. (1987); in other words
they have been concerned essentially with issues relating
to design of the means of work.

AIM OF THE PROJECT

   What the project sets out to achieve must be seen in
relation to the problems outlined above. Its aim is to
develop criteria and instruments for analyzing and designing work tasks and work organization on the basis of industrial psychology. Particular attention is given here to
work tasks in the clerical and administrative sectors which
are directly or indirectly affected by the application of
information and communication technologies.

   What Contrastive Task Analysis basically sets out to do
is to ask which parts of a work activity should be computerized, and which should not. In order to answer this
question, we must have some idea of the human strengths
which the computer is meant to promote and support (cf.
Volpert (1986a).

THEORETICAL BACKGROUND

   The concepts developed as part of the Action Regulation
Theory (cf. Dunckel (1986), Frese & Sabini (1985), Hacker
(1986), Oesterreich (1981), Oesterreich & Volpert (1986),
Volpert (1982, 1987)) help highlight basic features of
human action which, on a general level, are characteristic
of specifically human activities or strengths. These four
basic features are: goal-orientation, object-relatedness,
social nature and process-like nature of human action. The
following sections look briefly at these basic features and
go on to derive from them a number of aspects relating to
task analysis.

Goal-Orientation

In his activity, man takes issue with his environment
and changes it in accordance with his objectives. Goal-
orientation is a fundamental feature of human action, what
may be considered specifically characterisitic of human
activity (cf. Rubinstein (1977). Goal-orientation means
that man gears his action to future (desired) states of his
self or his environment. Hacker (1983) characterizes the
significance of goal-orientation in terms of three functions:

1. Goals stimulate and motivate human activity.

2. Goals organize and direct activity through sequences
   of sub-goals, thus requiring the anticipation of
   future conditions and the planning of the individual's
   own activity.

3. Goals or objectives provide a basis for comparison
   with the actual result of an activity.Goals are therefore essential for experiencing and evaluating an
   action.
   Characteristic of human action is the fact that human
beings
   - are able to set their own goals and alter them flexibly
     depending on the objective conditions,
   - pursue goals consciously and deliberately,
   - pursue not only immediate goals and actions, but also
     larger schemes of action and long-term objectives.

In connection with the basic feature of "goal-orientation", we can distinguish five different task aspects which
enable us to analyze work tasks with respect to the degree
to which they support or hinder goal-oriented human action.
Work tasks or working conditions are termed "humane" if
they support and promote human strengths.

First Task Aspect: Humane working conditions call for and
provide for scope of action.
   By scope of action, we mean the degree to which workers
are able to act self-reliantly at their workplace and make
their own plans and decisions with regard to goals and the
means for attaining them. Just how far the scope of action
extends is largely determined by the work task itself; in
other words, the work task determines the way in which
goals of action are established, how they are broken down

into sub-goals and ultimately attained by actions, operations and movements.

Another important consideration in the division of
labour between the human being and the computer is to
ensure that the human being retains responsibility for
decisions about
- the type of work procedures employed,
- the quantity and quality of the work results,
- the nature and scope of the information provided for
  performance of the work tasks,
- the nature and choice of the means of work.

Second Task Aspect: Humane working conditions call for and
provide for temporal scope.

The second task aspect is concerned with the provision
of temporal scope by a work task, i.e. the provision of
facilities allowing the worker to structure self-reliantly
his or her action with respect to time. Though closely
connected with the scope of action, temporal scope is
important in its own right and of practical significance,
since too tight a time schedule for performing a specific
task frequently nullifies an otherwise quite generous scope
of action.

Another important consideration in the division of
labour between the human being and the computer is to
ensure that the human being retains the responsibility for
decisions about temporal factors affecting task
accomplishment.

Third Task Aspect: Humane working conditions call for and
provide for structurability.

"Structurability" refers not only to the transparency of
a worker's means of work and work task, but also to their
structurability in accordance with his or her goals.

Prerequisites for goal-oriented action are that
- the technical conditions and relations,
- the organizational structures (the temporal and
  spatial relations between work tasks and their relation with respect to content),
- the events occurring in the working process, and
- the consequences of the worker's own intervention in
  the working process
are foreseeable and transparent for the worker.

Transparency is merely a prerequisite to goal-oriented
action. Going on from this, the worker must be able to
structure perceptible (transparent) conditions and events
in accordance with his or her own goals. While this is, to

some extent, a question of the information and qualification measures provided by management, it is, at the same
time, a question of the concrete design of a work system
(especially a computerized one) (cf. Spinas (1987), Ulich
(1986)).

Fourth Task Aspect: Humane working conditions must avoid
objective hindrances to the work activity.
    A question which should always be asked in practical
work task design is whether or not task accomplishment
(for a given scope of action) is impeded or hindered by
specific factors that are not inherent in the work task
itself. These organizational and/or technical factors (e.g.
input devices which are difficult to operate, information
which is difficult to make out) constitute an objective
stress factor - provided that they cannot in principle be
eliminated by the worker - since as a result of these factors task accomplishment requires additional effort (e.g.
an action may have to be recommenced following a "system
breakdown"). Humanely adequate work design means freedom
from hindrances.
    With regard to the question of computer system design,
this means above all that the computer system should not
produce any stress factors (e.g. interruptions caused by
malfunctions etc.).

Object-Relatedness

    The characteristic "object-relatedness" denotes both the
embodied nature of human action and its relation to the
external world.
    "Embodiedness" refers to the fact that activity and the
psychological processes behind it are invariably those of
an embodied, material ("object-related") actor. The body
thus forms the basis, source of supply and coordinative
centre of the (work) motor actions (cf. Gibson (1979), Turvey & Kugler (1984), the integrative centre of the different sense organs, and a genuine element in human communication (e.g. through facial expression, gestures).
    Two further task aspects follow from the characteristic
"embodiedness":

Fifth Task Aspect: Humane working conditions call for and
provide for bodily activity.
    It is particularly in connection with the mechanization
and automation of work that the question of sufficient
motor action demands for a specific work activity arises.

Insufficient motor action results in an impairment of mental processes, too: e.g. waning attention and alertness, decreased sense of well-being.

An important consideration in the division of labour between the human being and the computer is to ensure that a particular work task provides for changes in body posture (walking, standing, sitting) and allows for different forms of motor action.

Sixth Task Aspect: Humane working conditions call for and provide for the use of a wide variety of sensory capacities.

Human beings possess at least 13 sensory domains, each of which has its own specific sense organs or receptors (cf. Stadler et al. (1975). It may be assumed that the receptivity of these senses is impaired if no demands are made on them. (cf. Mander (1979), Rubinstein (1977); cf. also research on the so-called vigilance problem). The long-term negative effects of sensory deprivation are well-known (cf. for example Grüner (1981), Leontjew (1977).

In connection with the division of labour between the human being and the computer, it must be ensured that a particular work task makes demands on those sensory domains that are essential to human existence (in particular: sight, hearing and touch).

What we mean by human action's "relation to the external world" is the fact that the human being has a practical and active relation to objects "outside and independent of him- or herself". Practical relation is taken here to denote primarily the concrete, material handling of objects, and thus the direct relation to the productive process. This form of practical relation is almost non-existent in clerical and administrative work, which is primarily concerned with the use of characters and symbols. We should nevertheless demand that clerical work, too, remain related to the material production process (e.g. that the purchaser have direct access to production stock) and to social situations (e.g. that the insurance clerk have direct contact with the client). This leads us on to another task aspect:

Seventh Task Aspect: Humane working conditions must both call for and provide for a concrete relation to real objects and social situations.

A further characteristic of human action is the fact that the human being is able to react flexibly to changes in his or her environment. However, this presupposes that the person has experience of a variety of situational conditions and of the active mastering of these. What is known as expertise is based precisely on experience of this sort, on actively coming to terms with a variety of different situations, and on the ability to combine and integrate these into flexible basic patterns can only emerge where the worker's environment makes varying demands on his or her action (e.g. by providing a variety of work tasks and assignments) or where situational conditions are not too highly standardized. This leads to a further task aspect:

Eight Task Aspect: Humane working conditions call for and provide for variability.

With regard to the division of labour between the human being and the computer, it is therefore important to ensure that any existing variety of work tasks and assignments is preserved, and that too great a standardization of situations is avoided.

Social Nature of Action

The bases of human action (work objects, means of work, work processes, etc.) are shaped by socio-historical development, which itself is created through the action of other human beings. Human action is always related to other human beings; individual learning and action can only take place in direct social contact with others, in groups where each human being cooperates and interacts directly with others. These social relations are based essentially on the exchange of information, news, characters, etc., in other words, on communication. There follows from this a further task aspect:

Ninth Task Aspect: Humane working conditions must provide for and promote cooperation and direct communication.

In designing technical communication facilities, it must therefore be ensured that cooperation and direct communication are not impaired.

Process-like Nature of Action

Human action should be understood and investigated as a process. Action and its individual psychological processes acquire significance only when they are analyzed in the overall context of the acting human being and the conditions surrounding him. There follows from this, not a task aspect, but a methodological principle: Psychological work analyses must take as their point of departure the concrete work action and the conditions surrounding it.

To conclude, one further point should be mentioned: a
"contrastive task analysis" does not cover all evaluation
levels of work design measures (especially not the level of
"performability" or "harmlessness"; cf. Hacker et al.
(1987). It also proceeds from the following fundamental
assumptions:
- that the working persons have a say in work design
  measures,
- that they are sufficiently qualified, and
- that no checks are kept on the performance of the
  individual worker.

METHODOLOGICAL APPROACH

The guideline for contrastive task analysis enables work
tasks to be evaluated with reference to the above-mentioned
task aspects or human criteria. It is the work task, then,
that is the subject of analysis. The analysis is condition-
related (cf. Oesterreich & Volpert (1987)), in other words
it is concerned with the question of to what extent working
conditions conform with the human criteria. The method used
for investigation is the "observation interview", which
involves asking the user of the guideline questions about
the work task. The information required for answering the
questions can then be acquired by the user in an open
dialogue with the working person while observing the work
activity.
The guideline is designed
- to provide ideas for prospective work design from the
  point of view of industrial psychology;
- to be suitable for use in a variety of different
  industrial fields;
- for practical application.
Furthermore, the guideline is being developed in close
cooperation with industrial enterprises and administrative
organizations, i.e. with workers, their representatives and
industrial and administrative management.

THE GUIDELINE FOR CONTRASTIVE TASK ANALYSIS

The present initial version of the guideline - which is
currently being tested in a number of different industrial
enterprises and administrative organizations - comprises
two main parts: the general procedure, and the special
procedures relating to the above-mentioned task aspects.
Each of these parts contains a detailed manual and answer
forms. The manual provides information on the aims and

functions of the respective parts or sections, on the procedure to be adopted in the investigation, and on how to
deal with the answer forms.

The General Procedure

The general procedure is subdivided into four parts.
Part A, when processed, provides a general picture of the
department or organizational unit under investigation. The
aim of Part B is to supply general information about the
individual workplace and to give a clear definition of the
work tasks to be performed at this workplace. Part C is
designed to provide an initial picture and a more detailed
characterization of the individual work task. It contains,
in particular, the question whether information and communication technologies are of importance for performing the
work task, and if so which ones. Part D enables a rough
analysis of the work task to be made with reference to the
human criteria formulated above. Particular attention is
already paid here to whether any impairment of the human
criteria by the computer system is observable. Part D must
be processed separately for each different work task in a
particular department or organizational unit. By way of a
result, Part D indicates those task aspects which may have
to be processed in more detail by the special procedures.
At present, we are assuming that an informed user familiar
with the organization in question requires approximately 2
days to analyze a whole organizational unit of manageable
size (say: 20 workplaces) using this general procedure.

The Special Procedures

The other main part of the guideline comprises special
procedures which briefly cover the various task aspects
outlined above (Parts E to M of the overall guideline).
Here, too, the essential question is to what extent the
human criteria are either impaired by the computer system
or supported by it. In some cases, the individual procedures are condensed versions or adaptations of existing
instruments (TBS: Hacker et al. (1986); RHIA: Leitner et
al. (1987); VERA: Volpert et al. (1983); cf. also Resch et
al. (1984)) or recent developments. Depending on the particular questions or problems under consideration, specific
work tasks are selected for analysis using selected parts
of the procedure. The amount of time required in each case
varies accordingly. This second part of the guideline is
constructed according to the "modular design principle",

i.e. it also allows for consideration of each task aspect in isolation.

OUTLOOK

So far, our experience with the guideline has been promising. Most industrial practitioners concede the necessity of analyzing work tasks involving computers from the point of view of the human sciences. Findings have since become available to industrial enterprises and administrative organizations indicating that designing computer systems merely to meet technical criteria fails to take account of user needs. (This applies also, as far as the public administration is concerned, to an increasing extent to the needs of the general public.) Such design may therefore be considered dysfunctional. In many cases, considerable subsequent adjustments to the computer systems were necessary. Management experts, too, might find that by using the guideline for contrastive task analysis they will be able to eliminate in advance some of these problems.

ACKNOWLEDGEMENT

This paper was translated from the German by Philip Bacon.

REFERENCES

Bullinger, H.-J., Fähnrich, K.-P. and Ziegler, J., 1987, Software-Ergonomie: Stand und Entwicklungstendenzen. In: Software-Ergonomie '87, edited by W. Schönpflug and M. Wittstock (Stuttgart: Teubner), pp. 17-30.

Dunckel, H., 1986, Handlungstheorie. In: Psychologie, edited by G. Rexilius and S. Grubitzsch, (Reinbek: Rowohlt), pp. 533-556.

Frese, M. and Sabini, J., 1985, Goal Directed Behavior: The Concept of Action in Psychology, edited by id., (Hillsdale, N.J.: Lawrence Erlbaum).

Gibson, J.J., 1979, The Ecological Approach to Visual Perception, (Boston: Houghton Mifflin).

Grüner, U.F., 1981, Sensorische Deprivation. In: Handbuch psychologischer Grundbegriffe, edited by G. Rexilius and S. Grubitzsch, (Reinbek: Rowohlt), pp. 960-964.

Hacker, W., 1983, Ziele – eine vergessene psychologische Schlüsselvariable? Zur antriebsregulatorischen Potenz von Tätigkeitsinhalten. Psychologie für die Praxis, 15, 5-26.

Hacker, W., 1986, Arbeitspsychologie. Psychische Regulation von Arbeitstätigkeiten, (Berlin, GDR: Deutscher Verlag der Wissenschaften).

Hacker, W., 1987, Software-Gestaltung als Arbeitsgestaltung. In: Software-Ergonomie, edited by K.-P. Fähnrich, (Munich: Oldenbourg), pp. 29-42.

Hacker, W., Rudolph, E. and Schönfelder, E., 1986, TBS-GA – ein Analyse- und Bewertungsverfahren für Arbeitstätigkeiten mit überwiegend geistigen Anforderungen. Sozialistische Arbeitswissenschaft, 30, 351-354.

Hacker, W., Raum, H., Rentzsch, M. and Völker, K., 1987, Bildschirmarbeit. Arbeitswissenschaftliche Empfehlungen, (Berlin, GDR: Verlag Die Wirtschaft).

Leitner, K., Volpert, W., Greiner, B., Hennes, K. and Weber, W., 1987, Analyse psychischer Belastung in der Arbeit – das RHIA-Verfahren, (Cologne: TÜV Rheinland).

Leontjew, A.N., 1977, Tätigkeit, Bewußtsein, Persönlichkeit, (Stuttgart: Klett).

Mander, J., 1979, Schafft das Fernsehen ab! Eine Streitschrift gegen das Leben aus zweiter Hand, (Reinbek: Rowohlt).

Oesterreich, R., 1981, Handlungsregulation und Kontrolle, (Munich: Urban & Schwarzenberg).

Oesterreich, R. and Volpert, W., 1986, Task Analysis for Work Design on the Basis of Action Regulation Theory. Economic and Industrial Democracy, 7, 503-527.

Oesterreich, R. and Volpert, W., 1987, Handlungstheoretisch orientierte Arbeitsanalyse. In: Arbeitspsychologie (Enzyklopädie der Psychologie, Themenbereich D, Serie III, Band 1), edited by U. Kleinbeck and J. Rutenfranz, (Göttingen: Hogrefe), pp. 43-73.

Resch, M., Volpert, W., Leitner, K. and Krogoll, T., 1984, Regulation Requirements and Regulation Barriers – Two Aspects of Partialized Action in Industrial Work. In: Design of Work in Automated Manufacturing Systems with Special Reference to Small and Medium Size Firms, edited by T. Martin, (Oxford: Pergamon Press), pp. 29-32.

Rubinstein, S.L., 1977, Grundlagen der Allgemeinen Psychologie, 9th edn., (Berlin, GDR: Volk und Wissen).

Spinas, P., 1987, VDU-Work and User-Friendly Human-Computer-Interaction: Analysis of Dialogue Structures. In: Psychological Issues of Human-Computer Interaction in the Work Place, edited by M. Frese, E. Ulich and W. Dzida (Amsterdam: Elsevier), pp. 147-162.

Stadler, M., Seeger, F. and Raeithel, A., 1975, Psychologie der Wahrnehmung, (Munich: Juventa).

Turvey, M.T. and Kugler, P.N., 1984, An Ecological Approach
    to Perception and Action. In: Human Motor Actions,
    edited by H.T.A. Whiting (Amsterdam: Elsevier), pp. 373-
    412.

Ulich, E., 1986, Aspekte der Benutzerfreundlichkeit. In:
    Arbeitsplätze morgen, edited by W. Remmele and M. Sommer
    (Stuttgart: Teubner), pp. 102-121.

Volpert, W., 1982, The Model of the Hierarchical-Sequential
    Organization of Action. In: Cognitive and Motivational
    Aspects of Action, edited by W. Hacker, W. Volpert and
    M. v.Cranach (Amsterdam: North-Holland), pp. 35-51.

Volpert, W., 1986a, Contrastive Analysis of the Relation-
    ship of Man and Computer as a Basis of System Design.
    In: System Design for Human Development: Participation
    and Beyond, edited by P. Docherty, K. Fuchs-Kittowski,
    P. Kolm and L. Mathiassen (Amsterdam: Elsevier), pp.
    119-128.

Volpert, W., 1986b, Gestaltbildung im Handeln. Zur psycho-
    logischen Kritik des mechanistischen Weltbildes. Gestalt
    Theory, 8, 43-60.

Volpert, W., 1987, Psychische Regulation von Arbeitstätig-
    keiten. In: Arbeitspsychologie (Enzyklopädie der Psycho-
    logie, Themenbereich D, Serie III, Band 1), edited by U.
    Kleinbeck and J. Rutenfranz (Göttingen: Hogrefe), pp.
    1-42.

Volpert, W., Oesterreich, R., Gablenz-Kolakovic, S.,
    Krogoll, T. and Resch, M., 1983, Verfahren zur Ermitt-
    lung von Regulationserfordernissen in der Arbeitstätig-
    keit (VERA). Handbuch und Manual, (Cologne: TÜV Rhein-
    land).

IDENTIFICATION OF ERGONOMIC FACTORS
WHICH MAY HAVE INJUROUS EFFECTS

Kristina Kemmlert

National Institute of Occupational Health
Division of Applied Work Physiology
S-171 84 Solna
Sweden

INTRODUCTION

There is a great need for simple methods identifying postural stress, awkward movements and hazardous manual handling at workplaces (Kemmlert and Kilbom, 1988).

One of the underlying problems is the difficulty of defining exposure (Wallace and Buckle, 1987), another is the lack of scientific support for a relationship between short-term fatigue or discomfort, and long-term effects as injuries (Berguqist, 1984, Hagberg, 1987).

Thus resources for epidemiological studies of relationship between working posture, workload and health are poor. In consequence, the basis for assessment of ergonomic hazards at the workplace needs to be further substantiated.

During the last few years, however, detailed and extensive laboratory research has been performed to evaluate effects of different ergonomic stressors on the musculoskeletal system (Harms-Ringdahl, 1986, Jonsson 1982).

At the same time knowledge of the impact of occupational exposure on health and well-being is accumulated through epidemiological studies of shoulder-neck disorders in different occupational groups (cf. Hagberg, 1987).

In a literature review (Kilbom et al., 1986) eleven observation methods for registration of physical stress on the human body were studied and analysed. All methods were developed for the observation of an individual worker in his working conditions. Data are sampled directly at the work place or via a videorecording.

In the review the necessity of having defined the aim of the study is pointed out, when searching for an appro-

137

priate observation method for a certain object or target
group. For example epidemiological studies demand a broad
description of ergonomic exposure, while for basic
research at the laboratory, where in most cases detailed
studies are performed focusing one joint or limb at a
time, more advanced measurements are appropriate.

For the estimation of the likelihood of overexertion
injuries, however, the method chosen must be able to identify situations that may be hazardous.

IDENTIFICATION OF POTENTIAL RISKS

For a study of 200 work places a concentrated checklist
was developed (Supplement 1). It is selectively bringing
up factors documents to be potential risks for musculoskeletal injuries (Kemmlert and Kilbom, 1987).

The list of poential risk factors for stress on
different body regions had been compiLed from reliable
scientific documentation (Chaffin and Andersson, 1984,
Gamberale et al., 1981, Grandjean, 1988, Hagberg, 1987,
Harms-Ringdahl, 1986, Hunting and Grandjean 1980, Kilbom
and Persson, 1987, Westgaard and Aarås, 1984, and Winkel,
1982).

Each assessment in the study was summarized using words
and phrases collected from relevant parts of the flowchart. A statement could thus be given concerning ergonomic conditions that might lead to disorders.

The observer started his report by briefly establishing
if there was a risk for overuse syptoms. This was followed
by more specific information, opening with the most
serious risks. Individual and other circumstances not
mentioned in the form were taken into consideration but
also factors such as stress, noise and climate, which are
considered to have an additional negative effect on the
exposure as well as on the possible outcome in terms of
fatigue or pain. Two examples follow:

Street light electrician
The work tasks induce risks of overuse symptoms in the
fore-arms and hands, as the work entails repeated twisting
and forceful movements, but also unvomfortable postures
for fore-arms and hands. The tools are unsuitably designed
e.g. with regard to weight and handgrip. The working material is often difficult to handle. The work is sometimes
performed under stress which can lead to unusual or unexpected situations. When present, cold can add to the total
stress.

Telephone order clerk
    The work tasks induce risks for overuse symptoms in the
neck and shoulders, as similar movements beyond comfortable reach are repeated. The work place is unsuitably
designed and repeated keyboard work is performed when
reaching forward with one arm without support. There are
high demands on the visual capacity, but the visual conditions are troublesome. The neck is therefore often held
severely twisted, and extended backwards for periods. The
job is periodically performed under great time demand
which can add to the total stress.

Reliability

    Summaries from 8 eyperienced observers were analysed to
establish the inter-observer reliability. The contents of
the reports showed a concordance of 80 % (Kemmlert, 1986),
a percentage being acceptable according to Hartmann
(1977).

Validity

    The set of items can be looked upon as valid as it
derives from "a theoretical framework of available literature" (Carmines and Zeller, 1979).
    The validity in terms of random errors in the measure-
ment procedure was assessed (Kemmlert, 1986). Postural
angles of neck and trunk were estimated by 8 observers
and, for control of discrepancies, measured by means of a
goniometer. As found by other authors (Harris et al.,
1985, Keyserling, 1986) there was a lack of consistency
among analysts. But the study also showed random discrepancies between the estimations made by observers and the
registrations performed by means of a goniometer.
    As a result of the inability among analysts to define
boundaries between adjacent postures, the checklist classification of different neck and trunk postures was
expressed by wording such as "mildly flexed", "severely
flexed" etc., wording that is regarded as comprehensible
enough for establishing levels of hazards, thus forming
starting points for discussions about preventive strategies.

DISCUSSION

    For the purpose of work place assessments, and as
starting points for corrective activities at an actual

workplace, a checklist showing ergonomic hazards could probably be a sufficient tool.

Taking into account the weakness of the mentioned validity tests and the inconsistency among authors in indicating the measuring points for estimation of neck and trunk postures, it seems honest not to specify numerals for postural angles in the summarizing reports. Accordingly no illusion of exactness is given.

It seems important to bring up for discussion the value of detailed and time-consuming recordings of posture and movements, considering the difficulty of getting reliable registrations. The choice of different observation methods for different purposes also needs to be established.

The method presented above has proved to be an efficient tool for assessments of ergonomic hazards, and the summarizing reports designed for personnel responsible for health and safety at a plant or firm were easy to write. It is assumed that a similar structure of reports from different observers in a health team would result in more convincing messages. Reports containing a clear risk evaluation, supplemented by details, would probably be well received. Furthermore the repetition of defined risks for overuse symptoms in several reports would certainly have an educative effect in ergonomic matters.

REFERENCES

Bergqvist U. O. V., 1984, Videodisplay terminals and health. Scandinavian Journal of Work, Environment and Health, suppl 2, 10; 59-62.

Carmines E. G. and Zeller R. A., 1979, In: Quantitative Applications in the Social Sciences. Sage University Paper.

Chaffin D. B. and Andersson G., 1984, Occupational Biomechanics. John Wiley and Sons.

Gamberale F., et al., 1981, Människans tolerans för lyft- och bärarbete.(Summary in English). Arbete och Hälsa 1981:16

Grandjean E., 1988, Fitting the task to the man. (4th edition). Taylor & Francis, London.

Hagberg M., 1984, Occupational musculoskeletal stress and disorders of the neck and shoulder: a review of possible pathophysiology. International Archives of Occupational and Environmental Health, 53; 269-278.

Hagberg M., 1987, Occupational Shoulder and Neck Disorders. The Swedish Work Environment Fund, Stockholm.

Hagberg M. and Wegman D. H., 1987, Prevalence rates and odds ratios of shoulder-neck diseases in different occupational groups. British Journal of Industrial Medicine, 44; 602-610.

Harris S. R. et al., 1985, Goniometric Reliability for a Child with spastic Quadriplegia. Journal of Pediatric Orthopedics, 5, 3, 348-351.

Harms-Ringdahl K., 1986, On assessment of shoulder exercise and load-elicited pain in the cervical spine. Dissertation, Karolinska Institutet, Solna, Sweden.

Hartmann D. P., 1977, Considerations in the choice of inter-observer reliability estimates. Journal of Applied Behaviour analysis, 10; 103-116.

Hünting W. and Grandjean E., 1980, Constrained postures in accounting machine operators. Applied Ergonomics, 11; 145-149.

Jonsson B., 1982, Measurement and evaluation of local muscular strain in the shoulder during constrained work. Journal of Human Ergology, 11; 73-88.

Kemmlert K., 1986, Reliabilitetstest av plan för identifiering av belastningsfaktorer som kan innebära skadlig inverkan, Karolinska Institutet, Institutionen för fysikalisk medicin, Solna, Sweden.

Kemmlert K. and Kilbom Å., 1987, Method for identification of musculoskeletal stress factors which may have injurious effects. XIth World Congress on the prevention of occupational accidents and diseases, Stockholm.

Kemmlert K. and Kilbom Å., 1988, Besvär i nacke/skudra och samband med arbetssituation (Summary in English). Arbete och Hälsa, 1988:17.

Keyserling W. M., 1986, Postural analysis of the trunk and shoulders in simulated real time. Ergonomics, 29, 4, 569-583.

Kilbom Å. et al., 1986, Observationsmetoder för registrering av belastningar på rörelseapparaten (Summary in English). Arbete och Hälsa, 1986:21.

Kilbom Å. and Persson J., 1987, Work technique and its consequences for musculoskeletal disorders. Ergonomics, 30; 273-279.

Wallace M. and Buckle P., 1987, Ergonomic Aspects of Neck and Upper Limb Disorders. International Reviews of Ergonomics, 1; 173-200.

Westgaard R. H. and AArås A., 1984, Postural muscle strain as a causal factor in the development of musculo-skeletal illness. Applied Ergonomics, 15.3, 162-174.

Winkel J., 1982, En ergonomisk utvärdering av fotbesvär bland serveringspersonal (Summary in English). Högskolan i Luleå. TULEA, 26.

Method for the identification of musculo-skeletal stress factors which may have injurious effects.

Kemmlert, K. Kilbom, A. (1986) National Board of Occupational Safety and Health, Research Department, Work Physiology Unit, 171 84 Solna, Sweden.

Method of application:
- Find the injured body region
- Follow white fields to the right
- Do the work tasks contain any of the factors described?
- If so, tick where appropriate

neck/shoulder, upper part of back	elbow, forearms, hands	feet	knees and hips	low back	
1.		1.	1.	1.	**1.** In the walking surface uneven, slippery or non-resilient?
2.		2.	2.	2.	**2.** Is the space too limited for work movements or work materials?
3.	3.		3.	3.	**3.** Are tools and equipment unsuitably designed for the worker or the task?
4.				4.	**4.** Is the working height incorrectly adjusted?
5.				5.	**5.** Is the working chair poorly designed or incorrectly adjusted?
		6.	6.	6.	**6.** (If the work is performed whilst standing): Is there no possibility to sit and rest?
		7.	7.	7.	**7.** Is fatiguing foot-pedal work performed?
		8. a b c	8. a b c	8. a b c	**8.** Is fatiguing leg work performed eg: a) repeated stepping up on stool, step etc.? b) repeated jumps, prolonged squatting or kneeling? c) one leg being used more often in supporting the body?
9. a b c e				9. a b c d	**9.** Is repeated or sustained work performed when the back is: a) mildly flexed forward ? b) severely flexed forward ? c) bent sideways or mildly twisted ? d) severely twisted ?
10. a b c d					**10.** Is repeated or sustained work performed when the neck is: a) mildly flexed forward ? b) bent sideways or mildly twisted ? c) severely twisted ? d) extended backwards?
11. a b c d e f g	11. c f g			11. a b c d e f g	**11.** Are loads lifted manually? Notice factors of importance as: a) periods of repetitive lifting b) weight of load c) awkward grasping of load d) awkward location of load at onset or end of lifting e) handling beyond forearm length f) handling below knee height g) handling above shoulder height
12	12			12	**12.** Is repeated, sustained or uncomfortable carrying, pushing or pulling of loads performed?
13.					**13.** Is sustained work performed when one arm reaches forward or to the side without support?
14. a b	14. a b				**14.** Is there repetition of: a) similar work movements? b) similar work movements beyond comfortable reaching distance?
15. a b	15. a b				**15.** Is repeated or sustained manual work performed? Notice factors of importance as: a) weight of working materials or tools b) awkward grasping of working materials or tools
16.					**16.** Are there high demands on visual capacity?
	17. a b c d				**17.** Is repeated work, with forearm and hand, performed with: a) twisting movements? b) forceful movements? c) uncomfortable hand position? d) switches or keyboards?

Also take these factors into consideration:
a) the possibility to take breaks and pauses
b) the possibility to choose order and type of work tasks or pace of work
c) if the job is performed under time constraint or psychological stress
d) if the work can have unusual or unexpected situations
e) presence of, eg, cold, heat, draught, noise or troublesome visual conditions
f) presence of jolts, shakes or vibrations

EPIDEMIOLOGICAL ANALYSIS OF WORKLOAD DATA USING ERGONOMIC DATA BASES

R. Brauchler and K. Landau

University of Hohenheim
Federal Republic of Germany

INTRODUCTION

Problem analysis

The method of correlating job-related stress and workers' diseases has already been familiar to epidemiological
research in social medicine for many years. In most cases,
this was done by using simple chains of causation between
occupation and disease, or between stress, strain, and
disease, respectively.

Several studies that are based on existing data from
social and health insurance institutions show relationships between the different industries or occupational
groups on the one side and diseases on the other side (TÜV
Rheinland, 1986; Bundesverband der Berufskrankenkassen,
1981). These studies, however, are not able to give
detailed information on the relationships between stress
and disease since the designation of the occupation does
not allow precise conclusions to be drawn on the work content and the work situation. This information can only be
derived from job, stress, or demand analyses. Also, the
data delivered by social and health insurance institutions
do not allow statements as to the causes of the diseases,
particularly if they are induced by the job. Limited conclusions as to the cause of a disease are only possible if
information on present and former jobs, on the duration of
the individual occupations and on the social and habitual
situation of the person in question are available.

These findings lead to the assumption that monocausal
approaches, i.e. the simple correlation of job and health
impairment, have to be abandoned because a worker's health

and disease depend on a multitude of factors that can be
traced back to job conditions and private life. Since the
private sphere of the individual should be left untouched,
this project is aimed at assessing stresses resulting from
the habitual and social situation (habits such as smoking,
sports) as well as the health status of the imcumbent, in
addition to the stresses that are present at the workplace. The missing information about other aspects of private life (e.g. stresses resulting from marriage, family)
will thus be responsible for the expected residual variance in the correlation between stress data and medical
findings.

Job-related diseases and occupational disease

A disease is generally defined as malfunctions of normal vital processes in organs and organ systems that are
caused by a pathogenic stimulus. Type and extent of a disease are assessed and characterised by medical findings
and diagnosis. In particular, job-related diseases are to
be distinguished from occupational diseases. As proof of
occupational diseases, the pathogenic influence of specific noxious substances is prevailing. This does not
apply to job-related diseases where the often complex
cause-effect relationships are still unknown, which com-
plicates the proof of the cause of the disease.

METHOD

Concept of the investigation

Proving and predicting job-related diseases requires a
multi-causal model which links the determinants of the
occupational sphere to determinants of the private sphere,
in order to assess causes of disease that may lie either
in the occupational or in the private sphere.

The starting point of the concept to be elaborated is
the enlarged stress-strain concept (Rohmert, 1983) which
shows the complexity of the relationships between external
stresses and their impacts on the human being. This concept that lends itself both to physical and psychical
stresses, makes a basic distinction between an area that
is independent of the individual, the so-called object
area, and an area that is dependent on the individual, the
so-called subject area.

This distinction reflects the fact that objectively
identical demands may result in different impacts on human

beings. Differences in demands can result both from activity regulation and from individual characteristics and responses of the organ systems, being determined by the characteristics and abilities of the individual. In addition, apparently identical stresses can, through appropriate superposition of partial stresses, have different impacts on human beings. The combinations of partial stresses can result in compensation, indifference or cumulation effects (Rohmert and Luczak, 1979).

In the correlation of stress and disease, the psychical stress is of particular importance as a stressor. The original stress concept according to Selye (Selye, 1974) which defines stress as a physiological adaptation reaction of the organism to modified, adverse conditions is thus a partial aspect of the ergonomic concept of strain. Contrary to Selye's approach, however, this investigation does not focus on physiological adaptation reactions but discusses the reactions of problem management or coping strategies that result from psycho-social stress. In this context, Biefang (1985) distinguishes three conceptual hypotheses that are established to explain the relationship between stress and disease:

- the simple stress hypothesis that traces the outbreak of a disease back to life events while assuming the key role of both the number of events and the extent of the stresses related to these events,
- the interactive stress hypothesis that introduces social support and/or problem management behaviour as an additional variable in explaining the relationship between stressing life events and disease, and
- the additive stress hypothesis that assumes that social support and problem management behaviour have an effect on the disease that is independent of stressing life events.

Psychological research explains the different forms of psychical processing (stress reaction) with personality-specific influence factors as well as situation-related variables (cf. Udris, 1981). If, however, psychical problem management is considered as a result of personality-specific aspects, the subjective perception of a stress situation has a key impact on the relationship between stress and disease. Hackman (1970) replaces the concept of subjective perception with that of "redefinition".

As a conclusion, a model used to describe the hypothetical relationship between stress and disease should meet
the following requirements:
- Consideration of current situation in occupational and
  private spheres
  * Consideration of the objective external stress situa
    tion to which the human being as an individual and as
    a working person is exposed (object area). This in
    cludes stresses from work content and work environment
    as well as from leisure time outside of working hours.
  * Consideration of the redefinition of the work situa-
    tion, which is considerably influenced by the habitual
    situation (nutrition, way of life) and the social
    situation (characteristics, abilities, skills, and
    expertise).
- Dynamisation of the model
  * Consideration of former situations in the work and
    private spheres
The diagram in Fig. 1 is a greatly simplified representa-
tion of the hypothetical relationship.

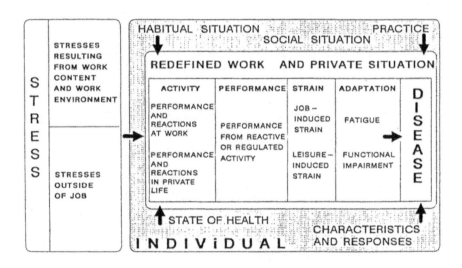

Figure 1: Hypothetical relationship between stress-strain
determinants and diseases

The discussion so far shows that two kinds of instruments will have to be developed in order to be able to
verify the described hypothetical relationship. One part
of the questionnaire will be used to assess the objective
stress situation in the job, while the second part will
assess several data items from the private sphere, in particular the health status and the habitual and social
situation of the working person.

The first partial questionnaire is a stress assessment
system ('Belastungs-Erhebungs-System', BES). Using a bottleneck-oriented job analysis approach, this questionnaire
assesses the objective stress situation in the job (see
below). The other partial questionnaire is an epidemiological assessment system ('Epidemiologisches Erhebungs-
System', EES); it is used to assess several data items
from the private sphere, in particular the worker's health
status and his/her habitual and social situation. This
medical questionnaire covers about 250 items and contains
a retrospective stress analysis that is, together with a
job, family, and social anamnesis, intended to minimise
the residual variance in establishing the correlation
between the medical findings (findings, diagnoses and
laboratory results) and the stress data. Completion of the
medical questionnaire (EES) is effected during the regular
preventive examinations carried out by physicians; owing
to the confidential relationship between the physician and
the test person, the data will also include the redefined
job and private situation.

Data assessment using these questionnaires is made
independent of the person. The data records are linked
through corporate job designations; processing of the
medical findings data is ensured by the use of different
classification schemes that allow complete encoding.

Linking of several data bases is made conforming to the
described concept of the hypothetical relationship between
stress and disease, using an epidemiological and stress
assessment system ('Epidemiologisches und Belastungs-
Erhebungs-System', EBES). This information system is
designed to assess the indicated data items from the
professional and private spheres and to evaluate them with
regard to their possible integration into an
epidemiological early-warning system.

The 'Belastungs-Erhebungs-System' (BES) was designed on
the theoretical basis of an objective bottleneck-oriented
job analysis which builds on the model of the man-at-work
system and the stress-strain concept. Its structure and
questionnaire has been derived from the existing job

analysis method AET (Rohmert et al., 1975; Rohmert and
Landau, 1979; Landau and Rohmert, 1981; Rohmert and
Landau, 1983). Owing to the particular requirement of a
strain-relevant stress description, the BES has to meet
the following requirements in addition to the requirements
of a job analysis method:
- Structuring of the method into strain categories (cf.
  Rohmert and Luczak, 1979)
- an at least qualitative graduation of the questionnaire
  items according to the psycho-physical strain described
  by them
- the possibility to allocate selected questionnaire items
  to characteristics of psycho-physical strain
- the provision of scaling and rating aids on the basis of
  physiological and psychological strain investigations
In addition, the findings of psychological job analysis
methods described in the literature (overview cf. Landau
und Rohmert, 1987) could be exploited.

When designing the BES, basic problems were encountered
with item selection and stress quantification or with item
scaling, respectively. The results of physiological and
psychological strain analyses documented in the literature
that included references to impacts on health contain
appropriate guidelines. Examples are the relationships
between different shift schemes and diseases of the
gastro-intestinal system and the cardiac/circulatory system as well as the proof of hypertension, headache, insom-
nia, anorexia and performance impairments as a result of
shift work (cf. Williamson and Sanderson, 1986; Knauth et
al., 1980).

The iterative development of the assessment method that
involved the cooperation of ergonomists, physicians, work
safety specialists and a psychologist ensured the objective selection of items. The iterative development of the
questionnaire focused on the following aspects (Landau,
1978):
- Improved ease of use
  * Clarity of the procedure
  * Comprehensibility of formulations
  * Congruence of the BES definitions with ergonomic terms
  * Implementation in a cost and time saving manner
- Tuning of directive and bridging examples
  and
- Objective selection of items
  or equalisation of author-specific weighing to improve
  the general applicability of the method to a larger
  number of jobs.

Only those items were considered that are task-specific
with regard to the fulfilment of a purpose, i.e. separated
from the characteristics of the imcumbent of the job to be
investigated. The accents of the theoretical concept
(philosophical-historical understanding of the work content) on which the BES is based are highlighted by the
basic structure:

Physical stress factors
                    - physical-situative stress factors
                    - energetic-effectory stress factors

Psychical stress factors
                    - Information reception   - Discover
                                               - Recognise
                    - Information processing   - Decide
                    - Information output   - Act

Information processing in human beings includes the
psychical stress factors, i.e. the stress resulting from
the conscious or unconscious comprehension, experiencing,
and processing of the task. The 130 items of the BES are
to be marked in an assessment interview and/or in an analysis of documents. This assessment technique offers the
advantage of highly cost-effective application, data processing, and data evaluation. The highly standardised
stress assessment system minimises the amount of discretion of the analyst. Appropriate training seminars will be
offered to familiarise the analyst with the technique of
detailed on-site observation and with the technique of
carrying out standardised interviews with incumbents and
superiors.

Quantification of the stress factors and evaluation of
stress height and duration, respectively, are made using
largely standardised rating indices (cf. Rohmert et al.,
1975). The multi-level indices are used to evaluate the
duration and height of stress as well as several design
aspects that influence the stress height.

Sample population

This investigation is part of a pilot project that
investigates the fitness of job analysis methods to predict job-related health impairments. The scope of this
pilot project is limited to the job-induced stresses and
possible impairments of the employees of one company division; this limited population is used to carry out initial

tests on the predictive value of assessment instruments
with regard to the implementation of an early-warning
system.

The stratified job and incumbent sample includes the
particularly exposed driving, controlling and supervisory
activities in brown-coal mining. These cover the whole
spectrum of the work types "light-heavy" and "easy-diffi-
cult". The deliberate selection of the job collective
allows, after modification of the bridging examples, the
applicability of the assessment instruments to all jobs of
this kind.

The pilot study considers the medical findings for 350
test persons and the job data for 40 different jobs.

Method of evaluation

From the ordinal ratings of the stress characteristics,
stress factors are derived that allow correct statements
as to the work content and the work environment for the
different jobs. The stress factors can be represented
graphically as a profile diagram to give a quick overview
of the height and duration of jobs. In doing this, the
classification of the individual items for the stress
factors is derived from the structure of the BES. Groups
of functions with regard to similar stress profiles can be
established through cluster formation.

The evaluation is intended to show functional relationships between stress data and data from medical findings
(disease = f(stress, habits, individual characteristics,
etc.)). Some relationships between stress and disease that
are already known to a large degree are initially proved
in order to verify the predictive value of the assessment
instrument. In this process, common statistical and sto-
chastic methods such as regression analysis and discrimi-
nance analysis are applied.

RESULTS

The stress factors which are taken at particular driving activities with the BES, are represented graphically
in a profile diagram (Figure 2).

BES – JOB ANALYSIS

DRIVING ACTIVITIES — % of maximum stress

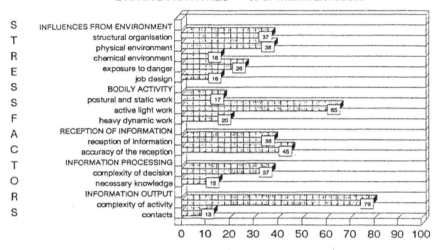

Figure 2. BES job profile "driving activities" - overview

The profile diagram shows the characteristics of the job "driving a vehicle (car, lorry)". The first part shosw the influences from structural organisation and physical environment. These stress factors obtain a few groups of characteristics like climate, noise, vibraiton and illumination, so it is advantageous to represent it in a particular job profile (Figure 3).

The analysis of the bodily activities show the importance of active light work (65 % of the maximum stress), while postural, static and heavy dynamic work comes only up to 20 %. When considering the work tasks, these results demonstrate that the motorist remains sitting the whole work day and that the main job operation is the transformation from information received to control of the steering gears with hands, arms and feet.

The explanation of the represented transaction needs the same kind of profile analysis which is shown as an

example of the stress resulting from the influence of
environment in Figure 3.

The profile column with 53 % of the maximum stress in
the temporal work organisation (shiftwork, breaks, etc.),
the fact that the stress resulting from low discretion in
taks contents comes up to 63 % of the maximum stress and
the importance of the structure of positions account for
the profile column with the characteristic "structural
organisation" at 37 % in Figure 2.

BES – JOB ANALYSIS

INFLUENCE OF ENVIRONMENT

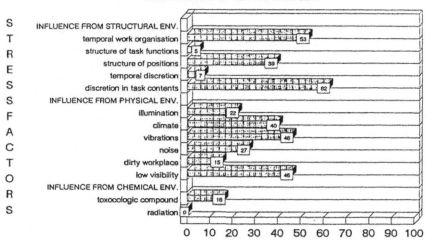

Figure 3. BES job profile "driving activities" for the
stress resulting from the influence of environment

The workload data for all groups of characteristics can
be represented and interpreted in this way and finally the
connection between these stress factors and the epidemiologic data base is possible. The connections between ergonomic and epidemiologic data bases are founded upon the
special number of task function and organisation units of

the company division. The results will be published in the
final project report by the German Bundesanstalt für
Arbeitsschutz und Unfallforschung.

ACKNOWLEDGEMENTS

We extend our respect and gratitude to our colleagues
in the research group that investigates the fitness of job
analysis methods to predict job related health impari-
ments: Dr. med. U. Blankenstein and Dip.-Ing. W. Ballé
from the Rheinbraun AG, Köln, for their helpful co-operation during the measurements both in the field and at the
physician centre and also to Dipl. Wi.-Ing. W. Brauchler
from the Universitiy of Hohenheim, whose part has been the
design of the epidemiologic and ergonomic data bases and
the evaluation methods.

REFERENCES

Biefang, S., 1985, Messung psychosozialer Erfolgs- und
  Prädiktorvariablen, Habilitationsschrift eingereicht
  bei der theoretischen Fakultät für Medizin der Univer-
  sität Ulm
Bundesverband der Betriebskrankenkassen (ed.), 1981,
  Krankheit und arbeitsbedingte Belastungen, Gesamtaus-
  gabe, Essen, Bundesverband der Betriebskrankenkassen
Hackman, J.R., 1970, Tasks and Task Performance in
  Research on Stress. In: McGrath, J.E. (ed.), Social and
  Psychological Factors in Stress, New York, Holt, Rine-
  hart & Winston, pp. 202-237
Knauth, P., Landau, K., Dröge, C., Schwittek, M., Widyn-
  ski, M., Rutenfranz, J., 1980, Duration of Sleep
  Depending on the Type of Shiftwork. In: International
  Archive of Environmental Health 46, pp. 167-177
Landau, K., 1978, Das Arbeitswissenschaftliche Erhebungs-
  verfahren zur Tätigkeitsanalyse - AET, Darmstadt
Landau, K. and Rohmert, W., 1981, AET - a new job analysis
  method. In: Proceedings 1981 Spring Annual Conference &
  World Productivity Congress, May 17-20, 1981, pp. 751-
  760
Landau, K. and Rohmert, W., 1987, Aufgabenbezogene Analyse
  von Arbeitstätigkeiten. In: Kleinbeck, U. and Ruten-
  franz, J., 1987, Arbeitspsychologie, Göttingen,
  Toronto, Zürich
Rohmert, W., 1983, Determination of Stress and Strain at
  Real Work Places: Methods and Results of Field Studies
  with Air Traffic Control Officers

Rohmert, W., 1983, Formen menschlicher Arbeit. In: Roh-
    mert, W. and Rutenfranz, J., Praktische Arbeitsphysio-
    logie, Stuttgart: Thieme

Rohmert, W. and Landau, K., 1979, Das Arbeitswissenschaft-
    liche Erhebungsverfahren zur Tätigkeitsanalyse - AET -
    Handbuch und Merkmalheft, Bern, Stuttgart, Wien: Hans
    Huber

Rohmert, W. and Landau, K., 1983, A New Technique for Job
    Analysis, London, Taylor & Francis

Rohmert, W. and Luczak, H., 1979, Stress, Work and Produc-
    tivity. In: Hamilton, V. and Warburton, D., Human
    Stress and Cognition: An Information Processing
    Approach, J. Wiley & Sons, Chichester / New York /
    Brisbane / Toronto

Rohmert, W., Luczak, H. and Landau, K., 1975, Arbeitswis-
    senschaftlicher Erhebungbogen zur Tätigkeitsanalyse -
    AET. In: zeitschrift für Arbeitswissenschaft, 29, 1975,
    4, pp. 199 - 297

Selye, H., 1974, Stress, München, Piper

TÜV Rheinland (ed.), 1986, Arbeitsmedizinische Daten als
    Basis für den Abbau von Belastungen, Abschlußbericht,
    Verlag TÜV Rheinland

Udris, I., 1981, Redefinition als Problem der Arbeitsana-
    lyse. In: Frei, F. und Ulich, E. (eds.), Beiträge zur
    psychologischen Arbeitsanalyse, Bern: Huber

Williamson, A.M. and Sanderson, J.W., 1986, Changing the
    Speed of Shift Rotation - A Field Study. In: Ergonom-
    ics, 1986, Vol. 29, No. 9, pp. 1085-1096

THE INFLUENCE OF SEAT ANGLE AND FURNITURE HEIGHT ON BACKPAIN

A. C. Mandal, M.D., Chief Surgeon

DK-2930 Klampenborg
Denmark

INTRODUCTION

There has until recently been a world-wide unanimity of opinion with respect to "correct" sitting posture, namely that the bodyshould be upright with a 90 degrees flexion or bending of thehip joint and with preserved lordosis of the lumbar region.However, nobody is able to sit in this posture while working.

No one has given any real explanation as to why this right-angled position should be better than any other posture. Nevertheless, it has quite uncritically been accepted by experts all over the world as the only correct one. Above all, the lumbar support has been considered to be the means to improve the seated postures (Aakerblom, 1948). But this is rather illogical as the lumbar support only carries about 5 % of the body weight - and only in reclined position (Branton, 1969).

Very little interest has been attached to the seat, which carries about 80-95 % of the body weight. Its influence on the posture of the body therefore must be much more important.

The sketches that follow, however, have absolutely no scientific background. They are nice looking, but entirely based on wishful thinking, aesthetics, morals and discipline from the days of Chancellor Bismarck and Queen Victoria. They are based on the false assumption that you are able to sit and work with a 90 degrees flexion in the hip joint and a preserved lordosis of the lumbar region.

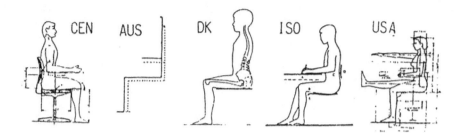

Fig. 1: Schematic models representing "correct right-angled posture" from various countries.

Nevertheless, they constitute the basis of:
1. International standardisation of school furniture (ISO) (1978).
2. European standardisation of office furniture (CEN) (1982).
3. Education of furniture designers (USA). Diffrient (1974).
4. Anthropometry (AUS.), Oxford (1969)
5. Instructions for "correct" sitting posture (DK), Snorrason (1968).

The Danish sketch by Snorrason may be the most interesting of them all, as it explains the origin of this type ofinstructions. This is simply a drawing of a skeleton sitting on a chair. But sitting problems of a skeleton have nothing in common with the sitting problems of a working person.

In Scandinavia enormous efforts have been made to teach people better sitting postures in schools, offices and factories, hoping this would reduce the great number of back-sufferers. In one local school authority (Gentofte) the pupils were given 90 lessons of posture training during 5 years. The poor results of these efforts can be seen in Figure 2.

The photos were taken with an automatic camera at 24 minute intervals during a four-hourly examination. All pupils are sitting in postures most harmful to the back.

Fig. 2: The results of intensive posture training with ISO school furniture. Table height 72 cm. All the pupils are sitting with quite unacceptable posture.

THE ANATOMY OF THE SEATED MAN

The conformation of a seated person has so far been unknown to most doctors, furniture designers, and physiotherapists; however, the German orthopaedic surgeon, Hans Schoberth, has carried out some excellent research on problems of sitting posture (Schoberth, 1962). Figure 3 is taken from his book.

When standing (A) there is almost a vertical axis through the thigh and the pelvis, and a concavity, or lordosis, is present in the small of the back. When a person is seated (B) the thigh is horizontal, the hip joint is flexed by about 60 degrees and the pelvis has a sloping axis. The lumbar region then exhibits a convexity, or kyphosis. Schoberth found from X- ray examinations of 25 people sitting upright that there was an average of 60 degrees flexion in the hip joint and an average of 30 degrees flexion in the lumbar region. When leaning forward over the desk, the increased flexion mainly took place in the lumbar region.

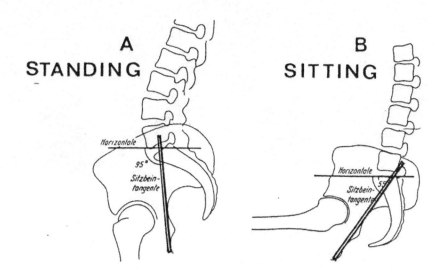

Figure 3: The normal anatomy of the lumbar region, standing, A, and upright sitting, B, (Schoberth, 1962).

This finding of Schoberths' has been confirmed by
Aakerblom (1948) and Keegan (1953). No scientific investigation has found a 90 degree flexion in the hip joint in
the seated work position. The sketches from Figure 1
should consequently be abandoned in serious ergonomic lit-
terature in the future.

The lumbar support will only have effect if the seat is
sloping backwards so that the point of gravity of the body
is forced backwards, behind the supporting areas. This,
however, leads to increased pressure under the knees and
will tend to tilt the axis of the pelvis backwards. In
this way the effect of the lumbar support is counteracted.
To avoid the knee- pressure the chairs and tables have
become lower and lower.

In the standing position you will automatically obtain
a lordosis, a concavity, of the small back. This also happens when sitting on horse-back or on the edge of a table
(Figure 4). All children know, that it is more comfortable
to tilt forward on the front legs of a chair when working
at a table (Figure 5). In all these ways you can sit with
thighs sloping about 30 degrees and this reduces the lum-

bar flexion to a similar degree, resulting in an upright balanced position, which needs no lumbar support.

Figures 4 & 5: Sitting with sloping thighs can preserve a straight back.

WHAT IS THE IDEAL HEIGHT OF FURNITURE?

During the 20th century the average height of man has increased about 10 cm and during the same period furniture height has decreased(!) about 10 cm. This will tend to give more constrained postures when working at a desk. Some years ago I investigated which furniture height a group of 80 people preferred when reading and writing. All preferred to have furniture 15-20 cm higher, provided the seat and the desk were sloping towards one another. At the preferred height most of them were able to sit in a balanced position with a straight back (Mandal, 1982).

To evaluate the influence of furniture height on flexion of the back a 171 cm tall person was asked to sit
reading / writing for a period of 20 minutes at:
    A. Traditional furniture with 5 degrees backward slop-
ing seat and a 72 cm high horizontal desktop, i.e. ISO-
standard.
    B. 20 cm higher furniture with seat and desktop sloping
towards one another, Figure 6.

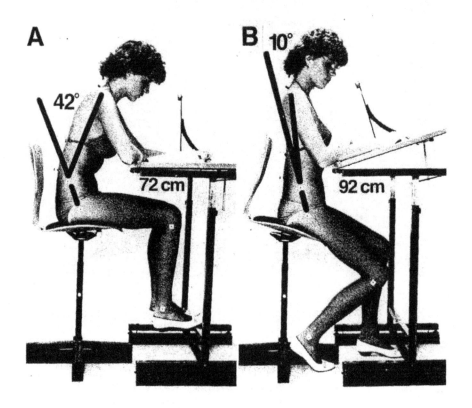

Figure 6:   Sitting on 20 cm higher furniture may result
in a reduction of 32 degrees of lumbar flexion. The girl
definitely preferred the higher position.

This experiment was repeated for ten days. By an automatic camera photos were taken at 4 minute intervals. To
control the flexion of the various parts of the body,
well-defined anatomical points were marked on the skin:
1.Knee-joint (capitulum fibulae). 2. Hip-joint (trochantor

major. 3. Fourth lumbar disc (midway between anterior and
posterior iliac spine). 4. Shoulder-joint (acromion).

At the end of the experiment 50 photos of the two situations were available. The skin marks were connected with
lines on the photos. The resulting angles between these
lines were measured:

A. Desk height 72 cm (ISO) showed an average lumbar
flexion of 42 degrees.

B. Desk height 92 cm showed an average lumbar flexion
of 10 degrees.

This means a reduction of lumbar flexion of 32 degrees!
The differences were highly significant (P<0.0001).

Besides this, the flexion in the hip joint was reduced
15 degrees when changing from 72 cm to 92 cm. Finally the
neck angle was measured and a reduction of 20 degrees was
found when changing from A to B. In all, this means a
reduction of the total back flexion of 67 degrees and the
girl definitely preferred the highert position. It is
obvious that the disc pressure is very low in this position, as it is half standing with preserved lordosis. The
majority of the new Danish school furniture is now conforming with this much higher construction.

THE ELECTRONIC OFFICE

In the modern electronic office height adjustment is
even more important as many will have to sit for many
hours with highly repetitive work and without the possibility of moving. The traditional solutions with low furniture and "effective" lumbar support have been prevailing. The result, however, have been disappointing.

Grandjean (1984) found that conversional terminal work
resulted in about 5 times more complaints (and data-entry
work in about 13 times as many complaints) from the neck
and shoulders as traditional office work. After 4-5 years
work with data-entry the number of back and neck sufferers
is evidently increasing rapidly. These figures are unacceptable and indicate that a reduction of hours spent with
data-entry work is necessary unless better working conditions are achieved.

Experiment with adjustment of furniture height

In a large bank in Copenhagen the data-entry personnel
were complaining of severe neck, shoulder and back problems. In a monthly magazine for the employees I offered a
correction of postures to those suffering from chronic

back-pain (daily). The13 who wanted to participate ranged
in height from 158 to 175cm and in age from 24-54.

On the first day they were positioned on a hydraulic
chair with tilting seat. While they were sitting and key-
ing-in, theheight of the chair and table were altered to
the height inwhich they felt the pain was least pronounced.

They all wanted to sit higher than before and most of
themwere sitting with a more upright position with a
straight back.

The height of the chair and desk was measured and their
daily workplace was adjusted to this height. They were
told only to sit in the higher position for 10-20 minutes
during the first days, as they would get tired.

After some weeks most of them preferred to sit in the
higher position most of the day. The furniture in the
workplace was easily adjustable but most of it had previously been used at standard height. Most of the participants had for several years used tilting chairs.

After a 2 month period, during which they could easily
change the height of the furniture, I compared what height
of the 13 participants had permanently been using. The
average preferred desk-height was 71.6 cm compared to CEN
(European Standardisation Organisation) recommendations
of 65 cm. Preferred chair height was 54.3 cm (CEN: 42-50
cm). Only 2 of the shorter ones, both 160 cm high, had
preferred to use the CEN standard desk height of 65 cm.
These 2 are not included in the following investigation,
as comparison of posture was not possible.

Registration of the postures of the remaining eleven
was done by means of an automatic camera. The participants
were asked to wear semi-tight sweaters and jeans and a 13
cm long white nylon ruler was stitched to the jeans with
one end over the hip joint (trochanter major) and the
other end over 4th lumbar disc (the point mid-way between
anterior and posterior iliac spine). Besides that, the 7th
cervical vertebra (vertebra prominens) and the knee joint
were marked on the skin and on the clothes respectively.

Firstly they were seated at their preferred height
while doing normal data-entry work for 15 minutes and photographs were taken by automatic camera at a rate of one
per minute. Immediately afterwards the furniture height
was reduced to CEN- standard i.e. desk height 65 cm and
chair height 50 cm. The seat was locked in a 5 degrees
backward sloping angle and the lumbar support adjusted.
This position was also maintained for 15 minutes and
another 15 photographs were taken.

During the investigation the participants were left alone in a shielded corner of a large office. Lines were drawn on the photographs between the marks on the clothes and the angles measured.

Results

In the higher, preferred sitting position the average flexion of the back (lumbar plus hip-joint) was 11 degrees less than in the CEN position (Figure 7. P<0.001). Pain indication with visual analog scale (Huskisson, 1974) was 35 mm in the higher position compared to 67 mm in the CEN standard position (Figure 8. P<0.001).

Seven out of eleven were able to sit permanently with a straight back or a lumbar lordosis in an upright balanced position without using the lumbar support (Figure 9). The position is similar to that when sitting on horseback. It will reduce the strain of the back and allow abdominal respiration. When they wanted to rest, they lowered the seat and leaned back against the lumbar support. This is the position normally considered a good working position.

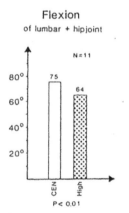
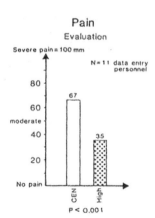

Figures 7 & 8: The CEN standard furniture resulted in increased flexion of the lumbar region and increased pain indication.

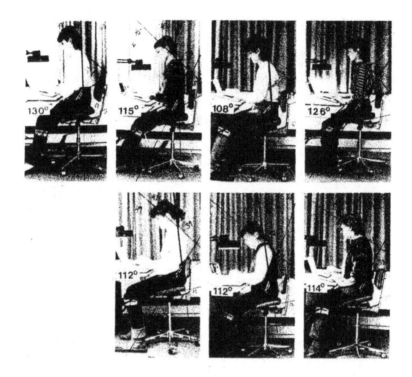

Figure 9: Seven out of eleven preferred to sit permanently with a straight back in an upright balanced position without using the lumbar support.

The four persons using lumbar support were sitting further back on the seat and with more pronounced flexion of the lumbar region than the rest. These four had all been instructed at the end of an eight hour working day. This proved to be a bad time as they were tired and more interested in getting home. For them the seat was sloping an average of 5.7 degrees forward compared to a 12.7 degrees forward slope with the 7 more upright persons. A forward slope of at least 10 degrees appears to be necessary to achieve a lumbar lordosis.

Three out of eleven had previous problems with swelling of the legs – they all reported improvement.

CONCLUSIONS

In an earlier experiment I had noticed that most people prefer to sit 10-20 cm higher when reading and writing, than recommended by the standards. In the higher position they were feeling considerably less backpain. The natural consequence of this was to invite the back-sufferers to adjust the furniture to exactly the height, where the pain was least pronounced.

For data-entry personnel this height proved to be a 6.6 cm higher desk, than recommended by CEN standards, after a two months trial period. In the higher position 7 out of 11 were able to sit with a straight back in a balanced position without using the lumbar support. The indication of pain was reduced from 67 mm (visual analog scale) on CEN furniture to 35 mm at the preferred height. Three had previously been suffering from swelling of the lower legs; they all reported improvement.

The present CEN standards will aparently result in unnecessary flexion, strain and pain of the back. As there is no scientific background for the CEN standards, they represent an unacceptable medical experiment with the health of millions of people. In the future we should probably rely more on the wishes of the consumers, as they often have to sit for many hours with backpain every day.

REFERENCES

Aakerblom, B. 1948: Standing and sitting posture. (Stock holm: Nordiske Bokhandeln).

Branton, P. 1969: Ergonomics, 12, 316-327.

CEN (Comité Europeén de Normalisation) 1982: Pr En, (Afnor, Tour Europe CEDEX 7, 92080 Paris, La Defense).

Diffrient, N. 1974: Human Scale. (USA: MIT Press).

Grandjean, E. 1984: Ergonomics & Health in Modern Offices. (London: Taylor & Francis), p. 447.

Huskisson, E.C. 1974: Measurement of Pain. The Lancet, p.1127.

ISO (International Organisation of Standardisation) 1978: TC 136/SC7, Cologne.

Keegan, J.J. 1953: Journal of Bone & Joint Surgery. 35A,3.

Mandal, A.C. 1982: Correct Height of School Furniture, Human factors, 24, 257-269. USA.

Oxford, H.W. 1969: Anhtropometric data for educational chairs, Ergonomics, 12, 140-161.

Schoberth, H. 1962: Sitzschaden, Sitzmîbel. (Berlin: Springer Verlag).

Snorrason, E. 1968: Tidsskrift for Danske Sygehuse. 22.

SAFETY DIAGNOSIS IN INDUSTRIAL PLANTS: CONCEPTS AND PRELIMINARY RESULTS

F. Ruppert
C. Graf Hoyos

University of Technology Munich
Federal Republic of Germany

THE BEHAVIOURAL APPROACH TO HAZARD ANALYSIS

Limitations of ex-post-facto methods

In recent years two lines of development in the world of work have intensified the application of behavioural concepts to accident control: 1. Progress in the design of safer machines and tools with the consequence that most accidents occurring can no longer be attributed to failures of technical equipment (e.g. a tearing rope) but are in some way caused by "unsafe" behaviour of the victim himself or of other people within the work system. 2. A dramatic increase in establishing complex systems operating tremendous amounts of energy (e.g. nuclear power plants, production of chemical and biological agents, weapons, aeroplanes and ships, buildings in high-risk environments) including the risk that even minimal 'human errors' may lead to catastrophic events.

If unsave behaviour evidently contributes to the occurrence of accidents and must be taken into account for accident prevention, "behavioural strategies" are urgently needed. First of all it is necessary to understand the mechanisms leading to safe and unsafe behaviour as well as to develop methods for analysing the relevant factors in a certain situational context. Indeed, there are models of (un)safe behaviour as well as promising approaches to an effective methodology (e.g. Burkardt, 1983; Hale and Glendon, 1987; Hoyos and Zimolong, 1988).

The most common method to explore the harmfulness of man-machine systems and to find out the role of the "human factor" seems to be the investigation of accidents already

happened. No doubt, this procedure has its benefits if
circumstances are carefully reported and people involved
in accidents can be asked in detail, but on the other hand
there are strong limitations of this method:
- Although the real number of accidents occurring per year
  in a country like the FRG (1.5 million) is too high to
  be neglected by the government and other responsible
  authorities, accidents – and also occupational diseases – must be called 'rare events' for statistical
  reasons with all the complications for computation and
  interferences. In the recent years the relative accident
  rate can be estimated as to be 32 accidents per million
  working hours.
- Very rarely, an accident can be explained by only one or
  two causes; in most cases many factors are effective and
  coincide into a chain of destructive events (e.g. sudden
  break of a machine, poor lightning conditions). A certain combination of factors coming together in an accident causation might be unique or even at random. For
  these reasons, it seems to be very difficult or even
  impossible to find laws of accident causation from an
  retrospective analysis of accidents.
- To analyse accidents means necessarily to consider
  things ex-post-facto: the events to be avoided in the
  future must already have been happend – an intolerable
  condition especially when consequences of an event are
  fatal.

Attemps have been made to overcome some of these limitations by analysing critical incidents ('near misses')
(Flanagan, 1954; Vollmer, 1978), but the purpose of hazard
control should be to avoid even near misses and not to
reckon upon them. Also it is not clear what a 'near miss'
would be in a case where the hazard is noise and can
result in deafness for the next 20 years. Therefore, there
is beyond all consideration of accident studies a strong
need for approaches to explore the work situation without
looking back to bad events in the past. Of course, what we
need is a predictive analysis of hazardous situations
which can show us
- how safe existing systems are,
- how safe a restructured system will be, and
- how safe new but not yet established systems will be.

Hazard analysis and/or job analysis

Looking for adequate methods to study the contribution
of humans to the safety of work situations of all kinds

but particularly of modern production systems one will, of
course, refer to methods of job analysis. This was the
situation we encountered when we went on to establish a
behavioural oriented safety diagnosis instrument. The
first step was to gain an overview of job analysis procedures written in German and to find out their potential
for hazard analysis. Unfortunately, this survey revealed
only deficits. While most of the procedures reflect on a
safety as a part of job tasks the proposed surveying of
safety aspects is marginal.

The 'Tätigkeits-Analyse-Inventar' (TAI) by Frieling et
al. (1984) contains about 2,200 items, 22 (1 %) of them
dealing explicitly with aspects of safety: 'sources of
hazards', 'training of safe behaviour', 'responsibility'
and 'degree of care'. About 6 % of 221 items in the 'Fragebogen zur Arbeitsanalyse' by Frieling and Hoyos (1978)
refer to safety: modes of exposition to danger and some
principles of safety measures. 15 of 390 items in the
'Arbeitswissenschaftlicher Erhebungsbogen zur Tätigkeitsanalyse' by Landau et al (1975) concern safety aspects:
characteristics of being endangered by objects and work
equipment, likelihood of occupational diseases and responsibility. Also the 'Analysis of Jobs and Job Demand' by
Bürgi (1976) reflects safety only in one dimension: exposure to danger.

For some other instruments of job analysis published in
Germany it is difficult to evalute their potential for
hazard analysis. The 'Verfahren zur Ermittlung von Regulationserfordernissen in der Arbeitstätigkeit' (VERA) by
Volpert et al. (1983) as well as the RHIA-instrument
(Greiner et al., 1987) do not mention safety at all as one
aspect of job tasks, but the proposed method of analysis
might also be applied to work situations with dangerous
task sequences. In the same way applying the 'Tätigkeits-
bewertungssystem' (TBS) by Hacker et al. (1983) safety
might be one aspect in evaluating jobs, particularly their
potential for injury, but this is not explicitly mentioned. Nevertheless, theoretical concepts of information
processing which are fundamental for the TBS such as
'behaviour-regulations by signals and indications' and
'incomplete or false use of existing information' are
quite stimulating as well for safety analysis.

Genuine procedures of hazard and safety analysis

Obviously, procedures for analysing hazards and those
for analysing safety seem to have been developed quite

independently. But until now standardized and established
procedures of hazard analysis only exist for the investigation of technologically controlled hazards.
The following main procedures from this country to be mentioned are:
1. The 'event tree analysis' to explore and foresee bottom
   up consquences of system breakdowns (DIN 25 419)
2. The 'fault tree analysis' to investigate top down
   possible causations for critical or catastrophic events
   (DIN 25 424)
3. The 'failure mode and effective analysis' to inquire
   the effects of a failure in a single component of a
   system (DIN 25 448)
   Similar methods exist also in English versions (see
Hoyos and Zimolong, 1988). Furthermore, the 'Guide to Hazard and Operability Studies' should be mentioned because
of its growing importance in the chemical industries.
Some efforts are observed to use these procedures also for
investigating the human factor in safety. Denny et al.
(1978) applied the event tree method to investigate major
accidents in underground mine systems including also
behavioural errors. Monteau (1977) developed a practical
method to describe the net of circumstances leading to
accidents. For that purpose he classified the task accomplishment into four components: person, task, material,
and environment. The goal of analysis is to make a list of
all relevant variations of normal operation conditions to
foresee the coincidence of alterations possibly leading to
accidents. Other questionnaires or checklists to mention
here are the 'Diagnostic Safety Form' by Tuttle et al.
(1974) and a 'Guide to recognize Hazards' by Nohl and
Thiemecke (1988). Nohl and Thiemecke set up hazards, sub-
dividing and combining them with single job operations.
They also try to estimate different risks by evaluating
the probability of every single harmful event.
   While most of the attemps to develop instruments of
hazard analysis also consider psychological aspects, only
a few seem to be based on genuine psychological concepts.
One of these seems to be a 'question list' presented by
Hale and Glendon (1987). The authors propose to investigate every source of danger systematically under three
dimensions: 'hazard detection', 'danger assessment' and
'action against danger'.
   In the following, problems of safety analysis with
special emphasis on behavioural aspects will be discussed.

BASIC CONCEPTS OF BEHAVIOUR-ORIENTED SAFETY DIAGNOSIS

Hazards and hazard control

It is common to speak of traffic safety, work safety, safety at home as well in public buildings such as schools. This classification shows us that safety issues are raised in different areas but also that safety is a very ubiquitous affair because people have to do with hazards on the road, at work, at home and in other places, in fact, people may get involved in hazardous situations everywhere. In most hazardous situations people are protected from injuries more or less by technical equipment and/or organizational measures, but to some extent people must take care of themselves. They must have more sophisticated control of hazards around them. Therefore methodological considerations with respect to safety which are the main concern of this paper should be discussed on a fairly general level as shown in the following.

Hazards as we like to understand them are considered to be latent amounts of physical energy which may hurt the human body if energy potentials are released. This kind of energy we have to deal with is of course related to the equipment at hand and procedures applied as well as environmental conditions. A car driver is exposed to the kinetic energy of a moving car which cannot be absorbed by the human body in case of collision. Workers are confronted with moving parts, heavy goods, electrical current, radiation etc. etc. Hazards of this type are lurking at home, too. In all the places mentioned and in general if a person stands upright, walks or climbs he or she is exposed to energy which is stored in the human body.

Of course, hazard should be eliminated whenever it is possible. This is the ultimate goal of any safety measure. It is impossible that men and hazards are to be separated effectively by devices of all kinds or people must be protected by helmets, glasses, gloves, and so on. After having done whatever is possible in this way people are in charge of controlling hazards if they come in contact with them, i.e. in case of danger (Hoyos, 1980; 1987).

The "Safety Diagnosis Questionnaire"

How do you understand hazard control? Hazard control or safe behaviour respectively means to maintain a reasonable state of safety within a system where a person is acting, for instance a worker on the shop floor. In order to strive for this goal the worker must perceive hazards,

judge physical dimensions, decide on certain actions and
act in accordance with norms and standards. In other
words, maintaining safety can be defined as a task which
consists of goals and a set of behavioural demands which
the worker has to cope with - mostly parallel to his main
work task. This definition causes us to consider hazard
control to be a secondary task with its typical competition with the primary task, i.e. the work task a worker
has to accomplish.

If safety officers and other safety experts want to
improve the human factor in safety which is seen today the
most important aspect of safety and accident prevention
than they must be enabled to describe demands on safe
behaviour in detail and in a systematic way. To provide
safety experts with an appropriate instrument to achieve
this goal we have begun to develop a questionnaire which
is suited to common job analysis procedures. This instrument (which also takes organizational aspects into consideration) is geared to preventive application and is en-
titled the 'Safety Diagnosis Questionnaire' (SDQ). It
regards human behaviour in hazardous situations as the
most crucial point in the intended diagnostic activity; it
is ment to enable safety officers as well as supervisors
to analyze level of safety in their factory or workshop
and to obtain indications of safety-related problems. The
SDQ represents an attempt to make psychological theories
of safe behaviour applicable to practice in the organization of work. Available knowledge about factors which
determine behaviour in hazardous situations - this knowledge is obviously limited - has been collected, systema-
tized and made usable for safety officers (Hoyos and Bernhardt, 1987).

The first step in this direction was to adopt a fairly
simple and popular model of human behaviour encompassing
processes of perceiving, judging, deciding, acting, for
instance in terms of stress cycle designed by McGrath
(1976). Results from the field of accident and safety
research were transposed into a set of questions which
describe types of demands for safe behaviour. In general,
in finding an appropriate format and mode of answer for
questions we were oriented to the "Position Analysis Questionnaire" (McCormick et al, 1969.) Table 1 shows chapters
of SDQ.

Table 1. 'Safety Diagnosis Questionnaire' (SDQ): Titles of
chapters and samples of items (Lehrstuhl für Psychologie,
1988)

Title	Sample
1. The organization	Does the job incumbent do shift work? (yes, no)
2. Hazards and danger	Which hazards (from an attached list) are present at the workplace? (for instance: moving parts, electricity)
3. Perceiving and attending hazard signals	Is it important for the worker facing this hazard – to keep his attention on work and hazard at the same time? (very important...unimportant)
4. Judging and foreseeing of hazards	Is it important for the worker to estimate distances of hazards? (very important... unimportant)
5. Planning and preventing	Is it important for the worker with respect to this hazard – to take preventive measures for cases of critical incidents (for instance: participating in First-Aid courses) (very important...unimportant)
6. Acting	Is it important for the worker facing this hazard – to accomplish task sequences in the right order and complete? (for instance: while mixing dangerous liquids) (very important...unimportant)
7. Cooperating and communicating	Is it important for the worker facing this hazard – to communicate reasons for suspicion to colleages? (for instance: unusual noise of machines) (very important...unimportant)

As you can see the analysis of safety related questions
(chapters 3-7) is preceded by chapters dealing with
descriptions of work tasks and hazard analysis. No doubt,

both chapters are basic for safety analysis: without going
into too much detail it should be mentioned that safety
related demands are to be analyzed separately for each
hazard identified at the workplace in question. It turned
out that in average a workplace is loaded with 6-7
hazards.

Table 1 also shows a sample of questions from the SDQ.
In general, a subject such as attention is preceded by an
introductory statement: "How important is it for the
worker facing the hazard -," followed by the specific
question: "to keep his attention at the same time on work
accomplishment and to cues for hazards." The investigator
has to rate the importance of this demand on a 5-point
rating scale.

From the sample in Table 1 it can easily be seen that
the questions of the SDQ refer to a broad repertory of
abilities and skills which are considered to be the basics
of hazard control by the worker.

The anticipatory character of hazard control

One of the basic ideas in the development of the SDQ
has been the assumption that safe behaviour is in essence
anticipatory behaviour. This is true of course for hazard
perception and hazard cognition. Effective processing of
hazard indicators leaves the person time for compensatory
actions. But there are also possibilities for controlling
hazards so that critical situations cannot arise. We call
actions of this type preventive or protective behaviour
(see Table 1, Chapter 5). Part of preventive behaviour is,
for instance, checking equipment and material on a regular
basis for defective parts, adequate storing etc. or lock-
ing dangerous liquids against unauthorized use.

Safety related conditions

The SDQ enables the safety expert also to examine the
workplace to see if the worker can satisfy norms of safe
behaviour easily or only against unfavourable conditions.
Of course, unfavourable conditions can be found within the
worker, for instance emotional disturbance or fatigue.
However, it is not the aim of this questionnaire to register person-related conditions. The SDQ deals with environmental conditions of different kinds. Very basic conditions refer to proper sight and hearing which can be
impaired by glare or noise. Other conditions can be found
in the practice of leadership which provides incentives as

well as feedback by supervisors. A third type of condition encompasses supporting devices (such as expert systems) as well as training measures.

POSSIBLE RESULTS FROM THE APPLICATION OF THE SDQ

After establishing a third and thoroughly revised version of the SDQ now containing 276 items we started a project[1] to analyse a greater number of positions across industry and service agencies.

The first step was to find an adequate sample of about 500 positions which would meet the following criteria:

- Number of employees doing a job should be taken into consideration: very rare jobs would not fulfill the aims of this project.
- Number of accidents and occupational diseases per occupation in question: only job with a certain amount of danger should be included in the sample.
- Workplaces with different levels of technological standard should be represented in the sample.

Until now about 300 analyses have been completed, but processing of the data collected has not yet been started. Therefore, only indications from this job which will go on during the next few months can be presented today.

1. Risk estimations: Because each hazard estimated to be relevant for a position is evaluated on the dimensions 'harmfulness', 'exposure' and 'likelihood of expected harm' it will be possible to establish rank orders of hazards for different jobs. This might later be of some use for practical purposes, e.g. to set priorities for urgent measures to be taken. The most important hazards in different spheres of production may be recognized more clearly on the basis of these rank orders.
2. Estimation of behavioural requirements (BR): As an index for the estimation of BR connected with a certain danger we propose the relation of maximum possible BR to BR really found in an analysis. On the basis of these computations we will be able to compare BR across different hazards to describe dispersions of BR on the different behavioural dimensions of the SDQ and to set up the variability of BR between different occupations. Correlations of BR and other safety factors like 'automation', 'shift work' and so on may provide further information.

3. Estimating negative conditions for safety (NC): Because
   for every single hazard rating about 63 possible negative conditions for safety are made, we can compare
   hazards, positions, professions and types of business
   with respect to chances for realizing safe behaviour.
   It may be of some interest to find correlations between
   BR and NC. Some preliminary statistics of 91 dangers
   found at 14 different positions show that a positive
   correlation can be expected. If this can be confirmed
   later it has to be clarified whether organizational,
   business or task-specific factors are dominant in this
   domain.
4. From our data we also hope to find more information
   about the importance of safety-relevant psychological
   factors (e.g. time pressure, incentives for unsafe
   behaviour).
5. At least, we will conduct some technical investigation
   of the SDQ, for instance to count reliability coefficients in terms of agreement of raters of the same job
   or to eliminate items from the questionnaire which are
   not able to discriminate between different positions.

ACKNOWLEDGEMENT

[1] This project is supported by a grant from the German
Federal Ministry for Research and Technology (dA 01 HK
786-5).

REFERENCES

Bürgi, A., 1976, Die Analyse von Berufen und Berufsanfor-
derungen (Stuttgart: Kohlhammer).

Burkardt, F., 1983, Arbeitsgewohnheiten und Einstellungen
im Lernprozeß zur Arbeitssicherheit. In Arbeitspsychologische Fortbildung von Sicherheitsfachkräften, edited
by BDP Sektion Arbeits-und Betriebspsychologie (Duis-
burg: Deutscher Psychologen Verlag), pp. 53-68.

Bundesminister für Arbeit und Sozialordnung (ed.), 1986,
Arbeitssicherheit '86. Unfallverhütungsbericht (Bonn:
Universitäts-Buchdruckerei).

Denny, V.E., Gilbert, K.J., Erdmann, R.C. and Ruble, E.T.,
1978, Risk assessment methodologies: An application to
underground mine systems. Journal of Safety Research,
10, 24-34.

DIN 25 419: Ereignisablaufanalyse (Berlin: Beuth-Verlag).

DIN 25 424: Fehlerbaumanalyse. Teil 1 und 2 Berlin: Beuth-
Verlag).

DIN 25 448: Ausfalleffektanalyse (Berlin: Beuth-Verlag.)

Flanagan, J.C., 1954, The critical incident technique. Psychological Bulletin, 51, 337-358.

Frieling, E. and Hoyos, C. Graf, 1978, Fragebogen zur Arbeitsanalyse (FAA) (Bern: Huber).

Frieling, E., Kannheiser, W., Facaoaru, C., Wöcherl, H. and Dürholt, E., 1984, Entwicklung eines theorie-geleiteten, standardisierten, verhaltenswissenschaft-lichen Verfahrens zur Tätigkeitsanalyse. Forschungs-bericht 01 HA 029-2A-TAP 0015 (Universität München).

Greiner, B., Leitner, K., Weber, W., Hennes, K. and Volpert, W., 1987, RHIA - Ein Verfahren zur Erfassung psychischer Belastung. In Arbeitsanalyse und Technik-entwicklung - Beiträge über Einsatzmöglichkeiten arbeitsanalytischer Verfahren bei technisch-organisa-torischen Änderungen, edited by Kh Sonntag (Köln: Wirtschaftsverlag Bachem), pp. 145-161.

Hacker, W., Iwanowa, A., and Richter, P., 1983, Tätig-keitsbewertungssystem (Berlin: Humboldt-Universität, Psychodiagnostisches Zentrum).

Hale, A.R. and Glendon, A.J., 1987, Individual behavior in the control of danger (Amsterdam: Elsevier)

Hoyos, C. graf, 1980, Psychologische Unfall- und Sicher-heitsforschung (Stuttgart: Kohlhammer)

Hoyos, C. Graf, 1987, Verhalten in gefährlichen Arbeits-situationen. In Arbeitspsychologie, Band 1 der Enzyklo-pädie der Psychologie, edited by U. Kleinbeck and J. Rutenfranz (Göttingen: Hogrefe), pp. 577-627.

Hoyos, C. Graf and Bernhardt, U., 1987, Fragebogen zur Sicherheitsdiagnose (FSD) - Konzeption, Erprobung und Anwendungsmöglichkeiten eines verhaltensorientierten Instruments zur Sicherheitsanalyse von Arbeitssystemen. In Arbeitsanalyse und Technikentwicklung, edited by Kh. Sonntag (Köln: Bachem), pp. 181-194.#

Hoyos, C. Graf and Zimolong, B., 1988, Occupational safety and accident prevention: behavioral strategies and methods (Amsterdam: Elsevier), p. 54 ff.

Landau, K., Luczak, H. and Rohmert, W., 1975, Arbeits-wissenschaftlicher Erhebungsbogen zur Tätigkeits-analyse. In Arbeitswissenschaftliche Beurteilung der Belastung und Beanspruchung an unterschiedlichen indu-striellen Arbeitplätzen, edited by W. Rohmert and J. Rutenfranz (Bonn: ohne Verlag), pp. 251-293.

McCormick, E.J., Jeanneret, P.R. and Mecham, R.C., 1969, The development and background of the Position Analysis Questionnaire (PAQ). Report No. 5 (Lafayette, Ind.: Research Center, Purdue University)

McGrath, J.W., 1976, Stress and behavior in organizations.
In <u>Handbook of Industrial and Organizational Psycho-
logy</u>, edited by M.D. Dunnette (Chicago: Rand McNally),
pp. 1351-1395.

Monteau, M., 1977, <u>Praktische Methode zur Untersuchung von
Unfallfaktoren. Grundsätze und Anwendungen im Versuch</u>
(Luxemburg: Kommission der Europäischen Gemeinschaften)

Nohl, J. and Thiemecke, H., 1988, <u>Systematik zur Durch-
führung von Gefährdungsanalysen</u>. Fb 536 (Bremerhaven:
Wirtschaftverlag NW)

Tuttle, T.C., Wood, G.D., Grether, C.B. and Reed, D.E.,
1974, <u>Psychological-behavioral strategies for accident
control: a system for diagnosis and intervention.</u> Final
report for the National Institute for Occupational
Safety and Health (Columbia, Md.: Behavioral/Safety
Center).

Vollmer, G.R., 1978, Erfassung von sicherheitswidrigem
Verhalten mit der Technik der kritischen Ereignisse.
<u>Die Berufsgenossenschaft</u>, 2, 80-82.

Volpert, W., Oesterreich, R., Gablenz-Kolakovic, S.,
Krogoll, T. and Resch, M., 1983, <u>Verfahren zur Ermittlung von Regulationserfordernissen in der Arbeitstätigkeit (VERA)</u>. Handbuch und Manual (Köln: TÜV Rheinland).

JOB LOAD AND HAZARD ANALYSIS: A METHOD FOR HAZARD SCREENING AND EVALUATION

Markku Mattila
Tampere University of Technology
Occupational Safety Engineering
Tampere Finland

Pertti Kivi
Tampereen Työterveys (A Health Centre)
Tampere, Finland

A systematic method, Job Load and Hazard Analysis, has been developed to identify safety and health problems inherent in work. The method is a simple job hazard analysis, which consists of four stages: i) information collection; ii) evaluation of the findings; iii) development of preventive measures; and iv) follow-up. Information is gathered in two ways, by means of observations and interviews made by safety and health professionals and through worker questionnaire. Five items (physical hazards, chemical hazards, physical work load, mental stress factors and risks of injury) are assessed on a three-point rating scale indicating relevance to workers' health. Occupational health and safety personnel, worker representatives and management assess the findings cooperatively, whereafter measures for prevention are developed. The method produces an overall analysis of occupational hazards, which may be used to plan the content of occupational health care services or of hazard reduction programs. The method has been tested in several building industry companies. In this paper an experiment in repair construction is presented. In practice, the method has been successful in improving the contents of the occupational health care programme and in generating preventive measures.

INTRODUCTION

The Finnish Occupational Health Care Act obliges employers to provide occupational health care for employees to prevent health impairment caused by work. Occupational health care programmes consist of (Howe, 1975): 1) maintenance of a healthful work environment; 2) preplace-

179

ment examinations and/or screening; 3) periodic health
appraisals; 4) diagnosis and treatment; 5) immunization
programmes; 6) medical records; and 7) gealth education
and counselling.

According to the Finnish Occupational Health Care Act,
the maintenance of a healthful work environment is realized by means of what is called hazard survey of the workplace (e.g. workplace hazard investigation). This concept
of hazard survey of the workplaye entails the screening
and the analysis of hazards inherent in the work and evaluation of their impact on workers's health and well-being
(Mattila, 1985; Rossi and Vaaranen, 1988). The hazard survey of the workplace is the basis of occupational health
care, used to plan other aspects of occupational health
care services (Mattila, 1987).

The aim of the study was (Mattila, 1985): 1) to develop
a simple, systematic, standardized method for the analysis
of work load and hazards, to be used in occupational
health care and in occupational safety activities; and 2)
to test the new method in the actual occupational health
care and safety performance of a construction firm.

The purposes of the method for hazard survey of the
workplace are: 1) identification of the health hazards to
which workers are exposed in their work and by their working conditions; 2) to help determine the contents of the
occupational health care programme according to the real
nees that arise from jobs and working conditions; and 3)
to support the prevention of hazards and the selection of
appropriate preventive measures.

JOB LOAD AND HAZARD ANALYSIS

The theoretical framework of the method comprises the
stress-strain concept, the hazard-anger model, and the
risk behaviour theory. The approach used in job analysis
was applied because this approach makes it easy to connect
the information about work load and hazards with individual workers (Rohmert and Landau, 1979).

The Job Load and Hazard Analysis includes four stages:
i) information collection; ii) evaluation of the findings;
iii) conclusions and proposals for preventive measures;
and iv) follow-up. The identification of hazards is first
made through preliminary job analysis, in which five factors are considered: i) chemical hazards; ii) physical
hazards; iii) physical work load; iv) mental stress factors; and v) injury risk. Each item is assessed on a

three-point rating scale according to assurance and relevance to workers' health. Assessment guidelines are available (Mattila, 1985).

The information is gathered and the analysis is done:
i) by occupational health care and safety personnel at the
site, through worker observations and interviews; and ii)
by workers themselves on a questionnaire form (in which
the items are illustrated with several typical examples).

The findings are discussed job by job by the co-operation team, which consists of those participating in the
safety inspection (occupational health care personnel, the
safety manager, worker representatives, and supervisors)
and the line manager. The workers' own assessments were
analyzed before the meeting, and the results were presented to the group. The group made a joint assessment of
the hazards and stress of every job. After the meeting of
the co-ooperation team and on the basis of theses assessments, the occupational health care personnel or safety
personnel reached their conclusions independently and made
proposals for the future. The stages of the procedure are
presented in Figure 1.

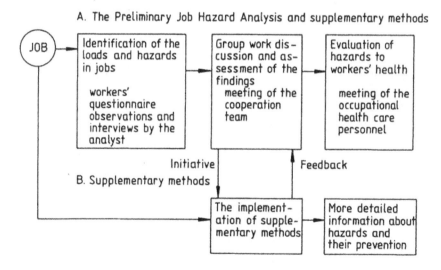

Figure 1. The structure of the method (Mattila, 1985)

To determine inter-rater reliability, the scores of two experienced raters, the nurse and the safety engineer, were compared. The two simultaneously rated 32 jobs. The reliability coefficient varied from 0.87 (mental stress) to 0.95 (work load) (Mattila, 1988).

A PC-programme has been developed for data storage and future use. It gives the following output: 1) a numerical and graphic summary of all assessments, for every job (means and deviations); 2) the changes in assessments made at different times, for every job; and 3) the ranking of jobs, listed in a priority order according to five different types of loads and hazards and based on the assessments of workers themselves and/or specialists (Mattila, 1987).

SUBJECT AND SETTING

The method was tested in this study, as part of the actual occupational health care in the building construction industry, for an 11 months period.

One repair con-struction site, a six-storey high office building completed in 1906, was chosen as the main subject. From 35 to 50 workers were employed at the site. The jobs were analyzed four times during the year. The information collected thus applied to different seasons and different construction stages. The response rate on the worker questionnaire varied from 90 to 97%.

RESULTS

The analysis yielded an overall assessment of job loads and hazards (Figure 2), which was summarized from the results for all the analysis. It illustrated the essential loads and hazards of different jobs and pinpointed the most critical jobs. This overall assessment was used as the basis for planning the content of the occupational health care program.

The analysis of worker questionnaires yielded priority orders according to five different hazards and loads, which were also analyzed for these factors together, i.e. the different ratings of workers themselves were added together. As an example of this kind of analysis, Figure 3 shows those jobs, for which the total sums of 5 items as rated by workers themselves were the highest. This may give some idea to the safety and health professionals about those jobs which have been recognized as most problematic by the workers and where the combined effects of health hazards have to be considered.

Object of analysis (job occupation, worksite)	Type of load or hazard														
	Chemical hazards			Physical hazard			Physical work load			Mental stress			Accident risk		
	0	1	2	0	1	2	0	1	2	0	1	2	0	1	2
1. CUSTODIAN			▲		▲			▲			▲			▲	
2. SURVEYER			▲			▲		▲				▲			▲
3. ROUGH CARPENTER		▲				▲			▲		▲				▲
4. OTHER CONSTRUCTION WORKER			▲			▲			▲		▲				▲
5. CARPENTER'S HELPER		▲			▲				▲		▲				▲
6. JACKHAMMER OPERATOR			▲			▲			▲		▲				▲

Rating scale: 0 = no load and/or hazard ▲
1 = some load and/or hazards; may effect health ▲
2 = much load and/or many hazards; definite effect
on health ▲

Figure 2. An overall assessment of some jobs at the repair construction site.

1. FITTER (VENTILATION PIPE)
2. PIPE DISMANTLING
3. MASON
4. JACKHAMMER OPERATOR
5. MASONRY DISMANTLING
6. CONCRETE LAYER

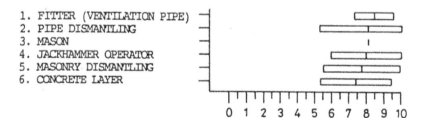

0 1 2 3 4 5 6 7 8 9 10

Figure 3. An example of the total priority order for some repair construction jobs according to the sums of 5 items as rated by workers themselves.

Another end result of this study was the new occupational health care programme compiled by the occupational
health professionals. The programme specified what type of
occupational health service was needed for each of the 28
jobs studied. Before this study the occupational health
care had the same content for repair construction as for
construction workers building new structures. The study
showed the differences in job loads and hazards, and thus
provided the basis for more specified occupational health
care. The written job analysis also serves as the basis
for health education and safety training given by occupational safety and health professionals.

The preventive nature of the hazard survey of the workplace improved. The occupational health care programme
consisted altogether of 63 proposals for preventive
measures. Many proposals specified the need for different
types of personal protection, but working methods and
conditions were also handled.

CONCLUSIONS

Job Load and Hazard Analysis has proved to function
well in practice. The simple job analysis seems to be an
appropriate approach to gather systematic information for
overviews about workplace risks as well as for the basis
of preventive measures.

The procedure of Job Load and Hazard Analysis includes
such features as worker involvement, group problem
solving, and the organized co-operation of health and
safety staff with the production management and with the
worker representatives, an approach which improves the
usefulness of the analysis. This procedure applies the
fact that the workers themselves know the most about these
jobs and have a lot of inside information about the safety
and health problems of their jobs. The occupational safety
and health professiovals have to be informed about these
facts, which are strongly recognized by the workers.

Job Load and Hazard Analysis offers one solution for
collecting work environment data as an essential part of
the company's safety information system (Successful Accident Prevention, 1987). This information can be connected
to practical PC programs with other occupational health
care and accident data, e.g. workers' records and accident
records.

ACKNOWLEDGEMENTS

This study was supported by a grant from the Finnish Work Environment Fund. The authors wish to thank the construction company Metsäpuro for good co-operation, the nurse Mari Mansikkamäki for practical help during the study and Sheryl Hinkkanen for correcting the English.

REFERENCES

Howe, H.F., 1975, Organization and Operation of an Occupational Health Program – Part I. Journal of Occupational Medicine, 17, 360–400.

Mattila, M.K., 1985, Job Load ad Hazard Analysis: a method for the analysis of workplace conditions for occupa tional health care. British Journal of Industrial Medicine, 42, pp. 656–666.

Mattila, M., 1987, Job Load and Hazard Analysis: a method to identify job safety problems and to produce preventive measures. In New Methods in Applied Ergonomics, edited by J.R. Wilson, E.N. Corlett and I. Manenica (London: Taylor & Francis), pp. 199–204.

Mattila, M., 1988, Job Load and Hazard Analysis: a co-operative approach to identify and to prevent ergonomic and other hazards at work. In Trends in Ergonomics/ Human Factors V, edited by F. Aghazadeh (New York: North-Holland), pp. 559–565

Rohmert, W., Landau, K., 1979, Das Arbeitswissenschaftliche Erhebungsverfahren zur Tätigkeitsanalyse (AET), Handbuch, (Bern: Verlag Hans Huber).

Rossi, K., Vaaranen, V.(Ed.), 1988, Occupational Health Care in Finland. Reviews 10, (Helsinki: The Institute for Occupational Health).

Successful Accident Prevention. Reviews 12, 1987, (Helsinki: the Institute for Occupational Health).

RISK ANALYSIS OF MOUNTING AND DISMOUNTING AGRICULTURAL VEHICLES BY MEANS OF A NEAR-ACCIDENT SURVEY

Heinrich Beutnagel and Wilfried Hammer

Institute for Production Engineering of the Federal Research Centre for Agriculture (FAL)
Braunschweig
Federal Republic of Germany

PROBLEM AND OBJECTIVE

The proportion of mounting and dismounting accidents in relation to all tractor accidents increased from 31 % to about 50 % in the years 1979 to 1985. This ratio is high also with other farm vehicles. Special interest must be paid to this accumulation of accidents though mounting and dismounting does not serve the direct aim, but is only an auxiliary to work. As a routine activity it is executed automatically most of the time. Acquired and subconsciously stored motion programs are called up and carried out without conscious attention. Therefore, the possibility to perceive danger signals and react to them is strongly reduced.

The objective of this study is the development and application of a suitable questionnaire method to gain information as comprehensively as possible on near-accidents from farmers and their co-workers.

Here it is advisable firstly to describe the undisturbed working system for mounting and dismounting which is defined as "standard condition". Then the causes, conditions and the procedure of accidents will be observed; this is defined as "actual condition". According to analyses of these data it is essential to show the cause-effect-relations by comparing the standard versus the actual conditions.

From the results measures can be derived to enhance awareness and the motivation for safe behaviour. Furthermore, recommendations may be given for the construction of related equipment – as far it is possible in the scope of this study.

METHOD

<u>Theoretical basis</u>

As a rule an accident is not only based on one single origin. Mostly there are several conditions interacting in a complex system and influencing each other. Therefore, in a study concerning work safety it is necessary to look at the system components man, machine and environment in their entity with their various interactions.

In the described man-machine-environment-system (Figure 1) the man plays a central part. Firstly he is the subject affecting and forming the system, secondly he as an object is affected by the system.

Figure 1: Presentation of the man-machine-environment-system

According to Leplat (1984) an accident is caused by a misfunction in the man-machine-environment-system. The causes of this are changes to the usual situation at the work place. They can be caused by man's behaviour or by equipment and work environment.

Therefore, in the study the determination of the normal, undisturbed work procedure comes first which is defined as "standard condition". In order to investigate the actual condition, which means the description of the disturbed and faulty work procedure deviating from the normal, the changes in the man-machine-environment-system must be observed.

In order to clarify these complex relations, a model was used which explains the action under risk conditions. Here the interaction of stress factors, risk perception, decision and performance is described (Figure 2). Starting point is the work situation. In order to accomplish the work objective the requirements of the task as well as those of the material and social environment must be reconciled to cope with the risk.

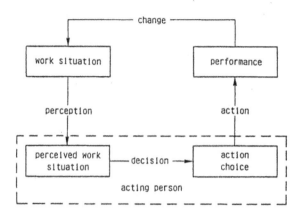

Figure 2: Control loop for acting under risk conditions using a model (Zimolong and Gresch, 1983, following McGrath, 1976)

The risk perception and risk evaluation are of special importance.

After the work situation has been perceived and assessed the person must decide on a certain performance. Mostly one can choose among several action alternatives. Now one must compare the advantage of an acceptable action alternative with the cost of an eventual risk. According to the individual risk acceptance each person will decide on a certain alternative.

With unconsciously performed actions like mounting and dismounting the risk perception and risk evaluation are sensitive weaknesses in the system, for the decision phase is strongly contracted or even totally eliminated. The choice of action alternatives has already been fixed.

Starting points for hypotheses of accident causes can be seen from the described model. Changes in the man-machine- environment-system principally can lead to a special risk, but also the perception of danger and devotion of attention must be investigated more closely.

Furthermore, starting points for measures become clear:
Perception:
The risk perception especially must be facilitated.
Decision:
The risk acceptance must be lowered, and the knowledge of alternative action possibilities should be improved.

Performance:
The mastering of safe performance methods must be
learnt.

Practical execution

Development of the questionnaire
Critical incidents and near-accidents should be investigated in order to get indications for disturbed work
procedures. This method was chosen, since it turned out
- that the causes of near-accidents and manifest accidents
  are similar, as was stated by Swedish authors (Lundqvist, 1982; Lindgren, 1975; e.g.),
- that far more near-accidents happen and thus empiric
  data can be gained more quickly and in a greater number
  and
- that questions concerning guilt and insurance are of no
  relevance and, therefore, the answers of the interviewed
  people are franker and more detailed.
A near-accident is defined as "one or several critical
incidents which occur unexpectedly and lead to a deviation
of the normal work procedure as well as to an acute risk
without resulting in a real or serious injury" (see also
Flanagan, 1965; Lundqvist, 1982; Carter, 1985).
It was necessary to gain comprehensive information as
to the facts before, during and after a near-accident.
Therefore, an interview should be carried out with farmers
and their co-workers. For this purpose a questionnaire had
to be developed.
The problem was which characteristics were to be in-
serted into the questionnaire. It was advisable to use the
model already described for the performance under risk
conditions as guideline and thus to develop a theory-based
questionnaire. In order to get references to such criteria
the authors went back to a post-accident study by Hankers
and Dieckmann (1982), who carried out inquiries about
tractor accidents. In their paper a multitude of characteristics - 154 variables - were examined. This led to an
abundance of information which was difficult to examine.
In order to avoid this problem in this study and to
isolate a clearly arranged structure of a least number of
independent criteria from the multitude of observed variables a factorial analysis was carried out (Beutnagel et
al., 1987). By these means the information of the data
matrix of Hankers and Dieckmann should be reproduced as
exactly as possible. Finally 33 factors were selected and
interpreted. They were included in the questionnaire in

order to produce understanding of possible causes of
accident origins.

Other references aso served as additional sources for
the selection of qualified variables (Bernhardt et al.,
1984; Segger et al., 1982; Gustafsson et al., 1980).

Procedure of the interviews

The interviews were carried out in the different farm-
ing regions of the Hannover Chamber of Agriculture. The
contact with the farmers was established via the local
agricultural extension services. Their advisors were asked
to inform the members about the accumulation of accidents
when mounting and dismounting and to announce the planned
project in their monthly periodical.

Next the farmers were contacted by telephone, and a
date was fixed for the interview. Only two persons carried
out the interview, that means each person separately
raised the questions to the particular farmer. On average
these conversations lasted one hour 40 minutes, respectively two hours representing the extrema. In total 237
interviews were carried out. The proportion of the persons
who could report on a near-accident was unexpectedly high
at 87 %.

Data analysis

Since the dependent variables, without exception, are
scaled non-metric the biometric analyses were carried out
by means of two statistical methods. With log-linear analyses of multiway frequency tables the effect of different
factors and their combination on the number of accidents
was determined and tested as to their significance. The
influence of certain variables on a dependent variable can
be determined by means of the logistic regression analysis
(Hammer et al., 1988), so comprehensive and significant
results could be gained.

Selected results

Of the described near-accidents about 1/3 happened when
mounting and 2/3 when dismounting. This also corresponds
to the relation of the accidents reported by the "Berufs-
genossenschaften" (= cooperative insurance groups). Dirt
and wetness on the steps are distinct hazards. This is
true especially in autumn and at tasks which are often
carried out under unfavorable weather (Fig. 3).

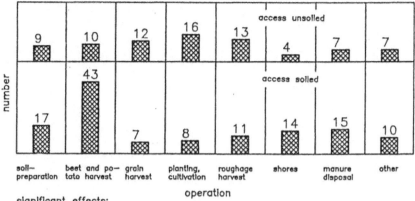

significant effects:

main effect:
  access condition

interaction:
  operation — access condition (p < 0.01)

Figure 3: Influence of the access condition and of the task on the number of near-accidents when mounting and dismounting

When mounting most accidents occur by slipping. This is true also for dismounting (Figure 4). But here also jumping and being caught by protruding parts must be mentioned as causes. Unfavourable weather and slippery soil were determined as influencing factors on the great number of slip accidents. Both lead to dirt on the steps.

Furthermore, many accidents are related to changes of behaviour, for 2/3 of the interviewed persons confirmed a deviation of their normal mounting or dismounting. These changes of behaviour can be caused by disturbances in the work procedure, time pressure and physical fatigue (Figures 5 to 7). These accident causes are explained in more detail as follows.

If the work procedure was disturbed 85 % of the farmers reporting about a near-accident changed their behaviour. If there was no disturbance only 56 % did not act as usual (Fig. 5).

With time pressure the behaviour was changed in 77 % of all near-accidents, without pressure only in 46 % (Figure 6).

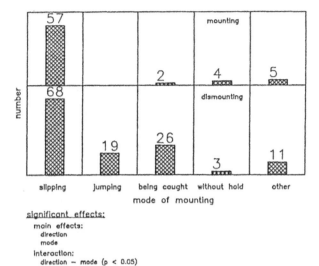

significant effects:
main effects:
    direction
    mode
interaction:
    direction — mode (p < 0.05)

Fig. 4: Influence of the motion type and direction on the number of near-accidents when mounting and dismounting

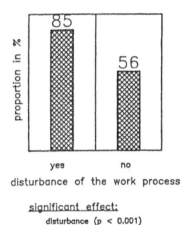

disturbance of the work process

significant effect:
    disturbance (p < 0.001)

Figure 5: Proportion of near accidents connected with change of behaviour in relation to all near-accidents either with or without disturbance in the work procedure

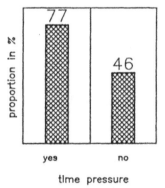

time pressure

significant effect:
    time pressure (p < 0.001)

Fig. 6: Proportion of near-accidents connected with change of behaviour in relation to all near-accidents either with or without time pressure

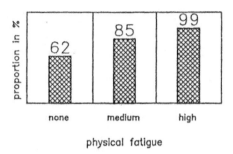

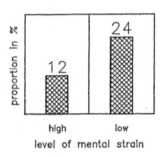

<u>significant effect:</u>
physical fatigue (p < 0.05)

<u>significant effect:</u>
level of mental strain (p < 0.05)

Fig. 7: Proportion of near-accidents connected with change of behaviour in relation to all near-accidents with the same state of exhaustion

Fig. 8: Proportion of near accidents if the risk is perceived in relation to all near-accidents with the same level of information capacity

The proportion of those changing their behaviour increased with the amount of physical fatigue and exhaustion suffered (Figure 7).

The described stress and the incidents imposed on man from the outside interfere mostly with the behaviour when dismounting. Many farmers, for instance, dismount forward in a near-accident though normally they do it backward.

Furthermore, it proved that dangers when mounting or dismounting often are not perceived. In particular if the main task asked for a high information capacity, that means high mental strain, only 12 % of the interviewed farmers were able to perceive risks (Figure 8).

Mounting and dismounting is mostly done automatically. Only 19 % of the farmers reporting on a near-accident during the tractor access paid attention to the access system. The proportion is a little higher with vehicles which are not mounted so often or have no access at all (Figure 9).

significant effect:

type of vehicle (p < 0,01)

Fig. 9: Proportion of persons paying attention to the
access in a near-accident in relation to all interviewed
persons using the same type of vehicle

The major risk potentials when mounting and dismounting are mentioned as follows:

External conditions

- unfavourable weather
- unfavourable ground

Technical conditions

- first step too high
- dirty steps
- missing access (especially on trailers)
- insufficient handles
- protruding parts

Behaviour of persons

- change of behaviour, especially by disturbance,
  time pressure and fatigue
- dismounting forward
- jumping
- without hold
- insufficient risk perception and risk evaluation.

CONCLUSIONS

The near-accident method offers good prerequisites for the goal of this study, that is to determine the causes of accidents and respectively near-accidents when mounting and dismounting, especially taking into account human behaviour and an overall systems approach. The necessary data could be acquired with reasonable effort. On this basis it was possible to gain statistically significant results about the influencing factors on the accident process and human behaviour when mounting and dismounting.

By means of these results proposals can be worked out aiming at an advancement in safety perception and in motivation for safe behaviour. References can be also given for some important technical and constructional changes.

However, it must be examined critically whether this method can successfully be applied also to other enterprises with respective types of risk. There are indications that equivalent, comprehensive and significant results cannot be gained with obviously dangerous work like handling a mower bar or operating a circular saw. With these activities a deviation from the normal work procecure mostly has fatal consequences. Near-accidents will hardly occur here, therefore, it will be very difficult to acquire sufficient data. Yet this method, indeed, can be applied for routine activities like mounting and dismounting or walking and carrying.

REFERENCES

Bernhard, U., Hauke, G., Graf Hoyos, C., Wenninger, G., 1984, Entwicklung eines Verfahrens zur Diagnose von Mensch-Umwelt-Systemen. Teil 1: Entwicklung und Erprobung des Fragebogens zur Sicherheitsdiagnose (FSD) Abschlußbericht zum Projekt Ho 182/11 - 1 u. 3 der DFG.

Beutnagel, H., Krone, W., Hammer, W., 1987, Verdichtung von Unfalldaten mit Hilfe der Faktorenanalyse. Bericht aus dem Institut für Betriebstechnik der FAL, Nr.153/ 1987.

Carter, N., Menckel, E., 1985, Near-Accident Reporting: A Review of Swedish Research. Journal of Occupational Accidents, 7, 41 - 64

Flanagan, J.C., 1954, The critical incident technique. Psychological Bulletin 51, No. 4, 327 - 358

Gustafsson, B., Lundqvist, P., 1980, Prevention of accidents in animal husbandry. Report 13, Swedish University of Agricultural Sciences, Lund, Sweden

Hammer, W., Thaer, G., Kemeny, P., 1988, Indirekte Gefähr-
    dungsanalysen mit Hilfe multivariater statistischer
    Verfahren. Journal of Occupational Accidents, Amster-
    dam, 10, 39 - 68.
Hankers, M., Dieckmann, J., 1982, Untersuchung psycholo-
    gischer Ursachen- und Hintergrundbedingungen bei land-
    wirtschaftlichen Unfällen durch Befragung der Unfallbe-
    teiligten. Diplomarbeit am Institut für Psychologie der
    TU Braunschweig.
Leplat, J., 1984, Occupational accident research and sys-
    tems approach. Journal of Occupational Accidents,
    Amsterdam, 6, 77 - 89.
Lindgren, G., 1975, Social Medicine in Agriculture,
    Summary of reports published 1970 - 1972. Jordbrukes
    Socialmedicin Meddelanden, 11, Lund, Sweden.
Lundqvist, P., 1982, Occupational accidents in animal
    husbandry. Proceedings of the Joint Ergonomic Symposium
    am 9.-11.09.1981 in Mainz, KTBL-Darmstadt, 125 - 133.
McGrath, J.E., 1976, Stress and Behavior in Organisation.
    In 7: Dunette, M.D. (Hrsg.), Handbook of industrial and
    organizational psychology, Chicago, 1351 - 1395.
Segger, R., Zimolong, B., 1981, Möglichkeiten zur Verhü-
    tung von Absturzunfällen. Forschungsbericht Nr. 314 der
    BAU
Zimolong, B., 1987, Gefährdungseinschätzung beim Rangie-
    ren. Forschungsbericht Nr. 194 der BAU, Dortmund.
Zimolong, B., Gresch, U., 1983, Ein handlungstheoretisches
    Schulungsprogramm für die Ausbildung im Arbeitsschutz.
    Arbeitspsychologische Fortbildung von Sicherheitsfach-
    kräften, Sektion Arbeits- und Betriebspsychologie im
    Berufsverband Deutscher Psychologen e.V.

FIELD OBSERVATIONS ON THE ERGONOMICS OF TYPEWRITING

D.L. Price
F. Fayzmehr
R. Beaton

Virginia Polytechnic Institute and State University
Human Factors Engineering Center
Blacksburg, Virginia
USA

INTRODUCTION

Short term and long term observations of typing work stations were made to investigate the ergonomics of typewriting. This goal required measurement of operator position and performance in the field.

SHORT TERM OBSERVATIONS - EXPERIMENT I

Posture Sampling. The short term observations methodology implemented for posture sampling of typewriting was an adaptation of "posture targeting" (Corlett et al., 1979). The posturegraph used was for a seated operator, with targets for the neck, upper back, lower back, upper arms, forearms, and hands. This method was selected among others, such as Labanotation (Hutchinson, 1970), Priel posturegram measurements (Priel, 1974), the Ovaco Working Posture Analysis System (Karhu et al., 1977; Karhu et al., 1981) and others, because it is easy to learn and it can be applied quickly.

The desire was for rapid recording. During one week of data gathering, the experimenter entered the subject's office and took five frames of super 8 movie film for each of three angles, the front, the side, and from above the typist. The experimenter left the office to return at a later time in the week and perform the same task. This procedure was accomplished three times. These films were reviewed by a film editor and the experimenter recorded the posturegraph targets identified above, using the procedure of Corlett et al. (1979).

Subjects. Nine subjects were used in the short term observations. They were all female. Mean age = 29.9 years (standard deviation = 8.41 years), average height was 163.6 cm (standard deviation = 7.9 cm), and the average years of typing experience were 6.2 (standard deviation = 3.1).

Results of Short Term Observation

The posture targets were scored and provided the basis for the following results.

Upper arm. The long axis of the upper right arm had an average angle (angle 1) from the frontal plane of 23.3 degrees forward, with a standard deviation and standard error of the mean of 8.24 and 1.62, respectively. The long axis of the upper right arm had an average angle (angle 2) from the sagittal plane of 1.73 degrees rightward, with a standard deviation of 8.83 and a standard error of the mean of 1.73. The upper left arm had an average angle (angle 3) from the frontal plane of 23.7 degrees forward, with a standard deviation and standard error of the mean of 8.2 and 1.6, respectively. The upper left arm had an average of 1.2 degrees angle (angle 4) from the sagittal plane leftward, with a standard deviation and standard error of the mean of 6.0 and 1.2, respectively.

Forearm. The angle "A" was between the long axis of the forearm and the frontal plane, with the angle measured on the side of the forearm which is away from the body (i.e. the left side for the left forearm and the right side for the right forearm), measured in the horizontal plane. This angle averaged 127.9 degrees, with a standard deviation of 10.6 and a standard error of the mean of 2.1 for the right forearm (angle A right). The angle "B" between the long axis of the forearm and the transverse plane, measured from the lower side of the elbow, measured in the vertical plane was 21.6 degrees, with a standard deviation of 14.4 degrees and a standard error of the mean of 2.83 degrees for the right forearm (angle B right). Angle A for the left forearm averaged 126.3 degrees, with a standard deviation of 12.6 and a standard error of the mean of 2.5 (angle A left). Angle B for the left forearm averaged 24.5 degrees, with a standard deviation of 21.7 and a standard error of the mean of 4.3 (angle B left).

Hand. The angle C between the long axis of the hand and the frontal plane was measured on the left side of the hand for the left hand and the right side of the hand for the right hand in the horizontal plane. The average was

117.3 degrees for the right hand, with a standard deviation of 15.8 degrees and a standard error of the mean of
3.1 degrees (angle C right). The angle D between the long
axis of the hand and the transverse plane measured on the
lower side of the hand in the vertical plane was 19.4
degrees average for the right hand with a standard deviation of 15.8 and a standard error of the mean of 3.1
(angle D right). The angle C for the left hand averaged
113.9 degrees, with a standard deviation of 15.3 and an
standard error of the mean of 3.2 (angle C left). The
angle D for the left hand averaged 18.0 degrees, with a
standard deviation of 8.5 and a standard error of the mean
of 1.7 (angle D left).

   Back. Only one angle could be obtained with this methodology. It was the angle of the upper back in degrees
pitched forward. The average was 20.5 degrees with a
standard deviation of 13.4 and a standard error of the
mean of 2.6.

LONG TERM OBSERVATIONS - EXPERIMENT II

   Long term observations of typing were conducted for
eight hours continuously at eight work stations. Three
locations were on the Virginia Tech campus, four at
various industry sites, and one at a local church office.

   Subjects. All subjects were female, aged 21 to 56
years, height averaged 163.8 cm, ranging from 157.5 cm to
182.9 cm, and weight averaged 55.8 kg, ranging from 47.7
kg to 68.2 kg.

   Equipment. A dual mount camera boom designed to allow
overhead and profile camera axes held two video cameras.
The camera for the profile field of view was equipped with
a zoom lens. A screen splitter received the camera output
signals and a VHS videocorder received and recorded the
signals from the splitter. A mechanical vibration micro-
phone was mounted to the typewriter to transduce machine
vibrations. Its signals were received and recorded by an
Optonica RT3300 dual channel cassette recorder. One channel was used for voice labeling and identification of each
recording. This equipment was controlled by an Apple II
microcomputer to activate a controller circuit at approximately 100 randomly spaced 90 second intervals during the
eight hour period. The total time for one period of cumulative off time and on time never exceeded five minutes.
The equipment used for data reduction included, in addition to that mentioned above, the follow-ing: An IMSAI Z80
microcomputer with a CAT 100 videodigitizer board, an

Information Systems 550 light pen, and software for motion
and posture data analysis. Signals from the Optonica
RT3300 were analyzed using PDP 11/10 and 11/53 computers
for Fast Fourier Analysis.

   Procedure. The equipment was transported to a given
location and set up to provide overhead and profile. Space
does not permit a description of the procedure for camera
alignment (see Price et al., 1982). The subject was instructed to ignore the presence of the equipment as much
as was possible, and to conduct work as if the equipment
were not present. Each was told that we were interested in
all activities at the work station, including non-typing
activity. Two circular white notebook reinforcement adhe-
sive rings were attached to the left hand for video-motion
analysis. One ring was attached on the back of the hand,
proximal to the knuckle of the middle finger; the other
was attached on the little finger side of the hand below
the knuckle of the little finger. The former presented a
target for the overhead camera; the latter, a target for
the profile camera. The equipment was activated, and the
subject was then told to conduct a normal day's work .

   Data Analysis. The video recordings were analyzed for
posture and motion. The posture data were analyzed by
measuring angles on the face of the display during videotape playback. These angles were then entered and stored
in the computer. The angles were then plotted over time
and linear correlation fits of the data were obtained for
each subject for each of the following angles.

   1. Approximate equivalents of angles 3, 4, A left, B
left, C left, and D left, as described above.

   2. Vertical upper body angle. This angle was formed by
the plane of the long axis of the torso with the horizontal axis.

   3. Horizontal upper body angle. This angle was formed
by the frontal plane of the torso with the plane of the
vertical axis.

   4. Vertical neck angle. This was the angle formed by
the plane of the long axis of the neck with the horizontal
plane.

   5. Horizontal neck angle. This angle was formed by the
sagittal plane taken through the head and the vertical
sagittal plane taken through the rest of the body.

   The motion data were analyzed for vertical and horizontal distances by measurements at the display of the video-
taped samples. The distance between two points was measured. These two points were the hand target locations at
one character activation and the hand target locations at

the next character location. Extreme motions beyond the overhead camera's field of view were counted for each sample during typing. The distance measurements were made using software conversions of light pen coordinates to actual distances in the workplace in centimeters. The data were plotted across samples and linear correlation equations fitted to the data.

The videotapes were also reviewed for the proportion of time occupied by actual typing. The vibration recordings were submitted to Fourier analysis as an indication of typing performance. This indicator was coupled with analyses of characters activated per second with "bursts". A burst was defined as a sequence of characters preceded and followed by intervals of two tenths of a second with no character activity.

RESULTS AND DISCUSSION OF LONG TERM OBSERVATION

Motion Analysis. The analysis of vertical and horizontal motions were well represented by linear equations for distance vs. sample number (i.e. approximate time of day). The correlations for vertical motions ranged from a low of $r = -.64$ to $r = -.97$, with a mean of $r = -.88$. Those for horizontal motions ranged from $r = +.49$ to $r = -.99$, with an average of $-.71$. There was only one positive correlation.

It is evident that as the time of day progresses, the motion distance between successive character activations shortens. This was a relatively consistent occurrence. The range of distance of motions in the vertical started with an average intercept value of 1.7 cm. The average minimum value was 0.68 cm. In the horizontal those values were 3.85 cm and 2.6 cm. The average vertical slope of the regression line was $-.013$, and of the horizontal, $-.014$.

The percentage of time spent typing ranged from 14.4% to 48.9%. The average was 30.1%.

The number of times per sample in the 100 samples per day, during which the subject rested her left arm, was counted. The count per sample was less than one. The linear fit correlation values ranged from $r = .44$ to $r = .99$. The average was $r = .79$. The intercepts ranged from .01 to .76, with an average of .24. The slopes ranged from .005 to .018, with an average of .013. Thus, resting of the left hand increased slightly throughout the day. The subject with the lowest correlation value also had the flattest slope and the highest intercept. Three subjects had correlations of .98, .99, and .99. They also had steeper slopes and lower intercept values.

The number of extraneous motions, that is the number of
motions off the keyboard and out of the field of view of
the overhead camera, increased throughout the day for all
subjects. The average correlation value was r = .72, with
an average slope of .022 and an average intercept of .23.

Posture. The variability of posture changes showed up
with the long term observations. Four of the angles which
were near approximates of angles taken in the short term
observations, showed relatively significant changes in
direction throughout the day of sample taking. These are
called near approximates because the short term sample
reference planes were body planes, but the long term reference planes were vertical or horizontal planes on the
display.

The four angles that showed significant changes in
slope in the long term observations which were also measured in the short term study were the left hand angle D
(binomial p = .035), the left hand angle C (p = .035), the
left forearm angle A (p = .145) and the left upper arm
angle 4 (P = .035). In addition, the horizontal neck angle
direction of slope was significant p = .109. Values of p
equal to or less than .20 were considered significant for
this application since it required six out of eight subjects to demonstrate the same slope sign. These angles are
discussed next. The average angles used are the average
intercept angle of the correlation equations from each
subject.

The vertical hand angle D had an average of 17.2
degrees and ranged from 2.3 to 32.2 degrees. The average
magnitude of change was an angle decrease of 9.8 degrees,
and a correlation of r = .61.

The horizontal hand angle C had an average of 96.4
degrees, values ranging from 68.5 to 129.8. The average
magnitude of change throughout the day was 16.4 degrees
increase. The average correlation was r = .52.

The forearm angle A had an average of 118.2 degrees and
ranged from 92.2 to 141.0 degrees. The average magnitude
of change was a decreasing angle of 15.3 degrees. The
average correlation was r = .70.

The upper arm angle 4 averaged 5.2 degrees, ranging
from 3.4 to 6.2. The average magnitude of change was 4.3
degrees increase. The average correlation was r = .43.

The horizontal neck angle averaged 40.2 degrees, ranging from 29.0 to 70.4 degrees. The average magnitude of
change was 13.2 degrees decrease. The average correlation
was r = .64.

These results indicate that the hand became more horizontal and rotated medially. The forearm rotated away from

the body in the horizontal plane. The upper arm rotated
medially in the horizontal plane, i.e. the elbows were
brought closer to the body. These actions appear to be
efforts to relieve the static loads of postures taken in
the day. The change in neck angle rotates the head
slightly to the left, or toward the typewriter and away
from the copy. This also is a relief of a static load.

Performance. Two measures of typing performance used
were characters per unit time within a burst, and the fundamental frequency of typewriter vibrations determined by
Fourier analysis. Both measures were taken over complete
work days.

The character activation rate within bursts and the
length of bursts did not change systematically during the
work day. In general the correlations showed a lack of
slope and were low. Therefore, these measures did not show
either an increase or a decrease in performance throughout
the day. The average characters typed within a burst at
morning data intercept was 5.6 characters per second, and
ranged from 5.0 characters per second to 7.8 characters
per second.

The fundamental frequency also did not change during
the workday for the six subjects analyzed. The fundamental frequency averaged 5.1 cycles per second for typing
text. These values ranged from 3.4 to 6.8. When the subjects were typing forms, the average dropped to 1.6,
ranging from 1.4 to 1.9 cps.

VALIDATION OF FOURIER ANALYSIS

The striking thing about the fundamental frequency
results is that this property of the Fourier power spectrum seems to indicate character activation rates when
derived from the vibrations of the typewriter. The impli-
cation of this finding is that it can be used for work
performance measurements, where the operator's actions
directly result in machine vibrations as they do in typing. In this case the average speed of the typist working
at a relatively constant pace should be proportional to
the fundamental frequency of the recorded waveform. Other
information to be gained from the Fourier power spectrum
could include the type of document being produced because
the shape of the power spectrum might very well differ
from a document containing only text compared with one
that is numerical in content or is a form to be filled in.

To validate the basic concept of this application of
Fourier Analysis a computer output a sequence of randomly

determined characters through an RS-232 port in an IBM
Selectric Typewriter. The characters were activated at one
of the following rates: 1.08, 1.24, 1.45, 1.74, 2.17,
2.90, 3.48, 4.35, 5.43, 7.25, and 10.87 characters per
second. The vibrations of the typewriter were recorded.

The recorded waveforms from each of the eleven rates
were analyzed and the linear correlation between typing
rate and the fundamental frequency was $r = .9986$ (P <
.0001).

CONCLUSIONS

1. The methodology used in the short term observations was
an effective means for determining working postures at the
typewriter for the angles measured.
2. The methodology used in the long term observations
provided useful data on changes over the working day in
hand and finger motions, parts of the body posture,
performance, and percentage time typing.
3. The use of Fourier Analysis to determine performance
for tasks such as typing is valid. It may be useful in
actually defining the type of work being performed.

REFERENCES

Corlett, E. N., Madeley, S. J., Manenica, I. (1979),
    Postural targeting: A technique for recording working
    postures. Ergonomics, 19, 357-366.
Huchinson, A. (1970). Labanotation, (2nd Edition).
    London: Oxford University Press. Karhu, O., Harkonen,
R., Sorvali, P. and Vepsalainen, P. (1981), Observing
    working postures in industry. Applied Ergonomics, 12,
    13-17.
Karhu, O., Kansi, P. and Kuorinka, I. (1977),
    Correct working postures in industry. Applied Ergono-
    mics, 18, 199-201.
Price, D.L., Fayzmehr, F., Haas, E., and Beaton, R.
    (1982). Ergonomics of Typewriting, Vols I and II.
    Report Number IBM/SP0-1,2, Virginia Polytechnic
    Institute and State University, Blacksburg, VA, 24060.
Priel, V.C. (1974). A numerical definition of posture.
    Human Factors, 16, 576-584.

BVA, A NEW METHOD TO INVESTIGATE COMBINED STRESS FACTORS

M. Bier

University of Technology, Darmstadt
Federal Republic of Germany

While a number of procedures to find out about job demands are available in ergonomics (Frieling, 1982; Hoyos, 1977), several standardized methods have been developed in the field of time sudies (Haller-Wedel, 1969; Pechhold, 1962).

Stress in the work place is usually determined by more than one stress factor. Being aware of that we found it to be of significant importance to combine demand analyses and time studies, in order to estimate more adequately multiple stress and the resulting strain. Knowing more about the temporal structure of multiple stress can help find the causes of high levels of work strain and that in turn can contribute to improving work conditions and the work environment.

This set of goals leads to the development of a new method of rating combined stress and strain. We named it BVA ("Beanspruchungsskalierendes Verfahren zur Arbeitsablaufanalyse) - a strain rating procedure to analyze sequences of operation. The following is a description of how our new procedure is conducted and an introduction to the options offered by its evaluation software.

Figure 1 shows the top part of the BVA record sheet. It allows the division of the job concerned into a maximum of twelve elementary jobs. These elementary jobs are then filled in to the left column of the BVA record sheet. They may be executed simultaneously or one after the other. From now on we will refer to them as "job elements".

1	moving about								
2	holding/transporting								
3	loading by hand								
4	assembling/dismantling								
5	operating manual tools								
6	operating powered hand tools								
7	operating stationary machine tools								
8	operating mining machinery								
9	controlling								
10	communicating by telephone/ radio								
11	planning/supervising/ educating								
12									

Figure 1: BVA record sheet, top part

13	cold/draft								
14	heat								
15	limited space								
16	lighting								
17	noise								
18	vibrations								
19	dust								
20	accident risk								
21	time pressure								
22	responsibility								
23									
24									

Figure 2: BVA record sheet, bottom part

In Figure 2 the lower half of the BVA record sheet can
be seen . It contains up to twelve features of the work
environment. We decided to call them "environment elements".

The total observation period is divided into intervals
during which the strain upon the worker, the environment
elements and the job elements all remain constant. If for
instance the strain level increases due to the worker's
progressing fatigue, a new interval begins. Consequently,
one specific combination of environment elements and job
elements and their respective stress levels is attributed
to each interval. Stress is rated on an ordinal scale from
"0" (= it never occurs) to "5" (= much above average).

The strain level and the length of each interval are
written into two lines in the centre part of the BVA
record sheet (Figure 3).

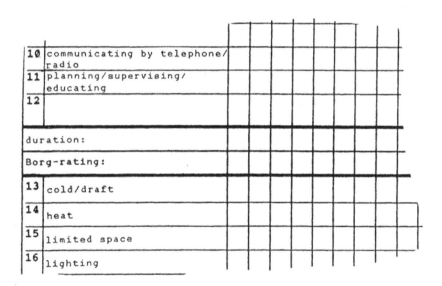

Figure 3: BVA record sheet, centre part

Strain is rated on the Borg-scale, whose explanation
can be found in the upper right-hand corner of every BVA
record sheet (Figure 4).

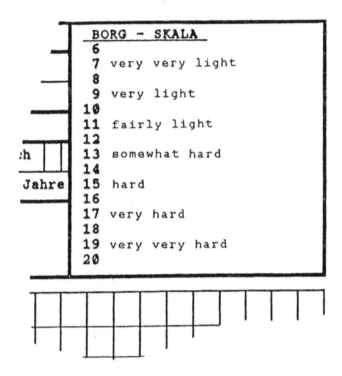

Figure 4: Borg-scale

Forming a series of consecutive intervals creates the
opportunity to expand the analysis time limits.

An example of a completely filled in BVA data sheet can
be seen in Figure 5. In this case the first interval
lasted four minutes and the strain recorded here rated "8"
on the Borg-scale. Two job elements occurred simultaneously, their respective stress levels were "2" (job element
1) and "4" (job element 11). During the first interval
three environment elements were recorded. They each rated
"2". Data for another nine consecutive intervals were
recorded in the same way.

job element/ environment element	1	2	3	4	5	6	7	8	9	10	11	12	13	14	15	16
1 moving	2	2	2	4	3			2	2							
2 pushing/pulling a cart		4	3													
3 holding/ tranporting								4	5							
4 paletizing/ moving palets				4												
5 putting cover/net on loaded palet				4												
6 containerizing																
7 fixation of packages																
8 positioning of packages						4		4	4							
9 executing simple manual jobs																
10 locating packages																
11 operating fork-lift truck	4		4													
12 break caused by changing work loads							5		5							
Zeit:	4	3	8	11	5	7	9	5	14	2						
RPE :	8	12	9	8	9	7	6	14	12	6						
13 cold/draft	2	2	2	2	2	2	2	2	2	2						
14 air pollution	2	2	1	1	1			1	1							
15 lighting																
16 noise	2	1	1	1	1	1										
17 limited space																
18 ground/standing conditions								2								
19 weather/rain								3	3							
20 time pressure																
21 accident risk																
22 responsibility																
23																
24																

Figure 5: Completely filled in BVA data sheet

Once all data are recorded they can be stored and
processed by a personal computer. If a computer is
available at the time and place of data-recording, the
BVA-sheet can be omitted. Currently several evaluation
algorithms are available within the BVA software, some of
will now be explained.

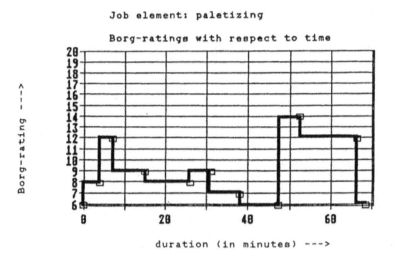

(Figure 6: Borg-ratings with respect to time)

Figure 6 shows a diagram depicting Borg-ratings with
respect to time. Changes in the Borg-ratings have been
found to correlate with changes of workers' heart rates.
What remains to be shown is how well the ratings correlate
with physiologial figures, such as the heart rate. In a
field study on coal mining the job element "moving along
below ground" was analyzed and a correlation factor of
0.76 between the recorded Borg-ratings and the miners'
heart rates was found. A correlation factor of 0.73 was
recorded between Borg-ratings and the conversion of energy
by the miners. Inter-rater-reliability plays an equally
important part in the evaluation of different methods of

job analysis. Inter-rater-reliability is a criterion that
states how great the similarity is in rating job elements
between independent raters. In four different field studies, in which both basic forms of human labour - predominantly physical and non-physical - were analyzed, correlation factors from 0.73 to 0.87 were found (Spearman,
1904). This means that the Borg-scale is indeed a useful
means of estimating strain.

Returning to BVA's evaluation algorithms, each job element can be classified either "predominantly physical" or
"predominantly non-physical". In consequence, every job
made up by classified job elements can also be rated
either one of the two or a mixture of both. The criterion
used here is the temporal proportion of the two basic
kinds of job elements. In Figure 7 you can see how frequently the twelve job elements occurred and their specific duration in proportion to the total time of observation. The black bars stand for relative frequency, while
the white bars represent relative duration. 23 different
jobs were examined throughout this study.

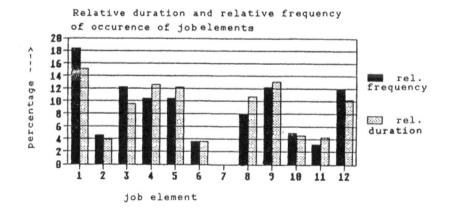

Figure 7: Relative duration and relative frequency of
job elements

Mean and maximum Borg-ratings of job elements

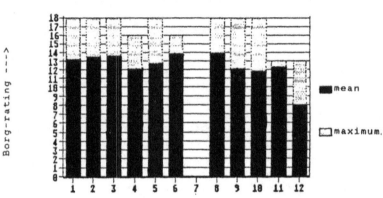

Figure 8: Mean and maximum strain levels of job elements

    With the help of BVA, job elements can also be analyzed
as to what their mean and maximum degrees of strain are.
An example of how this is done is shown in Figure 8. The
study from which the previous example has been taken,
deserves a wider space in this context. In 1986 the
Institute of Ergonomics of the Technical University of
Darmstadt was asked to analyze jobs in coal mining, in
order to give recommendations for the employment of
handicapped and elderly miners. It was found that moving
along the shafts of coal mines poses a major difficulty.
Walking was the most frequently recorded job element and
the strain level was in many cases higher than that
recorded for other job elements more typical of work in
coal mines. This becomes rather obvious in Figure 8: The
job element "moving along below ground", represented by
column 1, surprisingly not only creates a relatively high
average strain level, but also the maximum level recorded
throughout the study.

Finally a few of the options offered by our evaluation
software, which clarify the superposition of stress factors and its effect on the straining of a worker are
demonstrated by Figure 9 which shows a superposition
matrix (Haider, 1982). Its elements reflect the frequencies of the superposition of two particular stress factors. In the same way the duration of such superpositions
can be depicted and evaluated.

It seems that the superposition of job elements and
environment elements is critical when particular combinations last long and occur frequently. If these combinations also rate high on the Borg-scale, they should be
given priority in the process of work organization and
the designing of job conditions.

It is not possible to explain all the details of BVA here,
but it is hoped that some insight into our new method of
job analysis has been given.

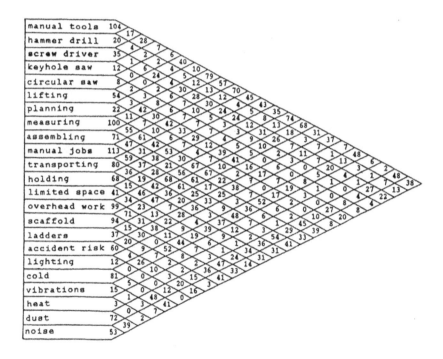

Figure 9: Matrix of frequencies of combinations of two
superimposed stress factors

REFERENCES

Frieling, E., 1982, Bestandsaufnahme arbeitsanalytischer Methoden in Forschungsvorhaben aus dem Bereich der Arbeitsorganisation, Universität München, Institut f. Psychologie.

Haller-Wedel, E., 1969, Das Multimomentverfahren in Theorie und Praxis (München: Hanser)

Haider, E., 1982, Ergonomische Ermittlung, Beurteilung und Gestaltung von superponierten Anforderungen. Exemplarische Analyse: Informatorische Arbeit und Klima (Düsseldorf: VDI)

Hoyos Graf, C., 1977, Handlungsorientierte Tätigkeits- analysen mit dem "Fragebogen zur Arbeitsanalyse". In: IfaA, Nr. 68, 4(1977).

Pechhold, E., 1962, Zeitmessung und Zeitmeßgeräte im Arbeitsstudium, Verband f. Arbeitsstudien REFA e. V., Darmstadt.

Spearman, C., 1904, The proof of measurement of association between two things, American Journal of Psychology, 15, 72 - 101.

STRESS AND STRAIN IN KITCHEN WORK

Clas-Håkan Nygård, Sirpa Lusa, Anneli Peltomaa
and Juhani Ilmarinen

Institute of Occupational Health
Vantaa
Finland

The work of kitchen helpers is one of the heaviest municipal occupations, especially among elderly women (Suurn£kki et al. 1985). The disadvantages appear as a high incidence of sickness and a decreased work capacity (Tuomi et al. 1985). There has also been a high turnover of kitchen helpers in recent years, and Finland's larger cities also now suffer from a clear labour shortage. The food delivery system in hospitals, institution homes and health care centres in Finland was redesigned some ten years ago, when the preparation of the meals and portions for patients was centralized to kitchens. Before the change the food was cooked in kitchens, but divided into portions in the wards by the nursing personnel. In the new centralized system the dishwashing, too, is done in the kitchens. Because of the centralized system, more conveyors were introduced into the kitchens, and the work became more standardized and repetitive. The aim of the study was to measure the stress and strain in these two different types of kitchen work.

MATERIAL

The subjects were chosen from two kitchens. One of them was a kitchen in a municipal service department (non-centralized food-delivering system), the other being a kitchen in a hospital (centralized food-delivering system). The subjects' mean age was 40 years (range 19-61 years; Table 1). The body weight, height and fat percentage were all higher in the non-centralized kitchen (NC-kitchen) than in the centralized kitchen (C-kitchen) workers. The difference in body fat percent was statistically significant ($p < 0.05$).

Table 1. Age, anthropometrics and maximal
oxygen consumption of the subjects by type
of kitchen

Type of kitchen			age yrs	weight kg	height cm	body fat %	VO2max ml.kg.min^{-1}
NC	10	M	39.7	71.4	163.1	30.0	28.2
		SD	13.6	11.6	6.6	8.5	5.6
C	10	M	40.9	63.1	162.5	22.8*	28.4
		SD	11.7	8.1	6.4	4.3	5.9
All	20	M	40.3	67.2	162.8	26.5	28.3
		SD	12.4	10.6	6.3	7.5	5.6

* $p < 0.05$
NC: non centralized kitchen
C: centralized kitchen

METHODS

The work profiles were done by the AET job analysis
method (Rohmert and Landau 1983). During one whole work
shift, a time budget of the main work tasks was prepared
minute by minute. Poor work postures (Suurnäkki et al.
1985) and time pressure were simultaneously registered by
minute by minute observations. Heart rate was measured
minute by minute, during the work shift, with an ambula-
tory device (Sport Tester PE 3000). Oxygen consumption
during the heaviest work tasks was measured directly for
five subjects, with a portable device (Morgan Oxylog;
Louhevaara et al. 1985). Oxygen consumption and heart rate
were measured during a stepwise increasing submaximal
bicycle ergometer test in the laboratory, and the maximal
oxygen consumption was estimated (Ilmarinen et al. 1985).

RESULTS

The main stress factors in kitchen work are found in
the physical environment (dirtiness, wetness, climate,
noise), in the physical work (static, repetitive work and
the use of forces) and in information reception (Figure
1). The main differences in the stress factors between the
two kitchens were in contacts with supervisors, visual
perception static and repetitive work, and in the fact

that the C-kitchen in part was like shift work occurring between 6.00 and 19.00.

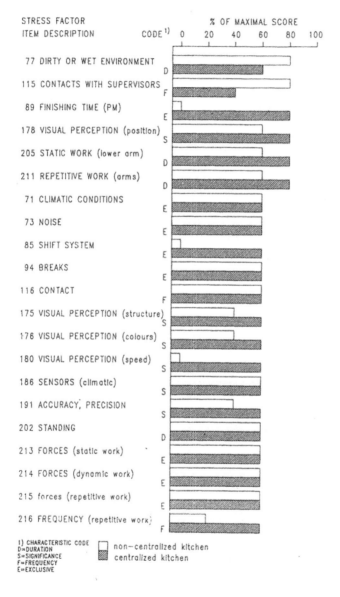

Figure 1. The main stress factors in non-centralized and centralized kitchen work.

Kitchen work included cleaning tasks an average of 11% of the work shift, being 13% in the C-kitchen and 8% in the NC-kitchen (Figure 2). Moving dishes and trays into and out of dishwashers averaged 8% for all; this task was more frequent in the NC-kitchen (12%) than in the C-kitchen (5%). Lifting and carrying goods weighing less than 5 kg amounted, on average, to 8% and maintenance tasks to 6%; there were no great differences between the time budget in the two kitchens. The work in the NC-kitchen involved more pauses than in the C-kitchen (29% and 19%).

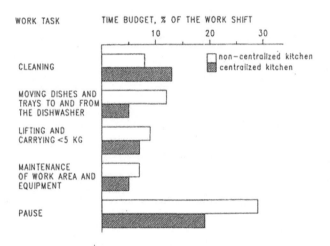

Figure 2. Time budget (% of the work shift) of the main work tasks in the centralized and the non-centralized kitchens.

Upper arms in the position between 30° and 90° was the most common work posture (38% of the work shift) in kitchen work. It was more common in the C-kitchen (48%) than in the NC-kitchen (28%) (Figure 3). The back bent less than 90° averaged 16% of the work shift, and was also more frequent among the workers in the C-kitchen (18%) than among those in the NC-kitchen (13%). The neck bent or rotated was also more common in the C-kitchen (7%) than in

the NC-kitchen (2%). The wrist twisted accounted for 4%
among those in the NC-kitchen, whereas this posture was
not found at all among those working in the C-kitchen.

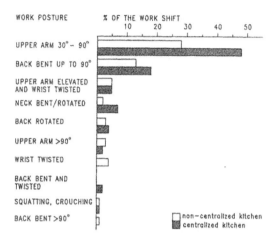

Figure 3. Poor work postures (% of the work shift) in the
centralized and the non-centralized kitchens.

Time pressure was observed for 9% of the total work
time in the NC-kitchen and 15% in the C-kitchen. More than
10% of the workday time pressure was observed for three
workers of the NC-kitchen and five workers of the C-
kitchen (Figure 4).

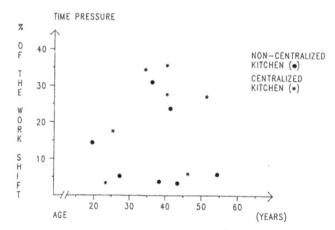

Figure 4. Time pressure (% of the work shift) among the
workers in the centralized and non-centralized kitchens.

Oxygen consumption during some main working tasks in the NC-kitchen averaged 0.87 $l \cdot min^{-1}$, which corresponded to 46% of the maximal oxygen consumption (VO_2max). The oxygen consumption ranged from 0.55 to 1.41 $l \cdot min^{-1}$, which corresponded to 24% and 70% VO_2max. The mean heart rate during these measurements was 102 $beats \cdot min^{-1}$.

The mean heart rate during the workday averaged 97 $beats \cdot min^{-1}$ in the NC-kitchen and 100 $beats \cdot min^{-1}$ in the C-kitchen. The mean heart rate ranged individually between 82 and 110 $beats \cdot min^{-1}$ in the NC-kitchen and between 92 and 112 $beats \cdot min^{-1}$ in the C-kitchen. Cleaning work increased the heart rate, on average, to 104 $beats \cdot min^{-1}$ in the NC-kitchen and 113 $beats \cdot min^{-1}$ in the C-kitchen (Figure 5). Moving dishes and trays also induced a higher heart rate in the C-kitchen (105 $beats \cdot min^{-1}$) than in the NC-kitchen (97 $beats \cdot min^{-1}$). In lifting, carrying and maintenance tasks the heart rate was, on average, on the same level (102 $beats \cdot min^{-1}$) in both kitchens.

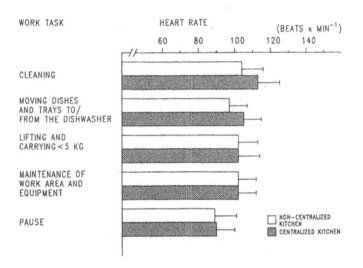

Figure 5. Heart rate (mean and standard deviation) among the workers in the main work task, by type of kitchen.

The cumulative distribution curve of the time spent in each heart rate class was slightly shifted to the right for those in the C-kitchen (Figure 6); this indicates a higher cardio-respiratory strain among those in the C-kitchen than among those in the NC-kitchen.

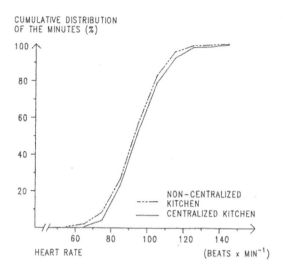

Figure 6. Cumulative distribution of the time\(%) spent at different heart rate levels, by type of kitchen.

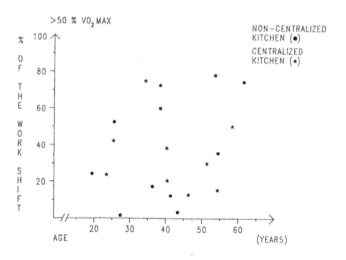

Figure 7. Time spent (% of the work shift) above the 50% VO_2max level plotted against age, by type of kitchen.

The 50% VO_2max level corresponded in this sample to a mean heart rate of 103 beats·min^{-1}. The time spent above that level was calculated and plotted individually against age (Figure 7). The time above that level ranged individually from 1 to 78% of the work shift. For half of the subjects it was above the 50% VO_2max level more than 30% of the work shift. In two subjects over 50 years of age working in the NC-kitchen and two subjects between 30 and 40 years of age working in the C-kitchen, the 70% VO_2max level was exceeded.

DISCUSSION AND CONCLUSIONS

The workers in the C-kitchen spend less time at the dishwasher conveyor moving dishes and trays to and from the dishwasher than those in the NC-kitchen. This could be because dish-washing in the centralized kitchen has to be done in a given time as group work. In the non-centralized kitchen the workers could regulate their working speed more freely. The upper arms between 30° and 90° and the back bent up to 90° were the most frequent poor work postures. These postures were noticed especially when subjects worked at the conveyor, because the height of the conveyor is not adjustable for different body anthropometrics. These postures were more frequent among the workers in the C-kitchen than among those in the NC-kitchen. The higher numbers of elevated arm postures among those working in the C-kitchen could partly be due to more repetitive work carried out near the conveyors.

Time pressure was found more often among the workers in the C-kitchen than in the NC-kitchen. This could be because the work in the C-kitchen involved more work at the conveyor than the work in the NC-kitchen. Observed time pressure for more than one quarter of the work shift was found for one worker in the NC-kitchen and for four in the C-kitchen. Time pressure usually occurred when moving dishes and trays to or from the dishwasher.

The mean heart rate during the work shift among the workers in the two kitchen was the same, and approximately the same as among kitchen workers on a passenger ferry (Tamminen-Peter et al. 1987), among cleaners (Louhevaara et al. 1983) and among women in municipal auxiliary work (Suurnäkki et al. 1985). Some of the work tasks (moving dishes and trays and cleaning), however, induced a higher mean heart rate among workers in the C-kitchen than among those in the NC-kitchen. This could partly be explained by the time pressure in the C-kitchen, especially when working at conveyors.

Seven subjects spend half of the work shift above a strain level of more than 50% VO_2max, which has been suggested to be the upper limit for work including breaks (Andersen et al. 1978). Notable also was that the strain level varied individually from 1% to 78% of VO_2max. This means that there could be great individual variation in strain among workers in the same kind of kitchen work, the differences being mainly due to differences in physical aerobic capacity and age.

It is concluded that the new centralized food delivery system has not improved the kitchen work with respect to the stress and strain factors of the work. This is partly in disagreement with the results of a Japanese study (Huang et al. 1988), where the strain on the musculoskeletal system, in particular, was found to be lower in an automated kitchen than in a traditional kitchen. Furthermore, our results indicate that job analysis and measurement of the strain on the worker are important when redesigning kitchen work.

REFERENCES

Andersen, K., Rutenfranz, J., Masironi, R. and Seliger, U., 1978, Habitual physical activity and health. World Health Organization, (WHO Regional Publications: European series no 6)

Huang, J., Ono, Y., Shibata, E., Takeuchi, Y. and Sanaga, N., 1988, Occupational musculoskeletal disorders in lunch centre workers. Ergonomics, 31, 65-75.

Ilmarinen, J., Luopajärvi, T., Nygård, C-H., Suvanto, S., Huuhtanen, P., Järvinen, M., Cedercreutz, G. and Korhonen, O., 1985, Kunnallisten työntekijöiden toimintakyky (Functional capacity of municipal employees). Työterveyslaitoksen tutkimuksia 3, 212-238.

Louhevaara, V., Ilmarinen, J., Nygård, C-H. and Pesonen, I., 1983, Siivoustyön fyysinen kuormittavuus (Stress and strain in cleaning work). Työterveyslaitoksen tutkimuksia 1, 34-45.

Louhevaara, V., Ilmarinen, J. and Oja, P., 1985, Comparison of three field methods for measuring oxygen consumption. Ergonomics, 2, 463-470.

Rohmert, W. and Landau, K., 1983, A new technique for job analysis., London, New York: Taylor and Francis.

Suurnäkki, T., Nygård, C-H., Ilmarinen, J., Peltomaa, T., Järvenpää, I., Järvinen, M., Nieminen, K. and Huuhtanen, P., 1985, Työntekijöiden kuormittuminen kunnallisissa ammateissa (Stress and strain in municipal work). Työterveyslaitoksen tutkimuksia 3, 239-261.

Tamminen-Peter, L., Suvitie, T., Nygård, C-H., Virtanen, T. and Saarni, H., 1987, Taloushenkilöstön fyysinen kuormittuminen matkustaja-autolautalla (Physical strain in catering work on the Baltic car ferries). Työ ja ihminen 1, 226-240.

Tuomi, K., Wägar, G., Eskelinen, L., Huuhtanen, P., Suurnäkki, T., Fahlström, P., Aalto, L. and Ilmarinen, J., 1985, Terveys, työkyky ja työolot kunnallisissa ammattiryhmissä (Health, work capacity and work conditions in municipal occupations) Työterveyslaitoksen tutkimuksia 3, 95-132.

MENTAL EFFORT IN PROBLEM SOLVING AS MANIFESTED IN THE POWER SPECTRA OF HEART-INTERBEATS INTERVALS

Jürgen Weimann

Humboldt-University of Berlin
Department of Psychology
Germany Democratic Republic

INTRODUCTION

A rising use of new information technologies in business and private life can be stated. The application of computers to aid mental routine work up to expert systems falls also into a widespread domain of psychological tasks. One field of interest shared by psychological and psycho-physiological research is the assessment of mental processing load or cognitive processing effort, respectively, during the solution of various task demands. Concerning a more macroscopic view of the analysis of mental load, that means by relative complex acting units, cardiovascular psychophysiology will be favoured progressively. Habcock et al. (1985) characterized studies of heart rate frequency and derived variables (e.g. sinus arrhythmia) as the currently most useful method for the estimation of mental load, in particular with respect to field application.

Some years ago we could find for the most part studies which involved phasic event-related analysis of heart rate changes.

At the present an increasing number of papers using tonic data analysis are noted. One of these is the power spectrum of the heart rate or interbeat-interval (IBI) time series, respectively. The power spectrum, as a rule calculated by the Fast Fourier Transformation, is a method splitting the whole variability of a time series in a defined frequency band. Commonly the band for IBI-spectra is defined in a range between 0 and .5 Hz, because this relatively small frequency band describes the majority of the time series variability (Kamphuis and Frowein 1985).

The spectrum includes three physiological relevant components which are believed to orginate from different regulatory subsystems. The main oscillation frequency at .03 Hz reflects thermoregulatory vasomotor activity. The frequency band about .10 Hz (band between .07 Hz and .14 Hz) reflects blood pressure regulatory vasomotor activity and the frequency band faster than .20 Hz seems closely linked with the respiratory activity (Sayers 1973, Mulder 1980, 1985).

A phenomenon that is interesting for psychological questions is the relationsship between the height of the .10 Hz component amplitude and the amount of mental processing load (e.g. Mulder and Mulder 1980, Mulders et al. 1982, Egelund 1985, Hatch et al. 1986).

It was demonstrated in different investigations that the employment of controlled processing leads to a reduction of the .10 Hz component. Increasing processing load, in comparison with lower demands on working memory in the same type of tasks, is connected with a reduced portion of variability of the 10 s oscillation (.10 Hz) regarding the total time-series variability.

I would like to emphasize that we discuss mental load in relation to changes of IBI patterns only in the sense of the amount or quantity of controlled capacity-limited information processing during the time of analysis based on the theory of controlled and automatic processing by Shiffrin and Schneider (1977, see also Schneider 1985). Mental load or cognitive effort, respectively, are functionally defined by the number of processing steps or processing demands for adequate task performance with particular respect to the time which is necessary for controlled processing in the working memory (Mulder 1980).

Schönebeck et al. (1985) investigated mechanisms of text processing. They constructed short texts with equal formal characteristics (70-75 words per text, 5-7 sentences, context representation by 36-44 propositions) based on the model by Kintsch and van Dijk (1978). The objective text difficulty was estimated as the sum of the numbers of reinstatements and inferences, ranging from 0 up to 5. A second classification concerns concrete and abstract text properties.

The subjects had to read and recall immediately. By means of the IBI power spectra, especially the .10 Hz components, it was possible to differ between the ranges of text difficulty. During the recall of difficult texts a convincing reduction of this spectral band was interpreted as a reflection of the increased cognitive demand. The

finding that the .10 Hz component explains the greatest
amount of variance was particularly evident for concrete
texts. Within the discussion of the use of inferences and
reinstatements by recalling "abstract" or "concrete" texts
the authors concluded that "the frequencies near .1 Hz
reflect only the cognitive demands which are placed on
working memory by the number of actually performed
cognitive operations,..." (Schönebeck et al. 1985, p.352).

First demonstrative results on the autonomic reflection
of emotional excitement in text comprehension suggest that
when cognitive processing demands are controlled (that
means in this case an equal weight regarding objective
difficulty) there are substantial effects of emotional
valence on text recall in a sense of a correlation of
performance and physiological activation patterns.

A second direction for work (of our group) was aimed at
the identification of different strategies in man-computer
interaction by means of performance data and additional
cardiovascular indicators, especially the IBI power spectra (Zimmer et al. 1985, Guguljanowa 1986, Zimmer and
Guguljanowa 1986).

Strategies were defined as different dialogue structures which could be used as a mode of man-computer communication to perform simulated commercial orders in a sales
division of a factory. The experimental studies with this
paradigm involved variations of controlled processes,
operational demands, motoric performances and motivational
factors. By means of the IBI power spectra it was possible
to separate strategies with different controlled processing effort (e.g. simple commands versus complex commands)
and between different levels of task difficulty too. There
were no contradictions with performance scores (e.g. time
of task solution). Generally increased cognitive demands
were connected with decreased power data.

The conclusion of all sketched studies were that the
.10 Hz component reflects the amount of controlled information processing in connection with a capacity-limited
working memory whereas motor operations and motivational
effort seems to be represented in the respiratory frequency band of the IBI power spectrum.

EXPERIMENTS WITH A SIMPLE ARITHMETIC PROBLEM

The reported experiments by Guguljanowa dealt with
different MCI dialogue strategies which involved varations
in cognitive demands and their external components (e.g.
computer commands).

The current question concerns with the differentiation of solving strategies or rules which are exclusively internally represented and did not involve various external operationalizations. That means strategies which have on principle the same start and goal situations and whose variations originate from the use of cognitive operations in their quantity and/or quality.

Based on a paradigm for the investigation of inductive inferences (Krause 1987) a task was realized where subjects were required to classify and predict.

The decisive information on the problem of the membership of the numerical items to special classes of numbers was masked in the divisibility of the test digit, e.g. divisibility by 5 with possible remainders 0 (class A), 1 (class B), 2 (class C), 3 (class D) or 4 (class E), therefore in the sense of algebra modulo classes.

For example: – presented item: "20"
                  solution   : 20 is divisible by 5 (=4)
                                  with remainder 0, that
                                  means class A
                                  (4x5+0=20);
              – presented item: "26"
                  solution   : 26 is divisible by 5 (=5)
                                  with remainder 1, that
                                  means class B
                                  (5x5+1=26) .

The subjects did not know anything about the classification mode in the beginning of the test. By means of an immediately right/false feed back and a "help" function (computer gives the right answer) they had to learn or to build up a system of classification rules to solve the task. In a series of experiments we used mod 4 and mod 5 tasks. Generally the first stage was declared as a "learning phase" where numbers from 2 or 3 classes were presented. This learning period was followed by "test phases" where the individual strategy had to be transformed to all numerical classes of the task.

Depending on the strategy used, the subject made differentiations or generalizations or had to change the rules to solve the task in the test period.

The following results are based on modulo 5 tasks. In the learning phase subjects of a first group (G1) had to process items of the classes A and B (that means divisible by 5 with possible remainders 0 or 1). A second group of subjects (G2) has items of the three classes A, B and C.

In the end of the learning phase the presence of possible
strategies was proved by a so-called "Invariance-test"
(based on Berg 1976). Following strategies or rules were
identified:

G1   strategy   K - divisible by 5 with attention to
                         remainders (modulo rules)
       strategy   L - divisible by 5 without attention
                         to remainders
G2   strategy   M - divisible by 5 with attention to
                         remainders (modulo rules like K)
       "strategy" N - no solution .

In the test phase both groups of subjects had to transform the individual solution paths on the whole possible
data set of 5 numerical classes. To solve this demand only
the modulo rules were needed. Therefore the strategies K
and M had to generalize their rule system (regarding
attention to remainder), strategy L should be differentiated (involvement of remainder) and the procedure N had
to change completely.

Dependent variables were answer (choice of class,
error, help), solution time (ST) and the heart-beat interval signal. Each learning period contained 30 items and
the test period 50 items, respectively. The classification
took place by special button pressing. The experimental
demands were enclosed by reference phases (silent backward
counting in three-step order from a given 3-digit number).

1. The use of solution rules showed the expected significant reduction of ST in the learning as well as in the
test phases. Note, that in the time period prior to a work
with a strategy no significant differences could be found.
We assume a decrease of effortful processes of searching
and comparisons by the use of rules. Figure 1 illustrates
ST's for one case.

Regarding the test period subjects with the strategies
K and M were able to solve the test problem by transformation in the sense of generalization. No differentiation
(strategy L) or change (procedure N) were provable, that
means no success in the test period. So we can here
summarize the solving process in successful strategies
(K,M) and failure (L,M, non-solver).

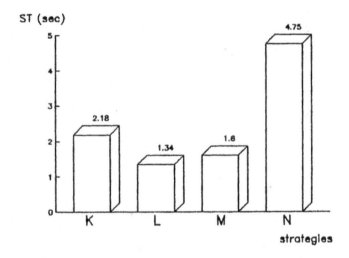

Figure 1. Time of solution (ST) for the solving strategies K,L,M and the unsuccessful procedure N in the learning period (after strategy using)

2. Additionally a formal description of strategies was done. A pool of production rules was constructed in accordance with elementary cognitive operations proposed by Klix (1985). Out of this pool an appropriate number of productions was taken to describe the different strategies. A formal numerical parameter was defined as capacity of information (Ebeling and Feistel 1982). Table 1 contains the indicators for the strategies K and M in the learning period. Remember, they have analogous rules but differ in decision number (numerical classes).

Table 1. Features of the strategies K and M
(ST- solution time, Pow(rel)- relative power of the .10 Hz
component of th IBI spectrum, FCap- parameter of the
formal description) in the learning period

Feature	K	M
ST (ms)	2182	1600
Pow(rel)	52.9	32.5
FCap (bit)	17.6	19.5

For M shorter time of solution is connected with
increased processing effort (expressed by lesser physiological value) and higher formal load. With consideration
of the same information circumstances we assume a comparable range of controlled attentional processing. That
means, the shorter the overall solution time, the higher
the portion of controlled processing of the total time. In
this sense the strategy M involves a higher degree of controlled processing expressed not only in the physiological
indicator but also in the formal production rules description.

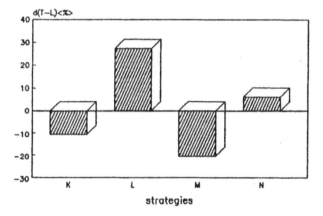

Figure 2. Differences of the physiological indicator
(.10 Hz component) between test and learning period
(positive direction indicates higher effort in the
learning period, see text)

3. Unfortunately, the spectra values of the time periods before and after the use of a solving strategy did not reflect the corresponding portions of the solution time. We suppose that the difference of processing effort between the search for a strategy (before rules were built up) and after the use of the strategies are too small to reflect in our physiological data, at least in this paradigm.

4. An alternative approach seemed to be the comparison of the difference regarding the physiological indicator between the two experimental demands (learning and test period). This result was striking (Figure 2).

By means of the strategies K and M (both are analogous modulo rules and in the test period are equal) the demands of the learning and test period could be solved. The procedures L and N did not have the same success. With respect to the psychophysiological reflection of cognitive processing effort in the .10 Hz component of the IBI power spectrum it offered that only the strategies with a solution in both phases show an adaquate "effort behaviour". The test period with increased cognitive demands is connected with higher processing effort expressed by the physiological tool. Both strategies which were not successful in the test period (L,N) indicated only the same or a smaller effort in the time of task despite the higher demands. We can only speculate if this portion of cognitive demand and inadequate processing effort or the reflection of this effort, respectively, seems to be a reason for non-solution.

CONCLUSION

The aim of an estimation of mental load or cognitive processing effort involves the search for a valid objective psychophysiological indicator. One candidate seems to be the .10 Hz component of the IBI power spectrum, also by reason of a possible field application.

Various results emphasize a relationship of reduced power of the component and raised effort in the sense of an increased portion of controlled processing (based on Shiffrin and Schneider 1977). According to Mulder (1980) the proportion of controlled and automatic processing will define an expenditure of time. In this sense of attention controlled operations the .10 Hz component can support psychological conclusions regarding mental load. Different functions of man-computer interaction will be considered as a good field of application.

REFERENCES

Berg, M., 1976, Die Invariantenanalyse – Entwicklung und Validierung einer Methodik zur verbalisationsunabhän-gigen Erfassung interner kognitiver Zustände. Probleme und Ergebnisse der Psychologie, 57, 5–23.

Ebeling, W. and Feistel, R., 1982, Physik der Selbstorga-nisation und Evolution. (Berlin: Akademie-Verlag).

Egelund, N., 1985, Heart-rate and heart-rate variability as an indicator of driver workload in traffic situa-tions. In: Psychophysiology of cardiovascular control: models, methods, and data, edited by J.F. Orlebeke, G. Mulder and L.J.P. van Doornen, (New York: Plenum Press), pp. 855–863.

Guguljanowa, B., 1986, Zur psychophysiologischen Differenzierung des kognitiven Verarbeitungsaufwandes unterschiedlicher Strategien: untersucht am Beispiel des Mensch-Rechner-Dialoges. Humboldt-Universität zu Berlin,(Promotion A, unveröffentlicht).

Hancock, P.A., Meshkati, N. and Robertson, M.M., 1985, Physiological reflections of mental workload. Aviation, Space and Environmental Medicine, 56, 1110–1114.

Hatch, J.D., Klatt, K., Porges, S.W., Schroeder-Jasheway, L. and Supik, J.D., 1986, The relation between rhythmic cardiovascular variability and reactivity to ortho-static, cognitive, and cold pressure stress. Psycho-physiology, 23, 48–56.

Kamphuis, A. and Frowein, H.W., 1985, Assessment of mental effort by means of heart rate spectral analysis. In: Psychophysiology of cardiovascular control: models, methods, and data, edited by J.F. Orlebeke, G. Mulder and L.J.P. van Doornen (New York: Plenum Press), pp. 841–853.

Kintsch, W. and van Dijk, T.A., 1978, Toward a model of text comprehension and production. Psychological Review, 85, 363–394.

Klix, F., 1985, Über die Nachbildung von Denkanforderun-gen, die Wahrnehmungseigenschaften, Gedächtnisstruktur und Entscheidungsoperationen einschließen. Zeitschrift für Psychologie, 193, 175–206.

Krause, B., 1987, Experimentelle Ansätze zur Kennzeichnung induktiver Lernfähigkeit. In: Neue Trends in der Psychodiagnostik, Bd.1, editiert von U. Schaarschmidt u.a., (Berlin: Psychodiagnostisches Zentrum), 143–151.

Mulder, G., 1980, The heart in mental effort. Rijksuniversitat Groningen (Thesis)

Mulder, G., 1985, Attention, effort and sinusarrhythmia:
    How far are we?. In: Psychophysiology of cardiovascular
    control: models, methods, and data, edited by J.F.
    Orlebeke, G. Mulder and L.J.P. van Doornen (New York:
    Plenum Press), pp.407-423.
Mulder, G. and Mulder, L.J.M., 1980, Coping with mental
    work load. In: Coping and Health, edited by S. Levine
    and H. Ursin, (New York: Plenum Press), pp.233-258.
Mulders, H.P.G., Meijman, T.F., Hanlon, J.F.O. and
    Mulder, G., 1982, Differential psychophysiological
    reactivity of city bus drivers. Ergonomics, 25, 1003-
    1011.
Sayers, B.Mc A., 1973, Analysis of heart rate variability.
    Ergonomics, 16, 17-31.
Schneider, W., 1985, A quantitative model of controlled
    and automatic processing. Annual Meeting of the
    Psychonomic Society, Boston.
Schönebeck, B., Zimmer, K.W. and Kniesche R., 1985,
    Cognitive strain in text comprehension and heart rate
    variability. In: Psychophysiological Approaches to
    Human Information Processing, edited by F. Klix, R.
    Näätänen and K. Zimmer, (Amsterdam: North-Holland),
    pp. 345-356.
Shiffrin, R.M. and Schneider W., 1977, Controlled and
    automatic information processing: II. Perceptual
    learning, automatic attending, and a general theory.
    Psychological Review, 84, 127-190.
Zimmer, K.W. and Guguljanowa, B., 1986, Assessment of
    mental load for different strategies of man-computer
    dialogue by means of the heart rate power spectrum. In:
    Man-Computer Interaction Research MACINTER I, edited by
    F. Klix and H. Wandke, (Amsterdam: North-Holland),
    pp. 357-363.
Zimmer, K.W., Weimann, J. and Guguljanowa, B., 1985,
    Phasic and tonic heart-rate changes related to
    different strategies of task completion. In: Psycho-
    physiological Approaches to Human Information Process-
    ing, edited by F. Klix, R. Näätänen and K. Zimmer,
    (Amsterdam: North-Holland), pp.357-369.

THE ASSESSMENT OF MENTAL WORKLOAD
IN DUAL-TASK PERFORMANCE:
TASK-SPECIFIC AND TASK-UNSPECIFIC INFLUENCES

Rainer Wieland-Eckelmann, Uwe Kleinbeck, Ronald Schwarz und
Hartmut Häcker

University of Wuppertal
Federal Republic of Germany

INTRODUCTION

Despite much disagreement about its nature, definition, and assessment workload is assumed to be an important and measurable entity. In particular, workload evaluation has become an important construct in operational or manufacturing environments, and in system design, since applications of sophisticated control and display technologies to modern systems can impose heavy demands on operator information processing capabilities. Such technologies often require the rapid sampling and integration of various kinds of information, and the resulting demands can approach or exceed the limited processing capacities of the operator. Therefore, a model of workload is especially of great importance early in the system conceptualization phase "... in order to predict which configuration will maximize performance efficiency and still leave some "residual capacity" to meet unexpected task demands" (Yeh and Wickens, 1988, p. 111). Thus, within the domain of Job Analysis research, workload measurement techniques may become a useful tool with regard to "prospective" system design and evaluation. It is evident, however, that a systematic attempt to minimize (mental) workload requires that the designers have access to adequate techniques for measuring workload.

Empirical assessment procedures of workload can be classified into three major categories:

This research was supported by a grant from the Federal Ministry of Research and Technology (BMFT).

1) subjective measures; 2) performance-based measures; and
3) physiological measures (for a review, see Wierwille
and Williges, 1978; O'Donnell and Eggemeier, 1986). This
paper focuses on performance-based measures and their usefulness in indexing workload in terms of task-interference
in dual-task performance. We rely on the dual-task technique, because it has been proven useful for the measurement and evaluation of mental workload in many experimental and applied research programmes (e.g., Wickens, 1984;
O'Donnell and Eggemeier, 1986; Hart, 1987).

However, in contrast to current approaches (for a
review, see O'Donnell and Eggemeier, 1986; Gopher and
Donchin, 1986), the present investigation differs with
regard to the following two aspects. The first refers to
the performance-outcome indices used in our analysis; the
second concerns an aspect which had been mostly neglected
in current workload research, and what we call "Task-Specificity". These aspects are described in detail next.

Performance-outcome measures

In principle, the following indices of performance-
outcome can be assessed: (1) accuracy or quality, e.g.
correct solutions per time unit, (2) speed of performance,
e.g., solution time, and (3) performance effectiveness
which can be defined in terms of the ratio between the
time and/or effort expenditure (Eysenck, 1979; Schulz and
Schönpflug, 1982) and quality of performance. Given the
assumption that in real workplaces performance errors have
to be minimized during task performance, we are likely to
argue that performance effectiveness is the most important
variable with regard to application-oriented measures of
workload and task-interference, respectively. To phrase it
differently, the time spent on task solution and the correct solutions per time unit should be the crucial criteria for the evaluation of the demands and requirements
imposed on the operator. Therefore, unlike the frequently
used performance indices, i.e. errors and correct solutions, in the present study the main focus is on solution
or reaction time. However, since solution time represents
only one part of what we designate performance effectiveness, it becomes necessary to control performance quality.
This could either be done, for example, using very easy
tasks or by training subjects extensiveley before the
testing situation until they reach an optimal performance
level. The latter seems to be the most favourable method,
since it represents a condition which is quite similar to
the one you will find in real work settings.

Task-Specificity

Although the dual-task methodology has been proven useful to measure task-interference, little effort has been made to examine and evaluate those origins of task-interference in dual-task performance that are due to individual differences (e.g., coping style) and situational demands (e.g., external goal-setting, motivational states) that is, task-unspecific factors. The term "Task-Specificity" is used to denote this important, but often neglegted issue in workload research, since it refers to the differentiation between **task-specific** and **task-unspecific** factors.

Task-specific factors refer on the one hand to the intrinsic features of the single tasks, such as difficulty, complexity, and data quality. On the other hand they are represented by the specific combinations of concurrently performed tasks. Within the conceptual framework of multiple resources, the overall level of competition and interference between concurrently performed tasks is considered to be determined by the degree of overlap (sharing) on four dimensions: modality of input (visual, auditory, or tactual); type of coding operations (spatial, verbal); stages of processing (encoding, central processing, responding); and responses (manual, verbal; see Wickens, 1984).

Task-unspecific factors refer to situational demands (e.g., task priorities defined by the experimenter) and/or individual coping dispositions, e.g., time-sharing ability (Ackerman et al., 1984) or stress- and anxiety-related coping styles, e.g., sensitive and defensive coping (Wieland-Eckelmann and Bösel, 1987). In other words, they refer to causes of single-to-dual task decrements or interferences that can not be directly related to the intrinsic features of the single tasks or their combination.

The importance of motivational influences on task performance derives from the dual-task method itself, since subjects are usually instructed to perform with graded changes in the relative priorities of tasks. That is, different emphasis levels which are indicated verbally and/or by feedback information lead to different motivational states and thus, performance is highly susceptible to subjective appraisals and interpretations. These may lead, for example, to the use of strategies such as (1) sequencing attention or executive control activities in a fixed order to either the requirements of the primary or

secondary task, e.g., working at first on the primary task
and then on the secondary task or vice versa, or (2)
switching with regard to the sequence in task performance
occasionally.

With regard to the latter, i.e. individual differences
in the use of strategies to deal with multiple task
requirements, there are - as far as we are aware - only
few studies in workload research that have explored the
impact of individual coping styles systematically. Mostly,
self-report data are used as dependent and not as an independent variable. An exception is M. Eysenck (1986) who
recently emphasized the importance of individual differences in coping style with respect to attention deployment
in a dichotic listening task in which pairs of words were
presented concurrently, one word on each ear. He found
that "facilitators (i.e. those high in trait anxiety)
responded very rapidly to the probe when it follows a
threatening word in the same ear, but they responded very
slowly when it followed a threatening word in the other
ear. In other words, they allocated processing resources
preferentially to the ear on which a threatening word had
been presented. In contrast, inhibitors (ie those low in
trait anxiety) showed exactly the opposite pattern, as if
they actively avoid attending to the ear on which a threatening word had just been presented" (Eysenck, 1986, p.
263). The author concluded that these biases operate at a
pre-attentive level, but they often affect subsequent
attentional processes, and thus performance-outcome.

The second part of this chapter summarizes findings
from a research programme developed to examine systematically the role task-specific and task-unspecifc factors
might play concerning the measurement and evaluation of
workload and task-interference, respectively.

METHOD

Subjects

Seventy-two students from the University of Wuppertal
participated in the experiment. All were paid for their
participation.

Apparatus

Subjects were seated in a light- and sound-attenuated
chamber. Tasks were implemented on an IBM-PC. A CRT-

display was approximately 90 cm in front of the subjects
and slightly below eye level. The subjects responded via a
usual typewriter keyboard on which some keys were specially marked.

Tasks

Primary task. The primary task consisted of identifying
the gender of a person from a business address. The
critical information was the first name. Subjects were
instructed that they had to complete the address by typing
either "HERR" (MISTER) or "FRAU" (MISS) and then finish
the task by pressing the Return-Key. After six seconds the
next address appeared on the display.

Secondary tasks. Three secondary tasks were used:
(1) A visual-spatial discrimination task which consists
of two parallel bars of different lengh. The lengh varied
in a random order with regard to the lower and upper bar.
By pressing either a red or a green button subjects had to
indicate the longer bar. The bars were permanently presented during the six second interval.
(2) An auditory signal detection task. The signal
consists of a tone of 1200 Hz or 1000 Hz. The tone was
presented for 300 ms via headphones at the beginning of
the six second interval. By pressing either a red or green
button the subjects had to decide which one of the two
tones had been presented.
(3) A tactual pattern recognition task. It consists of
two different spatial-temporal patterns of tactual
signals, which were presented with a frequency of 6 Hz
and 2 Hz, respectively. The stimulus was applied mechani-
cally by means of a specially constructed apparatus which
was fixed at the wrist of the left arm. The signal was
permanently applied during the six second interval.

Procedure

After an extensive training session on the first day,
subjects the next day had to perform 18 trials during the
test session, each consisting of 20 stimulus items within
the dual-task condition. Within single-task condition, 60
secondary, and 20 primary stimulus items were presented.
In the test session, each single-task condition was
performed once, follwed by 16 dual-task conditions which
were divided into four blocks. After each block subjects
completed a set of rating scales.

Priority-setting. The following priority-instructions
were given under dual-task conditions: (a) "Do your best";
(b) "Do 10% better" as compared to a defined individual
reference value; and (c) "Do 20% better" as compared to a
defined reference value. Instruction (b) and (c) were
additionally varied with regard to either primary or
secondary task emphasis; that is, subjects had to raise
their performance in one task (e.g., primary task) while
maintaining performance in the other (e.g., secondary
task) on the level they had reached under the dual-task
condition "Do 20% better" without priority-setting.

Independent variables

Within the 3x3x3 factorial design used in this study,
modality (visual, auditory, tactual) of secondary tasks
combined with the primary task, individual coping styles
(defensive, sensitive, non-anxious), and the three
priority-settings ("Do your best", "Do 10% better", "Do
20% better") were treated as independent variables. The
priority-settings represent the repeated measurement
factor.

Individual coping styles were assessed by means of an
inventory developed by Wieland-Eckelmann and Bösel (1987).
Previous studies provided evidence that these individual
ways of coping with task-related stress and anxiety correspond to differences in task performance and reported
states of stress (e.g., Wieland-Eckelmann et al., 1989).
Within the present study, participants were selected from
a total sample of 302 students, who completed the inventory during regular classes and were divided on the basis
of a diagnostic scheme from Wieland-Eckelmann and Bösel
(1987) into three groups : sensitive, defensive, and non-
anxious. Males and females were about evenly distributed
within the groups, and coping styles were evenly distributed within the experimental conditions.

RESULTS AND DISCUSSION

The first step in the analysis performed for the
present paper was to verify our assumption stated below
that performance effectiveness (ie ratio between time
spend on task-solution and correct responses) can be
defined in terms of task-solution time if the number of
correct responses reaches the optimal level. This was
accomplished by examining the number of correct solutions
with regard to all of the 18 trials of the test session,

as well as within the cells of our 3 x 3 x 3 factorial
design. Overall, we found for all trials a rate of correct
solutions of 95 %, and no significant differences were
found with respect to the experimental conditions. For all
analysis of variance reported below, a three-way analysis
(MANOVAs; regression approach) (Modality X Coping Style X
Priority) was conducted as well as univariate analyes.
Priority was used as a repeated measurement factor.

Task-interference in terms of performance effectivenss

To evaluate performance effectiveness of dual-task
compared to single-task performance, the following
parameter was calculated subject by subject:
$Ep = RTD - (RTS + RTP)$, where RTD denotes the total time
to solve the primary and secondary task under dual-task
conditions; RTS and RTP the solution time used under
single-task-conditions, for the secondary (RTS) and the
primary task (RTP).

The direct effects of secondary task-modality depicted
in Figure 1 indicate a significant difference in effectiveness for the secondary task-modalities under dual-task
performance ($F (2,55) = 27.99$; $p < .001$) as compared to
single-task performance. The effectiveness was significantly lower for the visual modality as compared to the
auditory and the tactual modality.

The result supports the assumption of Wickens (1984,
p. 303) and others that intra-modality (i.e. visual-
visual) interference is greater than cross-modality (i.e.
visual-auditory and visual-tactual) interference. Furthermore, given that poor dual-task performance would suggest
competition for the same resources, whereas effective
dual-task performance would suggest little resource competition (Wickens, 1984; Navon and Gopher, 1979), the high
effectiveness with regard to the tactual secondary-primary
task combination indicates the case where obviously only
few common resources are shared.

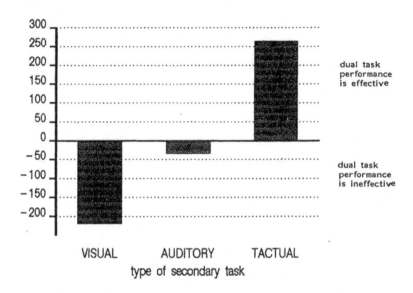

Figure 1. Performance effectiveness of dual-task compared to single-task performance, differentiated for secondary task-modality.

However, the picture becomes more complicated when, in addition to the direct effect of modality, task-unspecific factors, i.e. individual coping styles, are considered. In particular, the significant interaction between modality and coping style ($F (4,55) = 2.76$; $p < .05$) depicted in Figure 2 gives reason to assume that the auditory and tactual system seem to be more sensitive to influences deriving from sindividual differences in coping style. Without going into details concerning the mechanisms probably underlying these interaction effects (for a detailed discussion of the relationship between coping style and task performance, see Wieland-Eckelmann et al., 1989), it can be concluded that an important portion of variance of the results shown in Figure 1 is attributable to individual coping style. Thus, the interpretation of modality effects which play an important role in current workload research (e.g., Wickens, 1984) seems to be equivocal as far as we do not take into account individual differences. In the next paragraph further support of this notion will be reported.

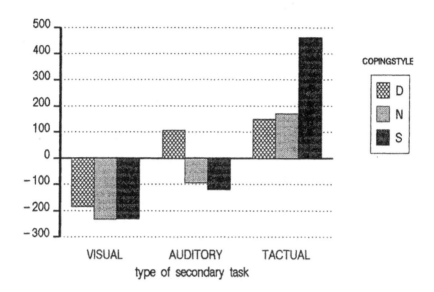

Figure 2. Performance effectiveness of dual-task compared to single-task performance, differentiated for secondary task-modality and coping style; D = Defensive, N = Non-Anxious, S = Sensitive.

Task-interference and priority (goal) setting

In Figure 3 solution time for the primary and secondary task in two different priority-conditions ("Do 10% better" and "Do 20% better") with secondary task emphasis is displayed. The performance level of the "Do 20% better" condition, in which subjects were instructed to enhance performance in secondary and primary task simultaneously, is used as a baseline.

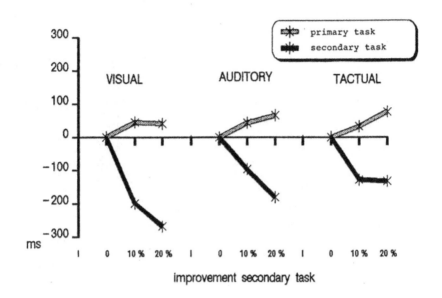

Figure 3. Changes in solution-time for the primary and
secondary task depending on secondary task emphasis, and
differentiated for modality. (0 = without priority, 10% =
"Do 10% better", 20% = "Do 20% better")

As expected, we found a significant main effect for the
manipulation of (secondary) task priorities; that is,
a significant decrement in secondary task solution-time
across the two conditions (F (2,126) = 11.79; p < .001)
and concurrently a significant increment in primary task
solution-time (F (2,126) = 4.61; p < .02). The observed
pattern of interference within the three pairs of tasks
revealed no signifcant differences across modalities.
Thus, this interference pattern corresponds to the framework of general limited (central) capacity models (e.g.,
Kahneman, 1973; Gopher, Brickner and Navon, 1982) and it
indicates competition for allocation of common resources.
This interpretation, however, might be too simple, since
these effects can be confounded with resource allocation
policies depending on the differential (attentional and

motivational) impact priority setting has on subjects differing in coping style. A further inspection of the data
concerned with this issue is described next.

As can be seen in Figure 4, there are remarkable differences between sensitive, defensive, and non-anxious
subjects (for the sake of simplicity, the averaged scores
for the two priority settings are displayed in Figure 4).
The interaction of Priority-Setting x Modality x Coping
Style ($F(8,126) = 1.84$; $p < .07$) revealed that sensitive
subjects increased their performance level under secon-
dary-task emphasis much more within the visual secondary
task as compared with the auditory and tactual tasks. For
defensive subjects we found the opposite pattern of performance levels. Non-anxious subjects showed almost no
differences across modalities. In contrast, with regard to
the performance level in the primary task no such interaction effects were found.

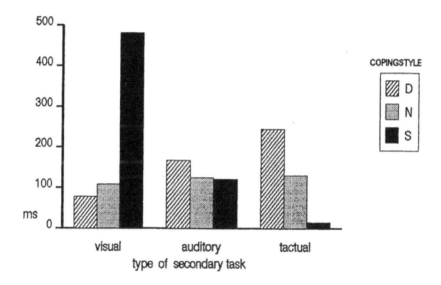

Figure 4. Solution-time decrement of secondary task averaged across "Do 10% better" and "Do 20% better" priority
condition with secondary task emphasis, and differentiated
for secondary task modality and coping style; D = Defensive, N = Non-Anxious, S = Sensitive.

It might be concluded from these results that the modalities moderate the allocation and availability or creation of additional resources (Kahneman, 1973) in a different way. The allocation policy seems to be more effective for sensitive subjects for the visual as compared to the auditory and tactual modality. In contrast, defensive subjects performed better in the tactual as compared to the visual condition. In a theoretical sense, these findings could possibly be interpreted in a way that there exists a modality-specific response-sensitivity that interacts with individual differences in coping style.

There might be, however, a third source of influence responsible for the findings described so far. Differences in secondary task performance as depicted in Figure 3 and 4 could be due to qualitative changes in processing as a function of strategy, or, in other words, active, top-down control (Rabbitt, 1979) This issue is discussed next.

Strategy and priority (goal) setting

In principle, in the present dual-task conditions, subjects can use at least two different stategies in task performance. They can first complete the secondary task and subsequently the primary task, or vice versa.

To analyse the data on a strategic level, we first examined, whether the sequence in performing the two tasks is correlated with task solution-time in the secondary and primary task, respectively. We found that secondary task solution time was negatively ($r = -.78$; $p < .001$), and primary task solution-time positively ($r = .81$; $p < .001$) correlated with task-sequencing. That is, in the case of performing the secondary task first, solution-time for the secondary task is shorter than in the case of completing it second.

Whether the use of such strategies is also systematically related to coping style is depicted in Figure 5. Using the order of task performance as dependent variable, the conducted non-parametric analysis (the data do not fulfil the criteria of analyses of variance) yielded the following results. Sensitive and non-anxious subjects performed in almost 16 and 12 cases (out of 20 possible cases), respectively, the secondary task first (see Figure 5). In contrast, defensive subjects changed their strategy depending on the priority (CHI-Square = 6.65; $p < .05$; Kruskall-Wallis). Since neither a main effect for modality nor for the Modality X Priority interaction was found, it can be assumed that the use of these strategies is mainly

controlled by top-down processes as described in resource-
strategy models. In this framework, resources are
"acquired information about the structure of particular
tasks and about the external world which are used by the
subject in order to control their momentary perceptual
selectivity and their choice of responses " (Rabbitt,
1979). Note that the subjects were well aware of tasks and
conditions, since they had a lot of practice during the
training session. This definition of resources is quite
similar to the conceptualization of coping style proposed
by Wieland-Eckelmann et al.: they stated that individual
differences in ways of coping – sensitive, defensive, and
non-anxious – "correspond to differences in pattern of
states which provide a potential source of information
with regard to the efficiency of self-regulatory activity
(i.e. compensatory state control and task-related attention demanding controlled information processing) and
related effectiveness of performance" (1989).

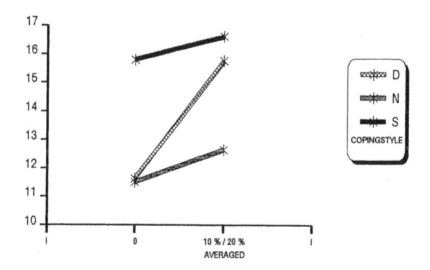

Figure 5. Number of cases in which the secondary task is
performed at the first place, depending on priority setting under secondary task emphasis (0 = without priority,
10 % / 20 % = averaged scores for "Do 10 % better" and "Do
20 % better" condition), differentiated for coping style;
D = Defensive, N = Non-Anxious, S = Sensitive.

The influence of strategy on task-interference in dual-task performance can be further decomposed by controlling these effects. Therefore, we conducted an additional analysis of the data depicted in Figure 3 and 4 which was based only on those cases in which the secondary task was performed first. The results of these "strategy-adjusted" analysis which were performed in analogy to those used for the data depicted in Figure 3 and 4, reveal for the main effect of priority as shown in Figure 3 almost the same results. That is, the subject's allocation policy was apparently not affected by the choice of strategy. On the other hand, since no interaction effect of Priority X Modality X Coping Style as depicted in Figure 4 was found, it can be concluded that the different strategies used by sensitive, defensive, and non-anxious subjects account for the effects presented in Figure 4. Or, in other words, individual differences in coping style lead to the use of strategies which in turn mediate the effects secondary task-modalities have in the three primary-secondary task-combinations.

CONCLUSIONS

In this paper, we have demonstrated that methods for the assessment and evaluation of mental workload in dual-task performance should be based on a combined consideration of task-specific and task-unspecific factors. The data presented so far (for a more detailed report and discussion, see Wieland-Eckelmann, Schwarz & Kleinbeck, in prep.) have made clear that there are strong influences of task-unspecific factors which should be considered more carefully in future developments of mental workload assessment and analysis techniques.

REFERENCES

Ackermann, P.L., Schneider, W. and Wickens, C.D. (1984).
    Deciding the existence of a time-sharing ability: A
    combined methodological and theoretical approach.
    Human Factors, 26, 71-82
Eysenck, M. (1979). Anxiety, learning and memory: a
    reconceptualization. Journal of Research in
    Personality, 13, 363-385.
Eysenck, M. (1986). Individual differences in anxiety,
    cognition, and coping. In G.R.Hockey, A.W.K.Gaillard
    and M.G.H. Coles (Eds.), Energetics in human information processing (pp. 255-270). Dordrecht: Martinus
    Nijhoff Publishers.

Gopher, D., Brickner, M.and Navon, D. (1982). Different difficulty manipulations interact differently with task emphasis: Evidence for multiple resources. Journal of experimental Psychology: Human perception and performance, 8, 146-156.

Gopher, D, and Donchin, E. (1986). Workload: An examination of the concept. In K. Boff, L. Kaufman, & J. Thomas (Eds.), Handbook of perception and human performance. Vol. II (pp. 41-1-41-49). New York: Wiley.

Hart, S.G. (1987). Research papers and publications (1981-1987). Workload research program. Moffet Field, Ca.: NASA technical Memorandum 100016

Kahneman, D. (1973). Attention and effort. New Jersey: Prentice-Hall.

Navon, D. and Gopher, D. (1979). On the economy of the human processing system. Psychological Review, 86, 214-253.

O`Donnell, R.D. and Eggemeier, F.T. (1986). Workload assessment methodology. In K. Boff, L. Kaufman & J.P. Thomas (Eds.), Handbook of perception and human performance, Vol II, Cognitive processes and performance (Vol. II, pp 42-1 - 42-49).New York: Wiley.

Rabbitt, P.M.A. (1979). Current paradigms and models in human information processing. In V. Hamilton & D.M. Warburton (Eds.), Human stress and cognition. New York: Wiley.

Schulz, P. and Schönpflug , W. (1982). Regulatory activity during states of stress. In H.W. Krohne & L. Laux (Eds.), Achievement, stress and anxiety (pp. 51-74).

Wickens, C.D. (1984). Engineering psychology and human performance. Columbus: Merril.

Wieland-Eckelmann, R. and Bösel, R. (1987). Konstruktion eines Verfahrens zur Erfassung dispositioneller Angst-bewältigungsstile im Leistungsbereich. Zeitschrift für Differentielle und Diagnostische Psychologie, 8, 39-56.

Wieland-Eckelmann, R., Bösel, R and Badorrek, W. (1989). Anxiety-related coping styles and the achievement process. In F. Halisch & J.H. van de Bercken (Eds.). International perspectives on achievement and task motivation. Lisse: Swets & Zeltinger.

Wierwille, W.W. and Williges, R.C. (1978). Survey analysis of operator workload assessment techniques. (Report No. 2, 78-100). Blacksburg, Va.: Symetric corporation.

Yeh, Y.Y. and Wickens, C.D. (1988). Dissociation of performance and subjective measures of workload. Human Factors, 30, 111-120.

THE MODULAR WORK ANALYSIS SYSTEM (MAS)

Klaus M. Groth

University of Technology, Darmstadt
Federal Republic of Germany

Numerous work analysis methods have been developed in recent years (Frieling, 1982). Most of them can be classified as 1. concerning specific analysis demands, and 2. being applicable to a great variety of work systems and analysis demands. The outstanding problem is that the latter lack the ability for highly differentiated results while the former lead to analyses which are hardly comparable to those of other methods. In many cases the available analysis techniques are either too unspecific or do not fit the actual problem, so that new or modified analysis procedures must laboriously be developed, or two or more systems have to be utilized in parallel.

One attempt to obviate this contradiction is, for example, the "Arbeitswissenschaftliches Erhebungsverfahren zur Tätigkeitsanalyse (AET)" (Rohmert and Landau, 1979) which is an all-purpose analysis technique with supplements (additional sets of characteristics) for the investigation of particular job groups.

A new approach to this problem is the Modular Work Analysis System (MAS), which has been developed since 1986 at the 'Institut für Arbeitswissenschaft der Technischen Hochschule Darmstadt'. The aim of development was to create a work analysis system able to analyse work systems with regard to any specific aspect and also to keep the results comparable to the results of AET and other MAS results as far as possible.

The MAS is based on theoretical models. Due to the complexity and variety of human work it is impossible to explain it with only one model. Models are used to deduce a 'complete' description of work; complete in a sense that every relevant aspect of work is covered. The ergonomic

scope leads to the stress/strain concept (Rohmert, 1984)
as a basic tool for the MAS to describe important aspects
of human work. The main theoretical model of the MAS is
the model of the man-at-work system, the value of which is
proved extensively. For the analysis of work demands the
model of human performance (Welford, 1965; Luczak, 1975)
is used. To meet new aspects of interest, the MAS is open
to new models or sub-models as long as they fit in with
the current hierarchical structure of characteristics.

   Work analysis with the MAS is done - like several other
systems - by investigating and rating a certain number of
characteristics; each characteristic describing a more or
less specific aspect of work. Rating is usually done by
selecting the appropriate level of the corresponding
multi-level classification code. Additional to standard
classification codes non-quantitative codes can be used
for verbal descriptions of aspects of the work. On the
other hand numerical (metric) scales can be used for the
coding of measurement results, for example, the temperature of the work place. One outstanding feature of the MAS
is, that the amount and selection of characteristics may
vary according to the purpose of work analysis.

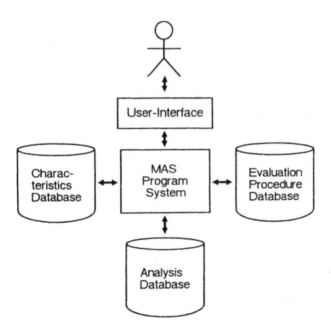

Figure 1. MAS system structure

The MAS is composed of mainly four parts, shown in
Figure 1. The elements are three databases (the characteristics database, the analysis database and the evaluation procedure database) and the linking MAS program system. The user can communicate with the program system via
an interactive graphic dialogue interface.

The characteristics database is an open hierarchical
database of characteristics; open in the sense that the
database can be extended for new characteristics; hierarchical in the way that superposed characteristics are
differentiated by subordinate characteristics (Figure 2).
Presently the database contains about 1200 characteristics
which describe the work system (worker, tools, objects,
environment), tasks, and work demands. To maintain compatibility with the AET, every characteristic of the
AET/d and its significant supplements (ADTV, B-AET, H-AET)
is also stored in this database. For every specific analysis demand a particular set of characteristics is hierarchically extracted from this database. Hierarchical means
that for every characteristic selected the selection of
all superposed characteristics is obligatory. The number
of included hierarchy levels determines the differentia-
bility of work analysis. The hierarchical selection guar-
antees a maximum compatibility within different sets on
the basis of common superposed characteristics.

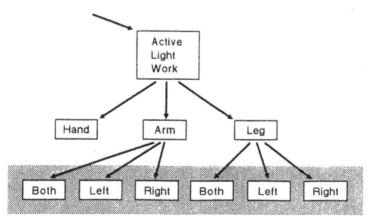

= Optional Characteristics

Figure 2. Characteristics hierarchy sample

The analysis database contains the coded ratings of those characteristics of the characteristics database used for the specific analysis. All analyses done with the MAS are stored in this database before evaluation and are kept for later access. This growing database as well as the existing AET analysis database can be used to get comparative groups of analyses, for example, to investigate changing work demands in worksystems using new technologies. The analysis database is kept at a central computer with copies on any decentralized computer working with the MAS. Storage is done according to the German laws (Bundesdatenschutzgesetz, Hessisches Datenschutzgesetz).

The evaluation procedure database is an open collection of evaluation methods used to evaluate the content of the analysis database in whole or in part. This collection contains methods of univariate and multivariate statistics, for example frequencies, means, medians, job profiles, superposition analyses and cluster analyses. The collection is open to new methods, so that any method satisfying special analysis demands can be easily integrated and accessed by the user via a homogeneous interface. Some interfaces to standard program packages like SPSS, BMDP, SAS, Lotus 1-2-3, dBase etc. are implemented to enable the use of external evaluation procedures.

The MAS program system enables an easy, uniform access to the databases described before. An easy dialogue is maintained by the mouse-based Graphics Environment Manager GEM (Digital Research Inc., 1985).

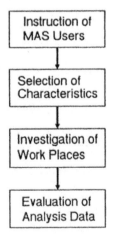

Figure 3. Steps of work analysis with the MAS

Work analysis with the MAS is done following four steps, shown in Figure 3. After the MAS user has been instructed, those characteristics of the database are selected, which are relevant for the aims of analysis. The selection process is detailed by the flowchart shown in Figure 4. For this selection a characteristics manual and a analysis data sheet can be printed. This set of characteristics is used to perform the analyses of the work places of interest.

Work analysis itself is done following Figure 5. After the work system is selected, the worker and his direct supervisor have to be informed about the purpose and modality of the work analysis. The investigation of the work is done by a combination of observation, interview, self-rating by the worker, measurements and document analysis.

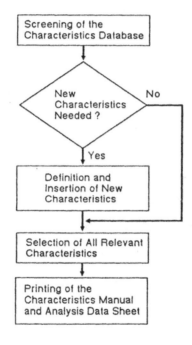

Figure 4. Characteristics selection process

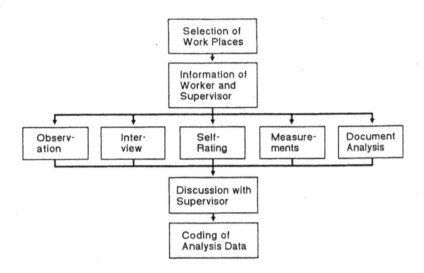

Figure 5. Work place investigation

The amount of each technique applied depends on the
type of work and the selection of characteristics. Measurements will be needed only if matching characteristics
are selected; Self-rating by the worker is neccessary only
if subject-related characteristics, for example, dissatisfaction, are included in the actual selection. Observation
is more important for investigation of mainly physical
work forms, while interview is emphasized for mainly non-
physical work. The data are controlled and completed by a
discussion with the investigated worker's supervisor.
Finally the data are coded either 'online' by entering the
ratings directly into a computer or 'offline' by filling
in an analysis sheet, which is transferred to a computer
later. The analysis of one work system will normally take
about two hours, but depending on the complexity of the
tasks and the degree of practice of the analyst the time
can range from one hour to one day. The coded data are
evaluated using methods of the evaluation method database.

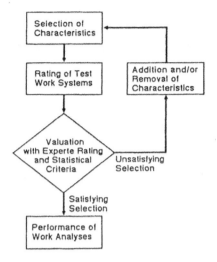

Figure 6. Iterative characteristics selection

The selection process is usually performed in an iterative process shown in Figure 6. The reason for this procedure is simply that the knowledge about the relevant characteristics properly exists only after the analysis of the work. It usually takes two or three iteration steps to get a satisfying selection. The iteration process includes selection, coding of a few test work systems and valuation of the characteristic selection by means of statistical test criteria (for example the reliability coefficient) and expert rating. Expert rating is very important because of low significance levels of statistical criteria due to the small number of subjects in the test phase.

The program system is implemented with the 'C' programming language (Kernighan and Ritchie, 1977) to maintain a maximum portability to other computer systems while getting maximum computer performance. The utilized hardware is a personal computer with Motorola's 68000 CPU, 1 MB RAM, 720 KB floppy disk, graphic monitor, alphanumeric keyboard and mouse. A 20 MB hard disc and a printer are recommended. A program version for IBM-compatible computers is in preparation.

The benefit of MAS is not only to enable work analysis; it can also be the resource for a structured approach to work systems. The characteristics database may be used to transfer ergonomic knowledge for example to the work designer. This database is a structured ergonomic knowledgebase and can be one step towards an ergonomic expert system.

The MAS was proved in several different studies. Some
of them are : the investigation of assembly of detached
ceilings (Rohmert et al., 1988b), the investigation of the
optimal width of work desks in private kitchens (Rohmert
et al., 1988c), the investigation of spatial binding to
the work place (Rohmert et al., 1989), ergonomic investigation of work places for coding street names of the German Bundespost (Rohmert et al., 1988a). Current projects
are the prevention of lower back pain of workers in steel
factories, the investigation of multipally-handicapped
workers and the investigation of stress and strain of
flight attendants in overseas flights.
     The MAS is designed as an evolutionary system, this
means that the characteristics database and evaluation
procedure database are growing over the lifetime of MAS.
The MAS can constitute the superstructure for integration
of known and intended ergonomic rating methods. Thus it is
a flexible tool and is able to match future interests of
work analysis.

REFERENCES

Digital Research Inc. (ed.), 1985, The GEM Programmers
    Guide Volume 1 and 2, (Monterey)
Frieling, 1982, Bestandsaufnahme arbeitsanalytischer
    Methoden in Forschungsvorhaben aus dem Bereich der
    Arbeitsorganisation, (Universität München, Institut für
    Psychologie)
Kernighan, B. and Ritchie, D., 1977, The C Programming
    Language, (Prentice-Hall)
Luczak, H., 1975, Untersuchungen informatorischer
    Belastung und Beanspruchung des Menschen, (Düsseldorf:
    VDI-Verlag)
McCormick, E.J., Jeanneret, P.R. and Mecham, R.C., 1969,
    The development and background of the Position Analysis
    Questionnaire (PAQ), (Lafayette, Ind.: Occupational
    Research Center, Purdue University)
Rohmert, W., 1983, Möglichkeiten und Grenzen menschen-
    gerechter Arbeitsgestaltung durch Ergonomie. In:
    Menschengerechte Gestaltung der Arbeit, Fürstenberg,
    F., Hanau, P., Kreikebaum, H. and Rohmert, W., (Mann
    heim, Wien; Zürich: Bibliographisches Institut)
Rohmert, W. and Landau, K., 1979, Das Arbeitswissenschaft-
    liche Erhebungsverfahren zur Tätigkeitsanalyse (AET)
    Handbuch, (Bern: Hans Huber)

Rohmert, W. and Landau, K., 1979, Das Arbeitswissenschaft-
    liche Erhebungsverfahren zur Tätigkeitsanalyse (AET)
    Merkmalheft, (Bern: Hans Huber)
Rohmert, W., Balser, D., Bruder, R. and Rückert, A.,
    1988a, Ergonomische Analyse des Arbeitssystems Straßen-
    namencodierung bei der Deutschen Bundespost, (Darm-
    stadt: Institut für Arbeitswissenschaft, not pub-
    lished)
Rohmert, W., Bier, M. and Ströder, M., 1988b, Entwicklung
    von Arbeitshilfen zur Montage abgehängter Decken,
    2. Symposium der Arbeitsgestaltung im Bauwesen,
    TH Leipzig, (in press)
Rohmert, W., Carstens, S., Groth, K., Haûkamp, C. and
    Helbig, R., 1988c, Ergonomische Analyse und Bewertung
    der Tiefe von Küchenarbeitsplatten, (Darmstadt: Insti-
    tut für Arbeitswissenschaft, not published)
Rohmert, W., Groth, K. and Ströder, M., 1989, Einsatz des
    Modularen Arbeitsanalyse-Systems (MAS) zur Untersuchung
    der örtlichen Arbeitsplatzbindung, (in preparation)
Welford, A.T., 1965, Performance, biological mechanism and
    age: a theoretical sketch. In: Behavior, ageing, and
    the nervous system, edited by Welford, A.T., (Spring-
    field)

THE P-TAI CONCEPT: AN INTEGRATIVE APPROACH

Werner Kannheiser, Roland Hormel & Robert K. Bidmon

Gesamthochschule Kassel
Federal Republic of Germany

INTRODUCTION

Present discussion in management literature concerning new technology focusses the necessity to take into account human factors in planning new technology as early as possible. This discussion confirms the recommendations made ever since by industrial psychologists to consider person-related aspects as early as the planning of technical systems starts. Industrial psychology speaks of a "human-centreed way of technique-implementation" (Corbett 1985), which leads to "complete working tasks" (Hacker 1986a).

The increasing emphasis on human resources management techniques in industry results from the fact that new production concepts require supporting steps in the personnel-planning sector: Attempts at "flexible automation" (e.g. FMS, Just-in-Time-Production, CIM) call for supporting strategies in the sphere of personnel planning to enable the personnel to show creativity, flexibility and a sense of responsibility in the handling of the expensive and partly trouble-prone machinery. Personnel experts and industrial psychologists agree that their attempts can only gain unmediated importance if these are linked to the technical planning in an early stage of technique implementation. Processes of technique implementation and especially integrated concepts are pushed ahead by technicians as "strategies for process control" (Hirsch-Kreinsen and Wolf 1987). The primary target is mostly the reduction, control or even elimination of the human factor. On the other hand personnel experts know the deficiencies of technocratic planning strategies and ask for comprehensive, integrating approaches. Future experiences will show

to what extent the opposing interests of technicians and
personnel experts can be reconciled.

THE P-TAI CONCEPT

Combining technical, economic, organizational and
anthropocentric planning approaches is a primary goal of
the P-TAI-project. Within the project "Entwicklung einer
arbeitsanalytisch-unterstützten betrieblichen Planungs-
und Entscheidungsmethodik im Bereich technisch-organisa-
torischer Änderungen auf der Grundlage des TAI-Teilverfah-
rens I" an attempt is made to adapt a scientific procedure
of job analysis (TAI, cf. Kannheiser 1987) to the requirements of the industrial world, i.e. to make it usable for
technical planners. Especially this practice-oriented version of the TAI (P-TAI) should convince technical planners
in the production sector and in production related sectors
of the necessities for and benefits of a <u>human-centred</u>
planning and implementation of new technology.

There are three basic assumptions of the P-TAI-proceeding:
* New technologies offer strategic choices for organizational design.
* Design options and especially human-centred alternatives are not used in practice in every case.
* Technical planners can only take advantage of these
  design options if human-centered planning approaches
  are integrated in the - mostly technically determined -
  planning-process as early as possible: Technique-
  centred strategies have to be completed by human-
  centered procedures; new systems have to be planned
  holistically, i.e. considering technical, economical
  and human-centred aspects.

A further starting point of the project was the consideration that a practice-oriented adaptation of methods of
job analysis can not only be based on further development
or modifications of analytical instruments. There is also
a necessity to specify conditions for using these instruments in the planning process. Based on these considerations the project not only develops practice-oriented
methods, i.e. analytic procedures or tools, but additionally establishes a <u>formal frame</u> for using the instrument.
This frame is to indicate how to integrate the specific
methods into the company planning processes and to support
this planning.

Moreover the method should not only be used to analyze and assess realized - and therefore hardly corrigible - design concepts, but primarily as a technique to provide a holistic and prospective job design.

The field of "classic" job analysis has to be exceeded therefore both in its methods and contents.

The practice-oriented adaptation of the TAI is done in cooperation with large-, medium- and small-scale enterprises of the metal-working and plastics-processing industries.

THE SPECIFIC STAGES OF THE P-TAI CONCEPT

The process of implementing new technology should typically be understood as a purposive, goal directed process. Therefore the single formal and substantial steps contained in the P-TAI as means for planning and deciding are constructed by analogy with models of problemsolving behaviour (Hacker 1986b): The following description of the reference of the P-TAI-concept to problems of the human-resources-management is therefore based on the sequence (1) Goal-setting - (2) Orientation - (3) Decision among particular variants - (4) Control of the execution. As Figure 1 shows, the "instructions for realization" and the "methods to assess the realized measures" in the P-TAI-concept are parallel to the four stages of the system:

By "realization" the "formal frame" is meant. Here all the developed instructions are summarized - in the figure labelled with an 'H' -, how to realize the implementation of new technology (e.g. formation of teams, hints for additional proceedings) and how the developed methods can be used in the enterprise.

As a creative and design-oriented methodology the P-TAI is proceeding from the assumption that evaluations - within the figure labelled with a 'B' - have to be made before implementing technical and organizational solutions: Therefore assessment-methods are part of every step from "goal-setting" to "decision".

A final assessment (control), as it is a traditional field of job analytic techniques (Kannheiser and Frieling 1988), can be made additionally.

Structure of the P-TAI-Concept

	Formal Frame	Substantial Methodology
(1) Goal-Setting	Planning Frame * Sceneries (H) * Integrated Planning (H)	* Goal-Assessment-Methods (B) * Goal-Interaction-Analysis
(2) Orientation	Method and Idea Store (H)	* Goal-Realization-Analysis (B) * Weak-Point-Analysis (B) * Target-Analysis
(3) Decision	Method and Idea Store (H)	* Analysis of Function Allocation * Assessm. (Relation to the Goals) (B) * Assessment (Tasks complete? (B) * Work Load and Stress Analysis (B)
(4) Control		e.g. Weak Point Analysis Analysis of Function Allocation Work Load and Stress Analysis Goal-Analysis

Figure 1.

The Stage of Goal-Setting

In the stage of goal-setting the foundations of an integration of technical-economic and organizational and person-related points of view should be laied. The users should
1)   reveal all pursued goals,
2)   examine whether these are all goals to be pursued and
3)   evaluate the interaction of the goals.
Planners should realize the far-reaching consequences of technocratic or only technical oriented planning concepts for the enterprise and the individual.

For the planning team (cf. Realization) the first step should be to analyze the importance of different goals for the planned technical and organizational innovation. The goal-levels are subdivided into
*   technical-economic goals,
*   organizational and personnel-related goals,
*   additional (e.g. position-specific, corporate identity) goals.

Using a goal-checklist it is possible to list the most important goals on each of the three levels and to argue for the the specific choice (method of goal assessment). By this means an extended survey of all possible goals and their values is obtained. At the same time the unreflected pursuance of - for example - position-specific goals should be prevented: Certain goals, e.g. extending the autonomy of the production area, are often not considered because they would reduce the competences of the department the planner belongs to. By specific assessment methods it is possible to recognize priorities and interests of the planning team in a short time. Conflicting, complementary or indifferent interactions become visible at the latest while assessing the goals.

In the P-TAI-concept such interactions are examined systematically. By a method called Goal-Interaction-Analysis (Zielbeziehungsanalyse) the interactions between the important goals are developed and evaluated. The concrete proceeding was taken from the "Sensitivitätsmodell" (cf. von Hesler and Vester 1980, Vester 1983).
While evaluating the goal-interaction-analysis four different types of goals can be distinguished:

Active Goals have the greatest influence on all the other
goals, but they are the least influenced. Pursuing such a
goal is simple: as you have almost no feedback, side-
effects are easily to appraise.
Reactive Goals have the least impacts on the other goals,
but are influenced the most. These goals change already
with the smallest external impulse.
Critical Goals affect all other goals the most and are
affected by the other goals the most at the same time.
Critical goals have to be pursued very cautiously, because
they have the strongest overall effects.
Buffering Goals have almost no influence on the other
goals and they are affected the least. Buffering goals
neutralize, are insensitive or inert and head off side-
effects.

Because the goal-checklist has to contain goals of the
organizational and personnel-related field, the discussion
of the interactions of the goals enables a first appraisal
of the importance of person-related goals for the planned
change: For instance, it becomes evident whether questions
of qualification are active, reactive, critical or buffering goals within the intended project. Because of this
result, measures touching personnel-related planning can
be discussed and developed in an early state of planning.

Orientation: Actual-Analysis on the Level of Factory and Department

The second part of the P-TAI touches many personnel
problem complexities like personnel-planning, job design,
coordination or design of socio-technical relations. When
the initial goals have been clarified the possibilities of
realizing these goals should be estimated as in an orien-
tating stage. Additional informations about the department
where the changes will be made have to be collected. The
instrument to use for this purpose is a group of methods
called "Organizational and Technical Conditions" ("Organi-
satorisch-technische Bedingungen", otb). The specific
parts of this instrument deliver data about the possibilities of goal-realization, about weak points to be avoided
and about target-strategies to be chosen. The purpose of
the first otb-method (Goal-Realization-Analysis, Zielrea-
lisierungsanalyse) is to become capable of assessing the
limits and possibilities of the concepts found during the
goal-setting stage. A detailed appraisal is made of which
conditions of the actual state can enable or prevent the

goal-attainment. Specific conditions which are recorded in
this stage are as follows:

*   existing allocations of functions,
*   developed decision-structures,
*   the style of leadership,
*   procedures of internal qualification-strategies
    (times, trainers, location of the measures).

It is of main interest whether these circumstances
enable or prevent the goal attainment.

A second part, or step of interpretation, of the otb
should reveal design deficits while making them avoidable
in the planned project at the same time: a Weak-Point-
Analysis at department level is performed. For example,
kind and frequency of disturbances, reasons for changes in
the production program or characteristics of the production control are taken into account.

A third part consists of a "Target-Version" (Target-
Analysis). For example it can be found out which functions
the new system should be able to perform, which decision-
structures are planned for the new system, how the
production control should proceed, the range of the
planning periods in the department or what qualifying-
measures should be carried out.

Within traditional proceedings some of these questions
are considered only after implementing the technology.

Decision

Having established a mental representation of the
investigated part of reality, the user can evaluate design
alternatives in the sense of operating on the model as a
next step. This process is based on the set goals in connection with the determined weak-points and target-condi-
tions. An additional frame of reference are psychological
criteria for a human-centred division of labour. The analytic tool is another part of the P-TAI called Analysis of
Function-Allocation (Funktionsverteilungsanalyse, fva):
With this method alternatives of division of labour can be
found out and evaluated. The fva should help to find and
solidify design options for the technical and organizational area.

Alternatives for allocating functions can be obtained by
a) finding out what functions should be carried out
    manually, computer-aided or automatically;

b)   asking additionally whether the function could be
     carried out <u>alternatively</u> manually, computer-aided or
     automatically ("<u>dynamic allocation</u>", cf. Kantowitz and
     Sorkin 1987));
c)   allocating the functions to groups of employees who
     could be responsible for this function.

   The present version of the fva contains about 70 func-
tions/activities of the production and the production-
preparing areas. The functions are divided into eight
groups of activities.

The developed design alternatives can be <u>assessed</u> in
several ways:
−   from a psychological point of view there is the
     possibility to assess whether the function allocations
     − and due to that the work contents − are complete in
     relation to department as well as workplace level.
     Allocations that do not fit the requirements of a
     human-centred work design can thus be eliminated;
−   finally the remaining alternatives can be coupled back
     to the goals found in the goal-setting-stage. The
     decision on the alternative to take can be made by
     rating-methods as described in literature (cf. Kann-
     heiser 1989).

   If detailed information about function allocations is
needed already in the stage of orientation, the fva can be
used as an actual-analysis-technique.
   The fva as a target-method (Soll-Verfahren) provides
even additional information: The determination of the
function allocations for a <u>planned</u> area − or even better a
systematic simulation of design alternatives − provides
requirement-profiles of the expected activities, which can
be used for assessing requirements of the new jobs..
Assigning the results to the eight activity groups it is
easy to detect displacements of the task priorities (e.g.
from only executing to more preparing or controlling functions) if you compare existing with planned departments or
work-places. Existing qualifications can be compared with
the necessary ones. Qualifying measures can be started −
<u>before</u> the technical system is implemented and the usual
personnel-related starting problems delay or even prevent
an optimal application. The significance of a punctual and
reasonable qualification shown in the results of a study
in enterprises of the metal-working industry: The "start-
ing-problems as a result of training and qualification

deficiencies of the employees" turned out to be the greatest problem during introduction of new technology (Hormel,
Kannheiser, Bidmon and Hugentobler, in preparation).

A first comparison of function allocations in a more
conventional organized and in a highly automated system
showed differences in the following:

Evacuated functions: In the highly automated system more
functions are executed outside the production sector.

Foremen: In the conventional system foremen carry out many
more functions than in the automated system.

Operators: The number of functions and the distribution
over the different activity groups was almost the same in
both systems.

Assessment Methods

The following assessment methods have already been
mentioned:
-    In the stage of goal-setting the method of goal-
     assessment;
-    in the stage of orientation the method of estimating
     the possibilities for goal realization; a weak-point-
     analysis at department level;
-    in the stage of decision the method to assess the
     alternatives in reference to the discovered goals and
     the criteria of human-centred, complete workdesign.

After choosing one alternative the expected workload and
stress at individual workplaces can be rated by the "Work
Load and Stress Analysis" ("Verfahren zur Belastungs-
analyse", bea). This method contains fundamental stress
dimensions.

This method takes into account those organizational and
technical conditions at the workplace, which may have a
negative impact on the affected employees, i.e. which are
potentially straining (e.g. insufficient communication
opportunities, high time pressure, strong dependences).

There is a further possibility to make a preventive
analysis by rating the expected workload of planned
workplaces. As a result the planning can be modified early
in the stage of decision.

The method can be used also as an actual-analysis-
technique during the stage of orientation or after the
implementation of new technology for a correcting work
design. Using the bea-method during the stage of orientation can lead to measures of change as a result of dis-
covered deficiencies or work loads on work place level.

Realization: Characteristics of the Formal Frame

The formal frame should support a human-centred application respecting realization of the described substantial
P-TAI elements. Traditional instruments and methods
require expert knowledge while carrying out the analysis
and even more in evaluating the results. In many enterprises this kind of knowledge is not available. Therefore
additional supporting procedures are given within the formal frame.

The stage of goal-finding is especially supported by a
"planning frame" which contains (among other design aids)
various "planning sceneries" and descriptions of their
specific advantages and disadvantages. As the P-TAI is an
integrated planning method, additional concrete proposals
as to how and why there should be integrated planning are
given: determinants of the planning process are discussed;
it is explained whether experts or project teams should do
the planning; advice is given on what persons or departments (e.g. personnel planning, personnel development,
product construction) have to be involved while planning
organizational and technical changes.

In a further formal part, the so-called "Method and
Idea Store" ("Methoden- und Ideenspeicher"), additional
proceedings to support the stages of orientation and
decision are discussed: e.g. the "collective note book",
"cause-effect-diagrams" and many other methods.

Thus the methods and techniques combined in the formal
frame are additional supporting steps.

CONCLUDING REMARKS

Summarizing the most important characteristics of the
P-TAI-concept it can be stated:
- The methodology appeals to groups of people who plan
  new technology; these are usually specialized production planners or teams of technicians.
- A first important formal aspect of our approach is to
  enlarge the planning-group qualitatively - this
  enlargement can even include the affected employees.
- Moreover a supporting framework is offered which contains tools and proceedings leading to an early consideration of personnel-related organizational possibilities and the crucial points of design. Not all of the
  methods and instruments are to be used in every case or
  can be used due to the lack of time or personnel.

- To meet the different requirements in different enterprises several starting points are given: either in the
  meaning of an ideal - goal-oriented - planning process
  or proceeding from weak points at department or work
  place level which can be pointed out by means of
  specific analytical techniques.
- The methodology can not - and is not supposed to -
  replace scientific instruments of job analysis. Within
  the bounds of possibilities of enterprises (especially
  small- and medium-sized enterprises) it should extend
  the ways of thinking and proceeding.

The P-TAI is an offer to enterprises and individual
planners to use enlarged, integrated and human-centred
concepts. To what extent this approach will actually be
acknowledged depends - besides the quality and the detectable use for the enterprises - on several conditions. The
most important would be a change in thinking that would
understand employees indeed as "human resources", thus
recognizing the design of technical processes as "human
resources management".

ACKNOWLEDGEMENT

The project is sponsored by the German Ministry of
Research and Technology (Number: 01 HG 017-0). For the
content, however, the authors are responsible.

REFERENCES

Corbett, J.M., 1985, Prospective work design of a human-
    centred CNC lathe. Behaviour and Information Techno-
    logy. 4, 3, 201-214.
Hacker, W., 1986a, Complete vs. incomplete working tasks -
    a concept and its verification, in: G. Debus & H.W.
    Schroiff (Eds.): The Psychology of Work and Organiza-
    tion. North-Holland, pp. 23-36.
Hacker, W., 1986b, Arbeitspsychologie. Bern
von Hesler, A. and Vester, F., 1980, Sensitivitätsmodell.
    Frankfurt/Main
Hirsch-Kreinsen H., and Wolf H., 1987, Neue Produktions-
    techniken und Arbeitsorganisation. Interessen und
    Strategien betrieblicher Akteure, in: Soziale Welt,
    2/87, 181-196.

Hormel, R., Kannheiser, W., Bidmon, R. K. and Hugentobler, S.,: Ergebnisse einer Umfrage zur Einführung neuer Techniken in Betrieben der metallverarbeitenden Industrie (in preparation)

Kannheiser, W., 1987, Neue Techniken und organisatorische Bedingungen: Ergebnisse und Einsatzmöglichkeiten des Tätigkeits-Analyse-Inventars, in: Kh. Sonntag (Hrsg.), Arbeitsanalyse und Technikentwicklung, Köln, pp.69-85.

Kannheiser, W., 1989, Methoden der Ingenieurpsychologie, in: Hoyos, C.G. & Zimolong, B. (Hrsg.), Enzyklopädie der Psychologie. Ingenieurpsychologie, Band 2 der Serie Wirtschafts-, Organisations- und Arbeitspsychologie. Göttingen, pp. 43-63.

Kannheiser, W. and Frieling, E., 1988, Arbeitsstrukturierung und Arbeitsanalyse, in: Frey, D., Hoyos, C.G., & Stahlberg, D. (Hrsg.), Angewandte Psychologie. München, 1988, pp. 129-146.

Kantowitz, B H. and Sorkin, R.D., 1987, Allocation of Functions, in: G. Salvendy (Ed.), Handbook of Human Factors, pp. 355-369.

Vester, F., 1983, Ballungsgebiete in der Krise. Vom Verstehen und Planen menschlicher Lebensräume. München, pp. 84-134.

OFFICE COMMUNICATION ANALYSIS: ITS CONTRIBUTION TO WORK DESIGN

Jörg Sydow

Institute of Management
University Berlin
Federal Republic of Germany

Office work is increasingly characterized as communication work. This is, looked at cursorily, why office communication analysis is so popular among West German organizations. More importantly, communication analysis is used
to determine systems requirements so that office work can
either be automated or assisted by information and communication technology. In this way, it serves the information needs of manufacturers as well as of users of new
office information technology. The former are interested
in promoting the organizational usage of information and
communication technologies; the later are interested in
introducing these technologies successfully and in legitimating their investment decisions.

The widespread application of office communication
analysis calls for a critical assessment of this methodology. Since office automation is conceived as comprising
technological as well as organizational aspects (Sydow,
1987a), this methodology, above all, must not only contribute to the technical requirement engineering, but also
to the organizational design of office work. If it does
not, additional office analysis methodologies are needed.

The critical assessment of office communication analysis is based upon
- a survey of office communication analysis methodologies
  currently in use
- a differentiation of this kind of methodology from other
  office analysis methodologies
- a reconstruction of the theoretical propositions about
  man and work in organizations underlying this kind of
  methodology

- its final evaluation from an organizational communication perspective, a socio- technical understanding of
office automation, and a methodological point of view.

The critical assessment leads to some provocative conclusions on the value of this specific type of office
analysis methodology.

A short discussion of the economic and technical background of the development and spread of office communication analysis methodologies will precede the critical
assessment of this methodology. This background will be
best elucidated if it is contrasted with that of traditional systems analysis.

FROM SYSTEMS ANALYSIS TO OFFICE COMMUNICATION ANALYSIS

During the last decades, the development and implementation of information and communication technologies has
not only contributed to organizational changes in office
work; it has also been associated with the rise and fall
of methodologies used for the analysis of office situations, office procedures, and office functions as well as
for the design of information systems.

Traditionally, the design of comprehensive, mainframe-
based application systems (off-line or on-line) has been
preceded by a thorough systems analysis (Gane and Sarson,
1977). Starting with a crude analysis of the system and
its environment, systems analysis primarily focuses on the
interrelationships of elements and subsystems within the
system and and depicts the information flows. Based upon
this type of analysis "systems professionals advocate a
design principle that states that systems must be independent of the organizational structures in which they are
used" (Markus, 1984). The work structures, however, are in
most cases subject to a (more or less intentional) redesign; they are adapted to the systems needs and/or vice
versa.

During the late 70s many organizations started to
install office communication systems. In contrast to main-
frame-based application systems, office communication systems represent a further development of word processors
linked by a network, and, more importantly, are not
devoted to a specific purpose (e.g. manipulation of mass
data, text processing). Office communication technologies
are multipurpose technologies and are a manifestation of a
different strategy of office automation: it is not only
technologically but also organizationally different from
the strategy of host-centred computing (Sydow, 1987a). In

the case of office communication systsms, systems professionals do nòt have to develop specific application software; on the contrary, it is said that the system will
find its application itself by usage. At this period of
time, office communication analysis was developed and
became popular with many organizations.

The 80s are characterized by a convergence of traditional data processing, office system technology, and
telecommunications (Long, 1987). UNIX computers for
instance, although derived from traditional data processing technology, are, from a functional point of view, much
more similar to office communication systems: they allow
multi-tasking, multi-user operation and provide a graphic
user interface and standard software tools for text processing, spreadsheet calculations, data base access, electronic mail, and so forth. They may be built into large
communication networks (LAN, WAN), which sometimes even
include host computers as data base servers. Wollnik
(1988) characterizes these new information and communication technologies as follows:
- open for different usages ('infrastructure')
- technically decentralized
- multi-functional
- reduced user complexity
- tool character
- technically integrated (i.e. providing communication
  facilities).

Because of their openness for different usages, organizational effects of the technologies emerge only when
applied to concrete office work; either by systems professionals or - as in the case of personal computing - by the
end users themselves. The application of these new information and communication technologies is, again, associated with the widespread use of communication analysis,
which, however, has been refined in the meantime, and is
sometimes only part of a broader office analysis methodology.

CURRENT METHODOLOGIES OF OFFICE WORK ANALYSIS

An office analysis methodology is a recommended set of
philosophies, procedures, rules, techniques and tools for
analyzing office work. The main purpose is, generally
speaking, to provide information relevant to the design of
information systems. These usually consist of information
and communication technology, people and structures, and
may be best understood as sociotechnical systems (Pava,
1983; Sydow, 1984).

Scientist from different disciplines (e.g. work psychology, organizational communication, industrial engineering, ergonomics, management and computer science) as
well as commercial organizations (hardware and software
manufacturers, consultants) contribute to the continuing
development of methodologies for office analysis:
- time and motion studies (Hamill and Steele, 1973)
- office communication analysis (OCA) as documented in
  Schönecker and Nippa (1987)
- business systems planning (BSP) by IBM
- office analysis methodology (OAM) by Sirbu et al. (1984)
- task analysis VERA/B by Nullmeier and Roediger (1987)
- socio-technical systems theory based analyses such as
  ETHICS (Mumford and Weir, 1979), STA (Ulich, 1981), and
  analysis of office work, which is developed at the
  Institute of Management (Sydow, 1987b)
- user systems analysis (USA) by Glick and Beekum (1984).
   This survey of office analysis methodologies ist not
complete, but may serve as a starting point for developing
a typology. It explicitly does not include methods the
primary focus of which is ergonomics (e.g. Knave and Widebäck, 1987) or the configuration of technical systems (cf.
Bullinger and Niemeier, 1987).

A typology

   The purpose of the following typology mainly is to differentiate the above listed methodologies. Generally,
these methodologies could be distinguished according to
- the interests they promote
- unit of analysis
- types of jobs included in the analysis (e.g. clerical,
  professional, managerial)
- activities included (e.g. communication, manual work,
  thinking)
- contextual sensitivity (e.g. taking existing technolo-
  gy/personnel structure into account)
- static vs. dynamic orientation
- expertocratic vs. participative apporach
- focus on analysis vs. focus on design
- sensitivity towards organizational conflict
- pure office focus vs. CIM orientation
- manual vs. computer assisted
   (for further criteria, see Nippa and Schönecker, 1987)
   Above all, a macro and a micro approach to the analysis
of office work should be distinguished. The macro approach
focuses on organizational and interorganizational aspects

of communication and information processing. The micro approach, in contrast, embraces information and communication as related to specific work situations or work processes within an organizational subsystem (see Figure 1).

A typology of office work analysis methodologies

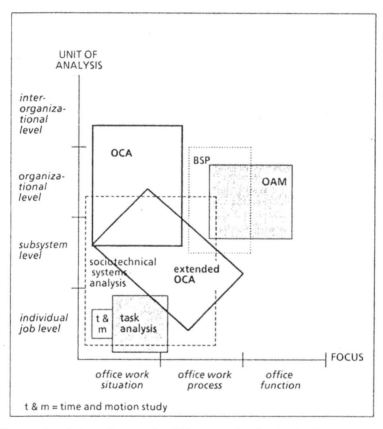

Figure 1. A typology of office analysis techniques

Furthermore, the above mentioned methodologies either focus on concrete office work or on more abstract office functions. The latter view concentrates on information content necessary to achieve organizational goals rather than on symbolic artefacts such as forms, files, and techniques. This is what the former does. It focuses on either work situations or work processes, i.e. work situations as related to each other in order to produce certain information. The work process view embraces the primary process

as it includes alternate paths for exceptional procedures,
all of which "are composed of a set of steps, each trig-
gered by the occurrence of some event" (Sirbu et al.,
1984).

Most of the current methodologies of office work analysis may be located within this two-dimensioned typology
(see Figure 1). The USA is not included in this as it
represents a multi-level methodology combining very different methodologies from sociotechnical systems analysis,
methods for investigating jobs and work flows, and social
network analysis (Lick and Beekum, 1984).

The interorganizational relations increasingly become
more important in the course of "systemic rationalization"
(Altmann et al., 1986). The other units of analysis, however, continue to be indispensable. This is particularly
true for job level analysis, since technological and/or
organizational changes at the other levels are apparent
also at the job level, where the work is finally done.
However, there are other methodological trends apart from
the possible shift towards interorganizational relationships.

Methodological trends

Generalizing from some of the above mentioned methodologies for office analysis, Niemeier and Ness (1986) do
not only observe an increased professionalization grounded
in systems theory, but use of phase models, project management techniques, and not least concrete office analysis
methodologies. For these methodologies they state the following trends:
- from general to situational application of a methodology
- from static to process orientation
- from analysis focus to design focus
- from one-shot to incremental information gathering
- from single methods to modules.
Only a few of these trends seem to be reflected within one
group of office analysis methodologies: Office communication analysis.

OFFICE COMMUNICATION ANALYSIS

Office communication analysis is a popular label for a
type of methodologies which are fairly heterogeneous.
Nevertheless, these instruments share some common objectives, features, and limitations.

Overview of current methodologies

Office communication analysis is included in almost all modern office analysis methodologies (Schönecker and Nippa, 1987; Anders, 1986). They are increasingly computer assisted. Some of them even share a common software package, serving as a tool for data analysis and presentation. Their common objective is to describe the organizational communication system in order to determine system requirements (see Davis, 1982; Galliers, 1987 for further methodologies for information requirement determination).

In detail, communication analysis methodologies have the following features in common:
(1) They aim at
- assisting the planning and design of information and communication systems (analytical and design-related function, which is explicit)
- promoting and implementing the information system, and legitimating the managerial decisions made (micropolitical function, which is implicit)
(2) They depict the status quo of
- internal communication flows and structures (who with whom, when, about what, using which media?)
- amount of external communication
- data bases/files in access
- information and communication technologies in use
- communication related activities/problems
(3) For these purposes, they
- are based upon standardized questionnaires
- produce mainly quantitative data on the status quo
- favour a graphic presentation of the results of the communication analysis
- are conducted by mixed teams of external consultants and internal professionals
- are, to some extent, adaptive to situational constraints.

Several communication analysis methodologies start with some kind of quantitative pre-analysis of primary tasks, organizational structure, formal rules and regulations, spatial situation, and preexisting information and communication technology. Almost all of them proceed with some kind of rudimentary network analysis depicting the internal communication structure of an organization, i.e. the office communication analysis. Some include methods which allow for an analysis of office work processes, e.e. of the sequential interdependence of office tasks (e.h.. KSA, MOSAIK). These latter do not only focus in a static manner

on the organizational level but also on subsystems and
individual units of analysis taking a process view. These
methods, which are mostly organized in modules, shall be
called extended office communication analysis: They extend
beyond communication analysis conceived as a technology-
focused adaptation of interactional analysis (cf. Tichy et
al., 1979).

Although biased towards the determination of technological requirements, office communication analysis must try
to analyze several aspects of the social system in order
to provide systems designers with the data necessary for
planning sociotechnical change. Schönecker and Nippa
(1987), among others, stress that nowadays every office
analysis methodology must emphasize the communicational
aspect of office work. Therefore it seems adequate to
assess office communication analysis methodology from an
organizational communication perspective. Furthermore, it
has been stressed that effective office automation implies
the analysis and design or re-design of work and job
structures, since technology must fit organizational
structures and processes, and vice versa. For this reason,
an assessment of this type of methodology from a sociotechnical point of view seems to be relevant.

A critical assessment from an organizational communication perspective

Communication in organizations relates a single job to
other jobs, one one functional department to another, but
also the organization to its environment. Hence, communication, which is a significant part of office work, serves
as a means for organizational integration and environmental adaptation. These functions are fulfilled in a sub-
stantive and in a symbolic manner.

The organizational communication perspective may be
related to any organization theory (Porter and Roberts,
1976; Euske and Roberts, 1987). Traditionally, however, it
has been heavily influenced by human relations, stressing
the importance of informal structures, communication climate, and communication behaviour. These aspects are taken
up by the most recent interpretative approach to organizational communication (Putman and Pacanowski, 1983; Gudykunst et al., 1985). Organizational communication is nowadays conceptualized as a transactional process (Luthans,
1985). The more transactional or interpretative the perspective, the more organizational communication is conceived as dependent on organizational members and their

construction of organizational reality rather than on
given techno-structures. A growing body of literature
indicates the need to integrate information and communication technology not only with organizational structure but
also with organizational culture (e.g. Morieux and Sutherland, 1988; Ogilvie et al., 1988).

Communication analysis methodology as described above
sticks to the techno-structural view of organizations,
ignoring the importance of organizational culture and the
social properties of organizational communication. This
type of methodology is restricted to what Wilson et al.
(1986) call the "digital level" of communication, neglecting the "analogical level" of meaning. Methodologies,
available for research on organizational communication,
such as social network analysis (Tichy et al., 1979; Richards, 1985) , include the transactional content (information, affect), the nature of links (e.h. intensity, reci-
procity), and structural characteristics (e.g. size, clus-
ters, openness, stability) of communication in their analysis. They investigate formally prescribed as well as
emergent communication relationships and try to grasp
their meaning for organizational members. With regard to
all these aspects, the technologically focused office communication analysis lags behind these research methodologies. Furthermore, its scope is even more restricted from
an organizational communication perspective, than that of
interventionists' communication analysis methodologies
such as OCD- or ICA-Audits (cf. Anders, 1986).

Above all, office communication analysis methodologies
have been developed in an engineering tradition and are
based upon assumptions central to Taylor's (1911) approach
management. Firstly, the planning and design of work has
to be separated from the operation of work, i.e. there is
no room for self-design, self-organization, or self-man-
agement. Secondly, the requirements for technological
and/or organizational change can be 'objectively' established. Neither interests, power, and micro politics nor
interpretative schemes, implicit theories, and cognitive
maps are particularly relevant to the design process.
Thirdly, if relevant at all, office work can be analyzed,
segmented, and composed according to any situational constraints but independent of personal abilities, cognitive
or motivational orientation.

A critical assessment from a sociotechnical perspective

The sociotechnical approach to work and organizational analysis and design calls for a joint optimization of the technical and the social system in a genuine participative manner (Trist, 1981). Therefore, it requires the subsystem and individual to be the central focus of analysis. Office communication analysis methodologies, apart from the extended modular versions, do not pay attention to this micro-level unit of analysis. Although some of them pay lip service to sociotechnical systems theory they all share an expertocratic approach to office analysis. None of them makes use of office workers' competence to self-design and self-organization. Implementation in their view does not seen to be the problem.

Due to these deficiencies, office communication analysis methodologies are unable to contribute significantly to the re-design of jobs, work situations, and work processes. This is an extremely critical aspect, since re-designing work
- does significantly contribute to productivity improvements
- is a means of office rationalization even without the introduction of information and communication technology
- is essential for office workers' perception of the work situation and hence, his/her behaviour.

Also, the introduction of modern office technology leaves a significant, even if not unlimited, scope of organizational choice to the designer (Sydow, 1987a). He/she should use it in order to maximize organizational effectiveness and the quality of working life by overcoming the widespread organizational conservatism (Child et al., 1987).

In contrast to both, the organizational communication view as well as the sociotechnical perspective, office communication analysis is entirely naïve with respect to the relevance of certain information for organizational conduct. Considering information as a fetish, they at best question the sociotechnical conditions under which it is produced. The organizational communication perspective, in contrast, explicitly includes the relevance of information under the heading of 'meaning', and the sociotechnical systems theory usually starts with the analysis of the 'private task'.

A critical assessment from a methodological point of view

Scientific research methods have to be valid and reliable. There is not method which absolutely fulfils these
criteria of rigorous research, and qualitative research
methods applied under the interpretative paradigm even
appear not to be strictly evaluated against these criteria
(Sanders, 1982). Methodologies used for initiating sociotechnical change in organizations are usually not blamed
for not keeping to the high standard of rigorous research.
Nevertheless, it must be somewhat clear what they measure;
and they must do it in a somehow reliable way.

As far as validity is concerned, it is not very clear,
whether office communication analysis methodologies depict
formal or informal, pre-existing or emerging communication
structures, or both. However, as they confine themselves
to artefacts (e.g. files sent and received) they are
likely to analyze this restricted section of organizational communication in a sufficiently valid manner.

The reliability of office communication analysis methodology has hardly been established. Conrath (1982) reports
low cross-check reliability for this type of methodology;
"On average, less than a third of each person's communication time was collaborated by the other parts." Therefore
he prefers a communication diary type of communication
analysis methodology with a cross-check reliability of
still about 50 per cent.

Summary of the assessment

In summary, office communication analysis methodologies
share some common features. In the main, they focus on the
analysis of the formal communication structure within an
organization. Only some of these methodologies go beyond a
macro analysis of organizational communication by analyzing office work situations and processes on a micro level,
too.

In trying to determine information systems requirements, they focus on productivity improvements by mainly
technological change. Those which go beyond the macro
analysis also contribute to the design of organizational
and work structures, although these too, by and large,
neglect the social system. This has been demonstrated from
an organizational communication pespective and from a
sociotechnical point of view. In any case, the use of
these methodologies promotes at best organizational efficiency, not organizational effectiveness. The short

assessment from a methodological point of view has raised
some additional doubts as to the value of office communication analysis methodology, In conclusion, there is no
reason to stick to this kind of office analysis methodology, if redesign of office work structure and processes
is of critical significance. This is not true for those
office communication analysis methodologies which extend
their scope to include the analysis of office work processes. These, however, assume tayloristic images of man
and organization even if they advocate some reintegration
of office work; but their process oriented analysis provides more information relevant to work design.

FROM OFFICE COMMUNICATION ANALYSIS TO...

This trend towards extended office communication analysis methodologies brings this type of office analysis
methodology closer again to classical systems analysis. As
such it is confronted with the same shortcomings and problems. Among others, these are: communication barriers
between systems professionals and users; lack of imagination concerning the new information system; deficiency of
theory based principles deriving design alternatives from
the analysis of existing situations; taking existing work
structures as given; no consideration given to cognitive
and motivational properties of systems users; emphasis on
"getting the requirements right" to the debit of "getting
the system working" (Nosek and Sherr, 1984).

Classical systems analysis confronted with these and
similar critiques is obsolete, at least in the view of
many social scientists and some scholars of informatics
(e.g. Briefs et al., 1983). They favour more participative
office analysis methodologies. These are often based upon
sociotechnical systems theory and include evolutionary
participative design techniques such as rapid prototyping
(Budde et al., 1984). These approaches are likely to be
accepted by systems professionals and management who seem
increasingly to follow a human research management
approach, an instrument of which is restructuring jobs
(e.h. Walton and Lawrence, 1985). Participation in this
activity is not only an instrument for developing human
resources but also a management strategy for responsible
autonomy which nowadays seems to be preferred to that of
direct control (Friedman, 1977).

Participative office analysis methodologies provide
systems professionals and management with the opportunity
to risk some more organizational experimentation with new

information and communication technology and new forms of
work organization. The use of participative techniques for
office analysis, however, does not guarantee innovative
sociotechnical systems. Firstly, there is a need for additional design-oriented methodologies enabling management
and systems professionals to discover the scope of organizational structures. "Only in such a way does it become
possible not simply to preserve existing social units, but
to create useful socio-technical units with meaningful
tasks. Without changing the boundaries, it is only possible to redistribute the tasks within the existing organizational units" (Ulich and Troy, 1986). Secondly, structural and cultural provisions for the effective use of these
methodologies are required.

Confronted with this methodological development and the
incessant tendency towards equipping almost every office
work place with a personal computer or a workstation, at
the very last a terminal, office communiction analysis
methodology will become unncecessary if no shift towards
office process analysis and towards a more participative
approach is initiated.

REFERENCES

Altmann, N., Deiss, M., Döhl, V. and Sauer, D., 1986, Ein
"Neuer Rationalisierungstyp". In: Soziale Welt, 37
(2/3), 189-207.
Anders, W., 1986, Die Gestaltung der organisatorischen
Kommunikation. Dissertation. Technische Universität
München.
Briefs, U., Ciborra, C. and Schneider, L. (eds.), 1983,
System design for, with, and by the users.
Budde, R., Kuhlenkampf, K., Madhasen, L. and Züllichen, H.
(eds.), 1984, Approaches to prototyping.
Bullinger, H.-J. and Niemeier, J., 1987, Analyse- und
Gestaltungsmethoden im Bürobereich. In: Paul, M. (ed.),
Computerintegrierter Arbeitsplatz im Büro,. München,
pp. 36-63
Child, J., Ganter, H-D. and Kieser, A., 1987, Technologi-
cal innovation and organizational conservatism. In:
Pennings, J.M. and Buitendam, A. (eds.), New techno-
logy: Needs, methods and consequences. In: Landau, R.,
Blair, J.H. and Siegman, J.H. (eds.), Emerging office
systems, pp. 139-157
Davis, G.B., 1982, Strategies for information requirement
determination. In: IBM Systems Journal, 21 (1), 4-30

Euske, N.A. and Roberts, K.H., 1987, Evolving perspectives
    in organization theory; communication implications.
    In: Jablin, F.M, Putnam, L.L, Roberts, K.H. and Porter,
    L.W. (eds.), Handbook of Organizational Communication,
    pp. 41-69.

Friedman, A., 1977, Industry and Labour.

Galliers, R. (ed.), 1987, Information Analysis.

Gane, C. and Sarson, T., 1977, Structured systems
    analysis: Tools and techniques.

Glick, W.H. and Beekum, R.I., 1984, A theoretical overview
    of user systems analysis. In: Hendrick, H.W. and Brown,
    O., Jr. (eds.), Human factors in organizational design
    and management, pp. 161-165

Gudykunst, W.B., Steward, L.P. and Ting-Toomey, St.
    (eds.), 1985, Communication, Culture and Organizational
    Processes.

Hamill, B.J. and Steele, P.M., 1973, Work measurement in
    the office.

Knave, B. and Widebäck, P.G. (eds.), 1987, Work with
    display units '86.

Long, R.J., 1987, New office information technology: Human
    and managerial implications.

Luthans, F., 1985, Organizational behavior. 4th ed..

Markus, U.L., 1984, Systems in organizations: Bugs and
    features.

Morieux, Y.V.H. and Sutherland, E., 1988, The interaction
    between the use of information technology and organiza-
    tional culture. Behavior and Information Technology, 7
    (2), 205-213

Mumford, E. and Weir, M., 1979, Computer systems in work
    design - The ETHICS method.

Niemeier, J. and Ness, A., 1986, Modelle zur Analyse und
    Planung von Bürosystemen. In: IPA-IAO (Hrsg.): Büroform
    '86. Informationsmanagement für die Praxis, pp. 241-271

Nippa, M. and Schönecker, H.G., 1987, Bedeutung und
    Einordnung computergetsützter Büroanalyse- und
    -gestaltungsmethoden. Inn: Schönecker, H.G. and Nippa,
    M. (eds.): Neue Methoden zur Gestaltung der Büroarbeit,
    pp. 9-37

Nosek, J.T. and Sherr, D.M., 1984, "Getting the require-
    ments right" vs. "getting the system working" -
    Evolutionary development. In: Bemelmans, Th. M.A.
    (ed.): Beyond productivity: Information systems
    development for organizational effectiveness, pp. 157-
    171

Nullmeier, E. and Roediger, K.-H., 1987, The limitations of task complexity through information technologies: Results of a field study. In: Frese, M., Ulich, E. and Dzida, W. (eds.): Psychological issues of human computer interaction in the work place. pp. 41-57

Ogilvie, J.R., Pohlen, M.F. and Jones, C.H., 1988, Organizational information processing and productivity improvements. In: National Productivity Review, 7, 229-237

Pava, C.H.P., 1983, Managing new office technology.

Porter, L.W and Roberts, K.H., 1976, Communication in organizations. In: Dunette, M.D. (ed.): Handbook of industrial and organizational psychology, pp. 1553-1589.

Putnam, L.L. and Pacanowsky, M.E. (eds.), 1983, Communication and Organizations. An interpretative approach.

Richards, W.D., Jr., 1985, Data, models, and assumptions in network analysis. In: McPhee, R.D. and Tompkin, Ph.K. (eds.): Organizational Communication: Traditional themes and new directions, pp. 109-128

Sanders, P., 1982, Phenomenology: A new way of viewing organization research. Academy of Management Review, 7 (3), 353-360.

Schönecker, H.G. and Nippa, M. (eds.), 1987, Neue methoden zur Gestaltung der Büroarbeit.

Sirbu, M., Schoichet, S., Kunin, J.S., Hammer, M. and Sutherland, J., 1984, OAM: An office analysis methodology, Behavior and Information Technology, 3 (1), 25-39

Sydow, J., 1984, Sociotechnical change and perceived work situations: Some conceptual propositions and an empirical investigation in different office settings. Office Technology and People, 2, 121-132.

Sydow, J., 1987a, Office automation - An organizational perspectiv. In: Frese, M., Ulich, E. and Dziga, W. (eds.),: Psychological issues of human-computer interaction in the work place, pp. 59-80

Sydow, J., 1987b, Office automation and work organization: Making use of the scope of choice. In: Knave, B. and Widebäck, P.-G. (eds.),: Work with display units '86. pp. 614-623

Taylor, F.W., 1911, Principles of scientific management.

Tichy, N.M., Tushman, M. and Fombrun, C., 1979, Social network analysis for organizations. Academy of Management Review, 4 (4), 507-519

Trist, E., 1981, The evolution of socio-technical systems.
    Issues in the Quality of Working Life No. 2
    Ontario Quality of Working Life Centre, Toronto,
    Ontario
Ulich, E., 1981, Subjektive Tätigkeitsanalyse als Voraus-
    setzung autonomieorientierter Arbeitsgestaltung. In:
Frei, F. and Ulich, E. (eds.): Beiträge zur psychologi-
    schen Arbeitsanalyse. pp. 327-347
Ulich, E. and Troy, N., 1986, Job organization and allo-
    cation of functions between man and work: II Job
    organization. In: Klix, F. and Wandke, H. (eds.):
    Macinter-I. pp. 421-427
Walton, R.E. and Lawrence, P.R. (eds.), 1985, Human
    resource management. Trends and challenges.
Wilson, G.L., Goodall, H.L., Jr. and Waagen, Chr. L.,
    1986, Organizational communication.
Wollnik, M., 1988, Reorganisationstendenzen in der
    betrieblichen Informationsverarbeitung - der Einfluß
    neuer informationstechnologischer Infrastrukturen.
    Handbuch der Modernen Datenverarbeitung, (142), 62-80

WORK ANALYSIS AS A TOOL FOR TASK- AND WORK-ORIENTED DESIGN OF COMPUTER-ASSISTED COOPERATIVE WORK SYSTEMS

Rainer Upmann
University of Aachen
Federal Republic of Germany

INTRODUCTION

Human working conditions in computer-assisted work systems are primarily determined by software design (Skarpelis 1987). Since software design invariably also means work design, extensive preliminary analyses are necessary. In order to create computer-assisted work systems which are both humane and economically efficient, the software/work designer requires a knowledge of all three relevant dimensions (organization, qualification, technology) of such socio-technical systems and of their mutual interrelationships. This entails organizational, work-psychology and (software-)ergonomic work analyses. In the past, software development has focused primarily on isolated technical and functional aspects, with little or no attention to impacts on work organization and the individual. In countless company analyses, personnel in the engineering design and operations scheduling departments of small and medium-sized mechanical engineering companies receive inadequate support in their work from currently available standard user software, owing to its lack of functionality and user-friendliness. In consequence, the spectrum of capabilities quoted for the standard software is not fully exploited; work flow and work organization are partially inappropriate to the tasks and the users. Not infrequently, they are oriented more towards the limited functionality of the standard software being used than towards the needs of users in the CAD/CAM/PPS systems or the requirements of their work tasks. This results in inapropriate and uneconomic work flows, which both cause long door-to-

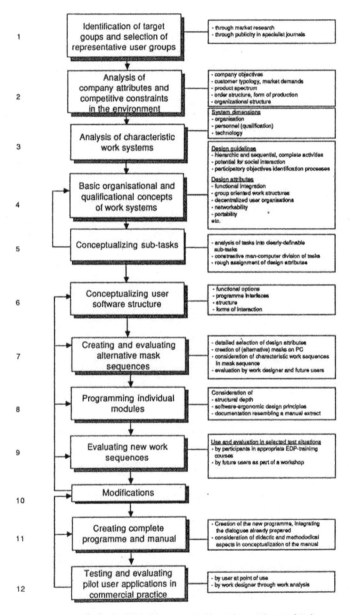

Fig.1: Procedure for the design of standard user software of computer-asssisted worksystems according to holistic criteria

door times and encourage greater division of labour (especially in the indirect areas).

A procedure developed by the Arbeits- und Betriebsor-
ganisatorisches Computerzentrum (abc centre) of the For-
schungsinstitut für Rationalisierung (FIR) and the Institut für Arbeitswissenschaft (IAW) of the RWTH Aachen, in
line with the design objectives outlined above, takes
account of competitive, organizational and behaviour
theory oriented design criteria, and can be used for the
corrective future-oriented design of standard user software for computer-assisted integrated work systems (Figure 1). This procedure has been tested and refined on the
basis of industrial studies in the indirect production
areas of ten medium-sized mechanical engineering companies. In our view, it is also applicable to software
development and work design for users in other sectors.

TWELVE STAGE MODEL FOR THE DESIGN OF STANDARD USER SOFT-
WARE ACCORDING TO HOLISTIC CRITERIA

In stage 1, the target groups and target group characteristics for the software and thus the work process are
roughly identified from market research studies. A representative sample from this group, ready to cooperate
actively in the operational work analyses and in software
development, is selected as a study field (e.g. by selecting the software manufacturer's customers or by announce-
ments in specialist and trade journals).

The object of stage 2 is the investigation of the overall context of the participating companies in which the
computer-assisted work systems are to be considered. This
covers both internal and external behavioural relationships (e.g. organizational structure and competitive factors), which are determined by questioning experts within
the company (executive management, heads of department,
workers' council) according to interview guidelines. This
enables important conclusions to be drawn for the subsequent consideration of working conditions (e.g. competitive factors: short delivery times; working conditions:
time pressure). Information is also obtained on constraints which have to be taken into account in the future
design measures from the point of view of the company. A
knowledge of company objectives and competitive constraints in the environment also make it easier to assess
the economic efficiency of software or work design measures correctly, since a cost-effectiveness calculation
oriented solely on costs has often proved inadequate or

inaccurate. Remembering that acceptance by company decision-makers of the practical implementation of such measures depends on this aspect, such criteria should not be
neglected in work analyses. Stage 2 is completed by a discussion of special company problem complexes and by the
selection and definition of company areas for which software is to be (re-)designed.

Stage 3 involves organizational, work-psychology and
(software-)ergonomic work analyses (Figure 2). The objective of the organizational element of the analysis is to
investigate the tasks of the personnel or the work systems, together with the task fulfilment situation and the
interrelationships between different work systems.

For this purpose, the formal organizational structure
(jobs, task areas, job relationships) is examined on the
basis of existing documentation (job descriptions, function diagrams, organigrams, etc.) and validated by expert
discussions (executive management, departmental heads).
This indicates the formally and informally legitimate
framework in which staff activity takes place. The subsequent organizational task analysis is intended to provide
a complete, systematic database (arranged in accordance
with the task attributes object, activity and (objective)
goal) within the framework of a structured interview
(Frese, 1980). The time scale of the individual tasks in
relation to the overall work activity of the personnel is
determined by questioning interview partners. A phase
analysis combined with the task analysis also provides the
work designer with a general view of planning, decision-
making, performance and controlling aspects of the work
content.

The constraint related task fulfilment situation is
determined by data on technical and organizational constraints (job order variability, technical equipment in
the work system, time fixing, cooperation and communication, etc.). Data concerning the information base on which
staff behaviours are based are of special importance in
investigating computer-assisted intellectual work. Here,
the input and output data for each work system and task,
the respective data media and the data archived at the
workplace are recorded by means of observation interviews
during the orientation phase and, if necessary, through
self-recording by the staff in the detailed analysis
phase.

The decision criteria or formal goals on which employees base behaviours directed at attaining objective goals
are determined through a decision analysis using observation interviews and through the reconstruction of opera-

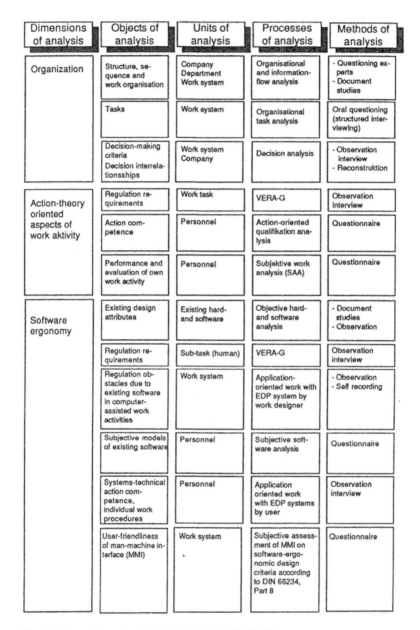

Fig. 2: Work analysis system for task- and work-oriented design
attributes of comuter-assisted cooperative work systems

tional flows.. This enables both structural and work-flow
organization data to be determined, together with deci-
sional interrelationships (Schreuder, Upmann, 1988), providing an indication of possible work design measures
(cooperation measures, functional integration, etc.).

The cognitive requirements imposed on staff by work
requirements are determined with the aid of VERA-G (Resch
1987). In the behaviour theory sense, these are a measure
of vocational personal development potential. The general
cognitive potential of the employees and their behavioural
competence (i.e. specialist, social, methodological and
learning competence) are determined by means of a qualification questionnaire in the individual-related section of
the behaviour-theory oriented work analyses. The first
part of the questionnaire contains questions on basic and
further training and present job activities and is completed by the employees themselves. The second part contains several scales covering each of the above-mentioned
dimensions of behavioural competence. For example, the
specialist competence dimension is assessed by means of at
least five scales covering the following knowledge areas:

- vocational and specialist knowledge,
- technology-specific knowledge (CAD, NC, etc.,),
- information technology related knowledge (e.g. basic
  EDP), and
- systems technology related knowledge.

Generally, non-specialist knowledge is measured using
scales for the dimensions of social and methodological
competence. The second part of the questionnaire is completed by the employees and their superiors. The qualification questionnaire is not intended to provide a comprehensive and detailed analysis of staff qualifications. It
does, however, provide indications of the potential scope
for changes in work organization (e.g. enlargement of job
content, introduction of autonomous work teams) and time
scales for their implementation. In addition, they form an
informative basis for a specific analysis of qualification
requirements by the personnel development planner. The
subjective work analysis (SAA) questionnaire is used to
determine general perception and evaluation of job activity (Udris, 1980). This provides indications of the extent
to which employees redefine their job tasks.

The work analyses described above are equally relevant
to conventional and to computer-assisted work systems. In
companies where computer-assisted systems are already in
existence, it is useful to carry out software-ergonomic

work analyses. The primary question is the extent to which the hard- and software currently in use supports or obstructs the user in the mental regulation of his job activity.

A complete survey of the design attributes* of the hard- and software in current use is necessary for this purpose. In computer-assisted work systems, these determine the extent to which objective freedom of action is influenced by technology (Heeg, 1988). Technical planning attributes are recorded through a study of system descriptions and by independent use of the data processing systems by the work designer (with experience in EDP).

For computer-assisted work tasks, a task micro-analysis (directly at the computer) is used to identify sub-tasks carried out by people, those carried out by the computer and those carried out in dialogue with the computer. Using VERA-G, the regulation requirements for the human sub-tasks are determined. If these regulation requirements are significantly lower than those of the corresponding work task, a Tayloristic division of labour between the operator and the computer is indicated. The work designer, who should be trained in software ergonomics, then has to examine whether and possibly why the performance conditions of the computer-assisted work flow established by the existing design attributes obstructs the attainment of objectives, i.e. whether obstacles to regulation occur (cf. Leitner 1987). In particular, he must examine whether:

- the division of tasks between the user and the computer corresponds to the requirements of contrastive work design (Volpert 1986) (e.g. avoidance of monotonous job activities, i.e. routine activities demanding attention),
- the mask sequence corresponds to logical human job steps or sub-goal planning,
- the information content of each mask corresponds to the information requirement for each job step (avoidance of unnecessary information reception problems),
- the presentation of information does not conflict with known features of perception psychology (avoidance of unnecessary information reception problems),

---

*Understood here in accordance with the design dimensions of computer-assisted work systems as forms of organizational, qualificational and technical realization whose impacts (if any) on certain system design criteria (e.g. those given in DIN 66234, Part 8) are to be assessed

- the dialogue and programme structure corresponds to the
  job variability and work-flow requirements (avoidance of
  additional effort, e.g. due to rigid dialogue structures) and
- the ergonomic design of the input devices is adequate to
  the task and user requirements (avoidance of motor
  problems).

   This work analysis is constraint-related, i.e. the
design attributes of the EDP systems concerned are evaluated by the work designer from the point of view of an
experienced user and in relation to the work tasks
involved. Only in the individual-related section of the
analysis can the design attributes be evaluated in relation to their suitability for the envisaged users. Here
the subjective models of the EDP systems held by the
actual users need to be determined. Individual knowledge
of the existence and potential applications of particular
design attributes of the EDP systems are elicited by means
of a questionnaire. Proper use of individual design
attributes by users can be established by means of an
observation interview, within the framework of application-oriented work with the EDP system. This also enables
individual work performance procedures to be identified.
These provide the software designer an indication of
whether and to what extent individual adaptability is
required in the redesign or modification of the standard
user software.
   In the final phase of software-ergonomic work analysis,
employees are given the opportunity to (subjectively)
judge the user-friendliness of their dialogue systems by
means of a questionnaire. The questionnaire contains
questions on particular operational design points deduced
from software ergonomic principles according to DIN 66234,
Part 8. Employees' answers provide the software designer
with specific information on the suitability of individual
design attributes or on the need to develop new design
attributes from the user's point of view.
   The evaluated results of stages 2 and 3 of the analysis
form the basis for deducing design attributes. Holistic
design of standard user software must pay continual attention to possible impacts on the three dimensions of organization, technology and qualification, and on the interactions between them. The resulting design process must be
oriented towards the two priority design objectives of
personal development potential and economic efficiency of
the work systems. The order of design of the dimensions is

determined according to the depth of their impacts on the
realizability of the desired objectives. Organizational
design must therefore take priority over software design;
in parallel with both processes, appropriate qualification
concepts need to be established (cf. Fischer, 1983). Competitive environmental constraints on the companies exercise a significant influence on the nature of structure,
scheduling and work organization. Data collected by the
Institut fÅr Arbeitswissenschaft (IAW) of the RWTH Aachen
(Schreuder, 1988, Kruhöfer 1988) have shown that over the
period from 1970 to 1985, one-dimensional organizational
structures (e.g. functional organization) have tended to
decrease, and that functional organizational divisions
have simultaneously been replaced by product or customer
oriented structures (as a consequence of adaptation to
altered market requirements). In a parallel development,
work organization within the individual departments has
changed. Thus, for example, an increase in group-oriented
work forms at the expense of individual work forms was
noticeable in the companies questioned (Kruhöfer, 1988,
Schreuder, 1989). This organizational transformation has
not only produced changes in the inter-personal division
of tasks, but has also influenced company hierarchy, vertical and horizontal division of decision-making powers
and communicative and cooperative relationships between
employees – with their impacts on software requirements.

At the beginning of the design process (stage 4),
software designers therefore need to determine the basic
organizational and qualificational concepts of the work
systems (in collaboration with organizational and
personnel planners). The primary question is whether
competitive requirements can be satisfied by means of
suitable organization concepts which simultaneously
provide employees with work activities allowing personal
development. The guideline here is the creation of
complete activities, in the sense used by Hacker (1987),
of possibilities of social interaction and of work forms
with participatory goal formation processes. The software
must support these (work-)organizational design
attributes. At this design level, software designers must
take account of aspects such as suitable organizational
forms for the use of EDP (e.g. decentralized direct
operation), software networkability, programme and data
portability and upwards compatibility of programming
languages (Schreuder, 1988) (Fig. 2). Neglect of these
aspects makes it impossible to exploit organizational
potential.

Stage 5 covers the division of tasks between the user
and the computer and the conceptualization of these sub-
tasks. The guiding principle is that the personal development task attributes created by the work systems should be
maintained and promoted through computer support. All sub-
tasks demanding and promoting human skills such as planning, assessment, empirical learning, development of solu-
tional strategies and heuristics, and relational thinking
should be reserved for the user. The computer should
relieve the user of routine work (e.g. searching for, con-
ditioning, ordering and outputting data) which can easily
lead to a feeling of saturation and to mistakes in the
work activity, especially where concentrated attention is
required. In industrial practice, for example, the engineering designer is frequently required to modify individual components in a sub-assembly (e.g. due to customers'
requirements, technical progress, etc.), which entail
changes in other components. Conventional CAD systems provide only inadequate support for the user in time-consuming routine tasks such as the acquisition of the necessary
geometrical and functional data, recognition of impacts
and mechanical implementation of resulting changes. In
this instance, rule-based computer assistance can contribute to work design with enhanced personal development
potential. With the aid of a system based on design rules
and technological knowledge, resulting changes and their
impacts can be identified by the compute. The more demanding task of evaluating the implications of the resultant
changes and deciding on suitable measures in the light of
pre-determined design criteria is reserved for the user.
The system performs the mechanical task of updating the
relevant data sets.

In stage 6, the structure of the user software can be
deduced from the concept design of the sub-tasks and the
qualifications of the users. Structure includes the spectrum of functions, programme flow structure, forms of
interaction and mask structure. Particular attention needs
to be paid to the harmonization of user interfaces and
forms of interaction. Particularly in work structures promoting personal development, such as, for example, autonomous design and production islands without rigid task
structures, users will be overtaxed if different dialogue
systems have to be mastered in addition to changing job
tasks. The computer integrated production (CIM) concept
demands the integration not only of data and functions,
but of the various user interfaces.

In stage 7, alternative mask sequences are created on a
PC, on the basis of the evaluated work analysis results,
so that characteristic computer-assisted job step
sequences can be presented to the future users. Following
an initial assessment of these sequences, individual
programme modules are realized (stage 8). The new work
flows are evaluated in pre-determined test situations by
representatives of the future user group (stage 9).
Experience has shown that participants in EDP training
courses are particularly able to provide design
suggestions which promote the learnability of the software
(Schreuder, 1988).

In stage 10, the insights gained from the preceding
phases are implemented in the software, so that a complete
programme results (stage 11). Before being introduced on
the market, this should be tested under real conditions in
normal industrial use by pilot users stage 12), to spare
future users the irritation of subsequent releases.

SUMMARY

The creation of humane and economically efficient
computer-assisted work systems demands a knowledge of all
three design dimensions (organization, qualification and
technology) on the part of the software designer. The
paper presents a behaviour theory supported procedure for
the analysis and (re-)design of standard user software,
taking equal account of competitive, organizational, work
psychology and (software-)ergonomic aspects.

ACKNOWLEDGEMENT

This project was sponsored by the Bundesministerium für
Forschung und Technologie (BMFT), Department for humanization of the working environment (project designation:
01HK467).

REFERENCES

Fischer, G., 1983, Entwurfsrichtlinien für die Software-
    Ergonomie aus der Sicht der Mensch-Maschine-Kommunika-
    tion. In: Balzert (Hrsg.) Software-Ergonomie 1983,
    Stuttgart, S.30-48.
Frese, E., 1980, Aufgabenanalyse und -synthese. In:
    Handwörterbuch der Organisation, Hrsg. v. Grochla, E.,
    2.Aufl., Stuttgart, Sp.207-217.

Hacker, W., 1987, Software-Ergonomie, Gestalten rechner
    gestützter geistiger Arbeit!?. In: Schönpflug,W.; Witt-
    stock,M. (Hrsg.), Software-Ergonomie `87, Nutzen
    Informationssysteme dem Benutzer?, Stuttgart, pp.31-54.
Heeg, F.-J., 1988, Empirische Software-Ergonomie, Zur
    Gestaltung benutzergerechter Mensch-Computer-Dialoge,
    Berlin.
Kruhöfer, S., 1988, Der Einfluß von CIM auf Aufbau- und
    Arbeitsorganisation sowie Mitarbeiterqualifikationen in
    mittelständischen Unternehmen, Diplomarbeit am Institut
    für Arbeitswissenschaft (IAW) der RWTH Aachen, Aachen.
Leitner, K. u.a., 1987, Analyse psychischer Belastung in
    der Arbeit-Das RHIA-Verfahren, Köln.
Resch, M., 1987, Die Handlungsregulation geistiger Arbeit,
    Dissertation TU-Berlin, Berlin.
Schreuder, S., 1988, Arbeitswissenschaftliche Gestal-
    tungsmöglichkeiten der rechnergestützten Arbeit in der
    Konstruktion, Dissertation RWTH Aachen, Aachen.
Schreuder, S.; Upmann, R., 1988, CIM-Wirtschaftlichkeit,
    Vorgehensweise zur Ermittlung des Nutzens einer
    Integration von CAD, CAP, CAM, PPS und CAQ, Köln.
Skarpelis, C., 1987, Software gestalten heißt Arbeits-
    bedingungen gestalten. In: Fähnrich, K.-P. (Hrsg.),
    State of the Art, Nr.5, Softwareergonomie, München,
    pp. 54-71.
Udris, I., 1980, Fragebogen zur subjektiven Arbeitsana-
    lyse, Lehrstuhl für Arbeits- und Betriebspsychologie an
    der ETH Zürich, Zürich.
Volpert, W., 1986, Kontrastive Analyse des Verhältnisses
    von Mensch und Rechner als Grundlage des System-Design.
    In: IfHA-Berichte Nr.11, Berlin 1986, pp. 1-16.

EVALUATION OF NEW WORKPLACES BY MODELLING AND SIMULATION OF OPERATOR PROCEDURES

Tom Bösser

University of Münster
Federal Republic of Germany

ABSTRACT

A methodology is described which is designed to support user-centred design of computer-based systems. The main concern is for a specific consequence of the design of computer-based systems, the procedural, device-specific knowledge required from the operator. The objective is to raise the efficiency of work by adapting the functional design of the device to the task requirements. The method is based on the formal language SL/R for the modelling of procedural knowledge and includes separate models of device functions and task requirements. Evaluation is based on simulated user procedures and should help to identify design deficiencies. Other application areas are the development of user support for defined tasks and systems.

INTRODUCTION

Innovation in modern information technology generates new configurations of workplaces: the worker may be faced with a new tool for an existing task, or even an entirely new task. Instances of the former are existing machines which are fitted with new computer-based controls, instances of the latter are entirely new installations such as automated storage and retrieval facilities, semi-automatic mailsorting machines or transport systems. Innovation in office systems effects both types of changes - text processors are new tools for existing tasks, but new tasks, for example electronic mail, emerge also.

Information-technology based systems affect the cognitive requirements on the worker, rather than physical workload. Systems of the type mentioned are effectively part-automated systems, where some of the control- and information processing functions are allocated to computers. The work of the human in systems of this type is defined by
- the tasks for the man-machine system
- the functions of the automatic computer-based system
- the man-machine interface.

By default all remaining, non-automated functions are allocated to the operator. Even if the design is not based on an explicit definition of the task for the total system and the operating constraints, the final result will determine the task allocated to the operator. Very frequently it is found that information-technology based systems do not just allocate part of the physical and cognitive functions of the human operator to automatic subsystems, but also generate new tasks for the operator, the exact nature of which often is not recognized before the system is used under realistic working conditions. The design of new workplaces using information technology is therefore largely a function of the design of computerised control systems functions (part automation). For low-volume IT systems the main costs are software development rather than production costs.

Two measures may be taken when deficiencies of the design are recognized late in the development cycle, or after the system has been put into practical use: 'patching' of the system and change of operator procedures. Patching means that ad-hoc changes are made to the existing system in the form of program patches, usually a short-term solution required by the urgency of the problem. Apart from the short-term costs it often has long-term effects by making the software-design much less systematic and orderly, and by lowering the quality of the software product.

Alternatively the operator may be instructed to change his procedures in order to compensate for deficiencies of the system. These may be additional instructions ('If event X occurs do A'), but can also include overrides of the automatic system and the instruction to enter into hand-operated mode. In this case effectively the design goals are not met, design deficiencies are remedied by requiring more complex procedures from the operator.

The design of workplaces using computer technology is determined to a large extent by the specification of the computer program. We consequently assume that it is much

more efficient to match system functions to the tasks
early in the design cycle in order to minimize the
requirements made on the human operator, rather than to
attempt person-centred solutions such as operator training
at a later stage (Shackel 1987). Systems produced and used
in large numbers should benefit most from improved human
factors design, but the added value must be made transparent to the customer in order to become effective as a market force, so reliable testing procedures are a prerequisite. User-centred design must minimize the requirements
on the operator by the tool used, and must affect system
design as early as possible. We present a methodology for
supporting design by modelling and evaluation based on
operator procedures.

Our evaluation methods are centred on the procedures
the operator uses to execute his tasks, which determine
the knowledge required from the operator. As discussed
further below, we define the task independent of the procedures used to execute the task; the procedures therefore
are a function of the task (the state changes to be
achieved) and the tool used, i.e. operator procedures :=
f(task, tool).

The design objective we consider is to reduce the complexity and learning requirements imposed by the user procedures, especially those which are imposed not by the
task, but by the tool, and which make the procedures more
complex. Task-related knowledge of applies to the work-
object only, e.g. the knowledge what a well-formatted document should look like, or the properties required of certain machine parts. This knowledge is the essential qualification for a worker and is complemented by tool-related
knowledge. The importance of tool-related knowledge
becomes apparent when new tools are introduced into existing jobs, where the task-related qualification of the personnel has to be retained and carried over to doing the
task with new tools. As we have shown, the change in working procedures due to the introduction of CAD or office
automation requires significant training of the operators
(2 weeks for text processing, 3 to 12 months for CAD;
Bösser 1987). Even with 'unskilled' machine operators in
the textile industry we have found that the training
required to operate machines with new computerized controls is significant.

SEPARABLE DESCRIPTION OF TASK, TOOL AND OPERATOR PROCE-
DURES

The general definition of a task in terms of what is to
be achieved is vague, and often it is much easier to
define a task by the procedure used to complete the task.
We define a task more generally by an initial state and an
end state of a work object, independent of the tool used
and the procedure required to bring about the state transition. This is easily conceivable for metal working, room
cleaning or text formatting, but abstract work-objects,
for example in database access or planning problems, are
hard to describe, even though initial state and acceptable
end states are clearly recognized.

An additional source of vagueness of task descriptions
is that a task, e.g. 'clean the room' is defined both by a
number of possible initial states, and a number of acceptable end states. It really describes a set of similar
tasks. In order to make complex tasks easier to understand, large tasks are generally described as a set of
part-tasks. A tool is any device used to effect changes of
the work object, but work effectively is only the change
in the state of the work object, not the state changes of
the tool. Part of the work may be, however, to transform
the tool into a certain end state. Although in many
instances difficult in detail, this concept permits us to
separate task- or tool-related knowledge. The design
objective for computer-based systems is to raise the efficiency of work by reducing tool-related complexity of procedures and knowledge prerequisites for the user.

In the application of CAD systems, knowledge of the
task domain may include knowledge about the design of
automobile parts or electronic circuits; tool-related
knowledge applies to the procedures to generate the appropriate design drawings. Technical drawing used to be a
craft, requiring considerable knowledge. CAD systems of
present-day technical standard are mastered after 3 to 12
months of training, i.e. acquisition of tool-specific
knowledge to reach the previous level of productivity.
This 'how to do it' knowledge - in this case how to produce CAD drawings - is called procedural knowledge, as
opposed to declarative or factual knowledge. It is
acquired by training and practice, (Bösser 1987). Well
trained procedural knowledge is called 'skill'.

The development of skills is costly in terms of learning time, the gain is a continuous improvement of performance and reduction of workload due to memorizing and

practice of procedures. The efficiency of work can be improved by minimizing the amount of procedural knowledge required from the operator, provided that the same task demands are fulfilled. This does not, as is often erroneously stated, imply a 'dequalification' of the operator, because the need for task-related knowledge is not reduced.

The recent spreading of 'desktop publishing' is a prime example: Typing used to be a skill requiring considerable training; corrections were difficult, formatting not possible at all with a typewriter. Formatting programs and laser printers available today allow anyone to produce formatted texts previously only possible with typesetting and printing equipment and by a skilled typesetter and printer. In reality we see that while the chores of typing, retyping, typesetting and lengthy corrections are made easy, the actual design of a well structured document is no easier and still requires considerable experience and knowledge. The advantage is that the learning effort can be invested into task-related rather than unproductive tool-related knowledge. The effective use of innovative user-interface elements (menus and icons, 'direct manipulation' and others) reduces the need for tool-related knowledge.

TASK ANALYSIS

Analysis of tasks is complicated by the fact that only existing working procedures are observable, but new tools require new procedures and also make new objectives achievable (for example better designed documents). Many authors call 'task-analysis' the description of procedures, which more appropriately is called 'work analysis'. The difficulty is to infer from observed working procedures which objectives are pursued, and the alternative solutions which would be considered with more efficient tools. A precise description of tasks must include the initial states, where the task occurs, and the acceptable end states which define task completion, as well as constraints in terms of costs, tool usage etc. Such a task analysis and description is quite tedious today and involves much inference and guesswork. Efforts not reported here are directed towards constructing more efficient methods for the generation of task models from observational data.

OBJECTIVES: TOOLS FOR EARLY EVALUATION OF SYSTEMS IN THE DESIGN CYCLE

We have constructed a method to support user-centred design of computer-based systems with the objective of optimising the efficiency of the user, and have implemented software tools for supporting the design process. As explained above, evaluation after the design is specified results in costly design changes and delays, and has generally the effect that human factors are not considered adequately in the design of systems. Norman (1986) stated that human factors deliver 'too little too late'. Instead, we propose to use formal models of the device functionality as a basis for evaluation, the result of which should be an improved match between the device and the tasks it is to be used for.

The advantage of the limitation to functional properties is that a useful evaluation is possible before all details of the user interface (menus, windows, screen masks etc) have been defined. The definition of the operational details in our opinion is easier when the functional architecture is well developed.

Good design is aspired to as a feature of the total man-machine system. The design of the device determines man-machine task decomposition, defines the job and the training the user requires. Ideally user-centred design should proceed in the following sequence:

1 tasks and design constraints are defined
2 the man-machine task-decomposition and device-functionality are specified
3 the user-procedures and training requirements are evaluated as a consequence of 1 and 2

SL/R - A LANGUAGE FOR MODELLING OF PROCEDURAL KNOWLEDGE IN WELL-DEFINED DOMAINS

The basis of our methodology for the modelling and evaluation of computer based man-machine systems is the formal language SL/R (Skill and Learning Representation) for the modelling and simulation of procedural knowledge in well-structured domains. In order to meet the requirements for an efficient support during the early phases of the design processes as outlined above, it was concluded that the method must become effective before the final product, or even prototypes, become available. Consequently evaluation is based on the design documents (specification) rather than a prototype. Empirical user tests are not possible at this stage, and in most cases by far too lengthy to be applicable. The principle is to model independently the device functions and the tasks, and to derive the user procedures by simulation. The user procedures are the basis of evaluation.

Modelling consists in the development of an executable device model and a task model from the design specification. Ideally the design process starts with a precise model of the tasks to be executed with the device under construction. Very often in system development the effort to develop a precise task model is avoided, but a precise model of the device is always generated (the specification).

DEVICE- AND TASK- MODELS

The principle adopted for modelling a hard/software system is to represent the device as a finite state machine, limited to the representation of the states and state transitions observable by the user of the device. This is adequate for a computer based device, and an extended ATN (Augmented Transition Network) formalism was chosen (Dunker et al. 1987). Specific is that, in order to make modelling more systematic, we identify states where the operator can apply the same set of commands. These are not identical states of the device, but are identical from the perspective of the user, they are called command-states.

The task model is the set of tasks to be executed with the device, where the tasks are described as a pair of [Initial State, End State]. By this definition independence of the device- and task model is achieved. An additional step is needed during modelling, the link process, where the changes of the work-object are linked to the device functions. Figure 1 summarizes the language elements of SL/R.

Independence of task model and device model is needed for formal reasons: a precise comparison of procedures for two devices is possible only when the same task is executed with both devices.

SOFTWARE TOOLS - THE SL/R TOOLKIT

In the initial stages of development it became clear that modelling of devices is complicated by the limited capability of the model author systematically to overview a complex system. Complex in this sense, it turned out, are devices like radios, telephones or controls of machine

---

SL/R : Language elements:

STC   State-transition class   IS   Initial state
Op   Operation   ES   End state
det   Determinator   tab Task Attribute
cond Condition

Device model (set of STCs):

STC [name N]   IS [deta = val ai, detb = val bi, detc = val ci, ...]
   Op A   [cond x, cond y, ...]
               ES [det a = val aj, det b = val bj, ...]
   Op B   [cond x, cond z, ...]
               ES [det a = val ak, det b = val bk, ...]
   Op C   [.....]

STC [name M]   IS [...]
   Op .....

Task model (set of tasks):

TASK [name]   IS [tab a = val ai, tab b = bi, ...]
             ES [tab a = val aj, tab c = cj, ...]

Link matrix:

If   device transition   IS [det a = val ai, ..] ES [det a = val aj, ..]
the   work object changes   IS [tab a = val ai, ..] ES [tab a = val aj, ..]

Figure 1

tools. Even more complex are CAD or office computer systems. It therefore became apparent that effective software tools are needed for making modelling practical. An overview of the set of software-tools, which is implemented in PROLOG on a SUN workstation, is shown in Figure 2. The advantages of the ATN formalism are exploited to help the model-author to avoid errors in the modelling process. With the support of these tools it becomes possible to construct working models of devices within a comparatively short time.

SL/R toolkit

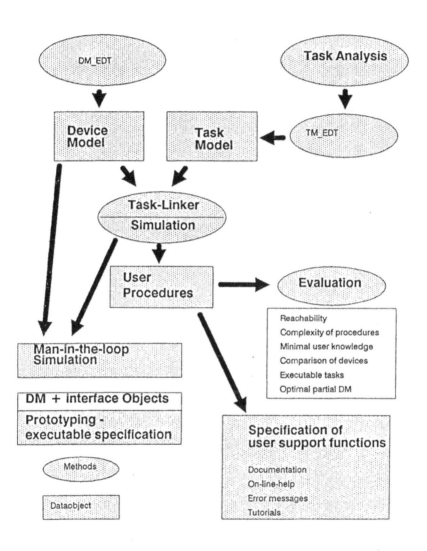

Figure 2

T. Bösser

Procedure for task [name]

	Current Determinators		Latent Determinators		Task Attributes	
	Det. c1	.....Det. cn	Det. l1	.....Det. ln	Attr. a1	.....Attr. an
INITIAL STATE	valuec1_1	valuecn_1	-	-	valueea1_1	valueean_1
← Command	-	-	-	-	-	valueean_1
STATE	valuec1_2	-	-	valueln_1	valueea1_2	valueean_1
← Command	-	-	valuel1_2	valueln_1	valueea1_3	valueean_2
STATE	-	...	...	...	...	...
← ...	...	...	...	...	...	...
...	...	...	...	...	...	...
END STATE	-	valuecn_2	-	-	valueea1_5	valueean_2

A *Procedure* is defined by the sequence of *Commands* which lead from the *Initial State* to the *End State*. Each state is described by *Determinators* of the device state and *Task Attributes*. Determinators are either
- *current determinators*, which determine to which subsequent state the command leads,
- or *latent determinators*, which will determine the state-transition effected by a command occurring later in the procedure.

Fig. 3

EVALUATION METHODS

Evaluation - from the user-centre point of view - pertains to the user procedures. Assuming that the task and the design constraints (standards, user population etc) are well defined, only devices are acceptable which permit the completion of the defined set of tasks. Given this, the objective is to select a design which minimizes the complexity of the user procedures and the tool-related knowledge required from the user.

Given task- and device models, the user procedures are derived by simulation. The result is a precise description of the procedures (shown in Figure 3 for example). A procedure is more comprehensive than a sequence of commands: The user must control the sequence of commands and for this purpose store intermediate variables which are preconditions for the later execution of subsequent commands.

Several evaluation processes are included in the SL/R toolkit, beginning with the capability to simulate the system in a step-by-step mode. This is limited to the functional level, because the operational details are not defined at this stage of system design. Further evaluative steps are
- design verification. This answers the question whether all intended tasks can be executed with the device as designed. In particular the analysis will show if all tasks can be executed succesfully from all initial states. It is also possible to test whether unwanted functions are excluded, for example the accidental destruction of the work-object.
- user knowledge model. User knowledge includes factual knowledge, in particular the determinators and task attributes, and procedural knowledge, the precise description of the operator procedures. Procedures include more than a sequence of commands, the device enforces a certain sequence on the execution of commands. The user must in addition to the commands have knowledge describing these procedures. The specification of user knowledge can be further used as the basis for designing user support functions (error messages, on-line help, documentation, tutorials, training simulators, computer based instruction).
- comparative evaluation of devices. In order to choose between design alternatives, complexity measures are calculated from the procedures to execute the set of tasks in the appropriate task model, which should indicate which device makes less requirements upon the user. Human performance, and also workload, are not static, but subject

to practice. Appropriate evaluation must therefore take
into account the effect of learning, and also the frequency of expected usage. Implementation of this aspect of
the method is currently under way. Details can not be presented here.

The result of simulation is not primarily a summary
evaluative statement, but a detailed simulation giving the
capability to identify design flaws and investigate the
consequences of design alternatives in detail.

VALIDATION

Validation of the method proceeds along two routes:
Firstly it is tested whether the simulated procedures
model the cognitive procedures of real users, and secondly
the predictive value of the evaluation is tested. The
first test is under way in experiments where models of
individual user's knowledge as a subset of complete tool-
knowledge are constructed on the basis of probing of individual knowledge, and the performance of model and human
subject are compared. The second route to validation is
more involved, it is similar to the construction of a psy-
chometric test and we consider this neither feasible nor
worth the effort. Rather, we compare in case studies the
results of modelling and evaluation with the experience of
end users of existing systems.

In comparison to the work of Kieras and Polson (1985)
and other authors following similar principles, a main
advantage of our approach is the capability ofstrictly
separating device- and task models. Compared to writing
models in the form of production systems we consider our
modelling tools to be considerably more efficient. Rapid
prototyping methods (Wasserman 1985) have the additional
advantage that they may generate code which can be
included in the final production system, but they do not
include methods for evaluation. Empirical user tests, even
when prototypes can be built very quickly, are prohibi-
tively time consuming.

Advantages to be gained by the application of SL/R are:
- Development of precise specifications of the system
  functions and task domain are enforced.
- Evaluation is done quickly and requires little additional effort.
- Computer based assistance for generating detailed descriptions of device, tasks and work procedures permits
  modelling of large domains. This is much easier than or
  not possible at all by paper-based methods.

- Programming is not required, usage is comparable to
using a speadsheet-program or expert-systems shell.

APPLICATION TO THE SPECIFICATION OF USER SUPPORT FUNCTIONS

We believe that in the design of computer-based devices
the preferable route is to match the design of devices as
closely as possible to the task. The actual design objectives and constraints depend, however, on the degrees of
freedom in a particular design task. Standardisation very
often defines constraints which preclude many design
options and do not allow a design to be generated which is
optimal for a given task.
In such cases SL/R can be applied for the precise formal description of user procedures and the design and
implemention of all types of user support functions.
This has not been applied to real-world examples so far,
but we have seen the demand for it. An obstacle here is
that the very high cost of training, and the added value
of a system due to good user support functions are hard to
recognize and to quantify. Therefore the high initial
effort to produce a formal description of task, device and
user procedures is not easy to justify.

RESULTS OF CASE STUDIES

. Case studies testing the SL/R methodology have been
conducted or are in progress for applications in office
systems (word processing), computer operating systems,
computerized terminals for machine tools and communication
devices for automobile applications.
Specific results reflecting the different problems in
these application areas can be summarized:
- The text processing systems under study have specific
differences in functionality tailored to different task
domains (office work, programming, technical writing), but
all have a very extensive and redundant functionality,
requiring extensive factual and procedural knowledge.
Incomplete knowledge still permits tasks to be executed.
- Operating systems for different types of computers provide all necessary functionality, but do not have much
redundancy and therefore require very precise and complete
factual and procedural knowledge. Modelling indicates that
user support functions can be effective in reducing operator workload and knowledge requirements.
- Communication devices for automobiles have been shown to
be unnecessarily complex for a domain where simple opera-

tor procedures are a major design objective. A task model
for many devices is conspicuously absent.
- Involvement in the design process of a computer-based
control terminal for a traditional textile machine lead to
a considerably simplified design. It was found that all
tasks can be executed with a reduced number of commands,
and the final design was found to be easier to use and
considered of higher quality.

The editing tools DM_EDT and TM_EDT proved to be efficient for editing models. It seems hardly possible to
develop models of complex devices with paper-based methods
only, and the result is a more precise specification. This
benefit alone may justify the use of the tools. In all
cases it was found that the task models of designers suffered both from a lack of data and observations, and from
adequate descriptive methods.

In our experience the design of systems suffers from
the fact that initially the design is started without a
precise description of the task to be done with the system, i.e. a task model. The task model usually seems to be
too simple, and excludes states and functions which occur
rarely. Matching of tasks to functions is attempted in
conjunction with the first tests of prototype systems. The
consequence is that more functions have to be added at a
late stage of development, and the overall design becomes
less well structured, in addition to the unforeseen cost
and effort required for these changes.

Recognizing that the software tools for generating task
models have not achieved the same level of sophistication
as the tools for generating and simulating device models,
further efforts will be directed towards building more
efficient tools for task analysis and modelling based on
observations of work under realistic conditions. Further
efforts are directed towards systems used in real-time
task domains like process control and vehicles (Bösser
1988), and man-machine systems which involve the interaction with partly autonomous systems.

REFERENCES

Bösser, T., 1987, Learning in Man-Computer Interaction.
  Research Reports ESPRIT Vol. 1. (Heidelberg: Springer
  Verlag).
Bösser, T., 1988, Assisting the drivers of automobiles
  with computer-based devices. In: Proceedings of the
  1988 IEEE International Conference on Systems, Man, and
  Cybernetics, Beijing and Shenyang, China, August 8-12,
  1988, Vol. 2. (Peking: International Academic Publish
  ers), pp. 845-857.

Dunker, J., Melchior, E.-M., and Bîsser, T., 1987, First prototype of modelling tool (Working paper B7.1a). Empirical methods for the validation of models of user knowledge (Working paper B7.2a). ESPRIT Project 385 HUFIT.

Kieras, D., and Polson, P.G., 1985, An approach to the formal analysis of user complexity. International Journal of Man-Machine Studies, 22, pp. 365-394.

Norman, D.A., 1986, Cognitive Engineering. In: User Centered System Design. New Perspectives on Human-Computer Interaction, edited by D.A. Norman and S.W. Draper (Hillsdale, NJ: Lawrence Erlbaum Associates), pp. 31-61.

Shackel, B., 1987, Human Factors for Usability Engineering. In: ESPRIT '87 Achievements & Impact. Part 2. (North-Holland), pp. 1019-1040.

Wasserman, A.I., 1985, Extending State Transition Diagrams for the Specification of Human-Computer Interaction. IEEE Transactions on Software Engineering, 11, pp. 699-713.

ANALYSIS OF CAD/CAM JOB CONTENT AND WORKPLACE CHARACTERISTICS (EXPERIENCES OF THE INTRODUCTION OF CAD/CAM SYSTEMS IN HUNGARY)

György Kaucsek

University of Budapest
Hungary

GENERAL CONSIDERATIONS

Real flexible manufacturing systems that allow not only a limited flexibility but also a great variety of products and technology can only be set up with the integration or combination of computer aided design and manufacturing systems. That is why the introduction of CAD/CAM in Hungary is considered to be an important stage, a preconditition of the formation of highly integrated flexible manufacturing systems.

The number of recent applications of CAD/CAM, counting also those of experimental character and those now being introduced can be not more than two dozens, but CAD/CAM in the real sense of the word can hardly be found in Hungary.

In the course of our research work we have conducted case studies with the help of interviews, observations and questionnaires in three large companies representing three different branches of industry (microelectronics, craneand ship building, bus production) and also three different kinds of approaches as to the introduction of CAD/CAM. Our investigations aim to explore the changes in the human factors involved in the introduction of CAD/CAM and also to call the attention of the administrative, management, trade union and educational organisations to problems that can only be outlined tday but must be solved in the course of applying information technology.

The analysis of work-places was conducted by comparison of an expert-checklist and some workers' questionnaire findings.

All the problems arising in the field of computer aided systems - according to Hatvany and Guedj (1982) - can be

319

grouped around three key-notions, namely: skill - style - comfort. The computer aided systems should give more and more possibilities for the constructors and the technological engineers using them to show their specific abilities and skills. The user requires also a work-style comfortable for him, i.e.speed, patience, easy access to the stored information, flexibility (so that it is possible to jump over any phase of the process of design, to discontinue it or to return to it later if necessary). In addition to that we can mention factors of comfort, namely: the quality of the display screen; the dimensions of the working space on the terminal table; the lighting for reading paper documentation; the possibility of avoiding unnatural, 'forced postures', etc.

Analysis of the changes in the work content is considered to be a key-factor of our research work. The problems appearing in this field on the one hand affect the functioning of the technological equipment and - as a selective factor - on the other hand have a considerable impact on all the outcomes of the given work situation in connection with the physical and mental strain, wages, social and labour market status of the workers.

Today the direction and extent of these changes are vague as these new technologies are still in the period of introduction and their influences have been exercised only for a short time. That is why they affect only a small number of workers, their dimensions are moderate, they operate on a small scale. At the same time a wide and inevitable spread of the so called information technologies can certainly be predicted

On the basis of our experiences of the possible influences of the application of CAD/CAM, there must be a certain distinction between companies where design and manufacturing can be carried out only with the help of CAD/CAM because of the characteristic features of the product itself (e.g. certain products of microelectronics) and where CAD/CAM replace an existing activity but on a higher level, providing more flexibility and speed in some operations (e.g. ship-building, bus-manufacturing, machine-tool industry). For this reason not only similarities can be observed but also considerable differences in connection especially with the conditions of introduction and influence on the existing labour power.

In the first case the problems of change to the new technology are of smaller scale as these companies have had no preliminaries without CAD/CAM and changes cannot take the organisation and labour by surprise, thus a char-

acteristic symbiosis will be formed. In this first case it
is characteristic for CAD/CAM in microelectronics that
when applied no battle is fought for their introduction,
their grounds do not have to be justified, the management
and the organization accept them right from the start. For
example at IC-design companies in California all the
organizational and technical conditions have been provided
for the designers practically from the beginning, thus the
determinant - the 'bottle-neck' - of productivity has
always been the designer himself or his capacity. Companies try to use their designers' knowledge as much as possible. As a consequence, it often happens (Hatvany and
Nemes, 1982) that these young IC-designing engineers work
with the CAD-system for quite a high salary and therefore
at a fantastic pace, but after about 5-6 years they 'burn
out' completely and become unable to continue their work.

   In the second case the new and old technology must
exist together for some time and the contradiction and
conflicts deriving from this situation extend the time of
a complete change and prevent the full use of possibilities provided by the new technology. In this case the
introduction of the CAD/CAM systems must often face the
resistance of the organization itself. It often has to
bear the burdens of interpersonal tension, as usually it
does not only change the traditional methods for design
and organization, but breaks down the existing framework
of the organization, too. The organizational factors -
including also the behaviour of the management - have an
increased importance in their influence on work content
and conditions at the beginning of the period of
introduction. When compared with the above factors a poor
provision of hardware and software quite often represents
a negligible problem.

   It is also characteristic that in the book of Majchrzak
et al. (1987) written about the human factors of CAD a
wider ground is given to the organizational questions of
its introduction than to all the rest of the field together. At one of the large industrial companies examined
by us, about a 10-year-long battle had to be fought for
the introduction of CAD/CAM, although - if considering it
from an objective point of wiew - it was a question of
vital importance for the company concerned. This battle
can be fought and won only by strongly motivated and
devoted people who are always obliged to prove everything
for the organization and the management. Therefore, under
such circumstances the psychological load on these people
is determined basically by the pressure of the organi-

zation and not by the more or less insufficient provision
of technical instruments.

In the order to determine practical measures and
further research activities in the field of work content
analysis to provide more effective introduction of the new
technology, we feel this kind of distinction necessary.

The impact of new information technologies in Hungary
with its two (JANUS) faces can be summarised as follows:
- it discontinues a certain scope of activities, but
  requires new ones;
- it releases from routine tasks, but can cause taylorization of mental work and aggravates the consequences of
  human mistakes;
- it improves the conditions of work but brings about new
  loads;
- it gives a relatively high social and professional
  prestige, but in spite of this there is no proper system
  for adequate financial incentives;
- it increases the autonomy, but can decrease the possible
  decisions and provides wider and closer management control of performance;
- the introduction of CAD/CAM systems is in the long term
  interest of the whole company nevertheless it is
  initiated by some 'zealots';
- it requires the standardization of knowledge, and as a
  consequence of this the 'tacit knowledge' of the workers
  will increase. This is the reason why the participation
  of the company makes sense.

This latter group of questions plays an especially
important role in the industrially less developed countries, such as Hungary. It is worth thinking over what can
happen when a lower organizational level suddenly has to
face a new information technology that 'tries to monopo-
lize' the individual and specific kowledge and 'wants' to
change those social-communication structures that have
been set up to organize and maintain the different processes of production up till now.

It is not difficult to realize that in these companies
on such a low organizational level there is a substantial
accumulation of information representing the so-called
implicit, secret, unrevealed (not documented), tacit knowledge of the manufacturing staff. In the case of an introduction coming from above, this knowledge can only be
learned and organizade with serious difficulty, therefore
can hardly be or cannot be put into the frames of any
algorithm.

Consequently, in our country, where the organization and culture of work is on a relatively low level, participation in the application and introduction of the new technology is even more justified than in other countries where the level of organization, the extent of documentation and production knowledge are higher. There-fore, when reconsidering the concept of 'initiating from above', it is necessary to provide that the yet unformalized and unformalizable elements of knowledge and thought are built into the planning and management of production.

It is not difficult to understand that in our country it causes a specific additional tension that the workers have objectively more to lose when giving up the monopoly of their tacit knowledge than in other countries where this process has been going on continuously, in steps of transition periods. This stress is influenced either favourably or unfavourably by the fact that the process of democratization initiated socially started parallel with the spread of the new technology.

JOB CONTENT CHARACTERISTICS

A survey was carried out by using questionnaires in the three engineering industrial enterprises ('A': public road vehicles, 'B': ship- and crane-manufacturing, 'C': micro-electronics) covering 45 persons total. Such 'screening' surveys were justified by the fact that in these cases the integration of CAD/CAM systems into the main production processes has already begun; certain patterns have already developed that can be generalized, facilitating the infor-mative overview of the predominating characteristics of jobs in CAD/CAM and promoting our further research activi-ties. In enterprise 'A' we found two, in 'B' three and in 'C' one such organizational unit where influences of the CAD/CAM system can already be registered.

The patterns examined by us have been homogeneous only in the factor of qualification (university graduation), however, they can be considered representative in spite of the small number of participants, because almost all the important specialists playing determining a role in the development and operation of CAD/CAM have been involved. On the basis of the analysis found in the international literature and of the experts' interviews, we have col-lected those factors of work content most likely influenced by the introduction of CAD/CAM. In the first part of the questionnaries we determined the characteris-

tic features of the various CAD/CAM jobs – with the help
of the workers involved evaluating the 19 factors chosen
by us as described above, using a four-grade scale (not
characteristic, hardly characteristic, characteristic,
very characteristic). Table No. 1 contains work content
factors and the global order of rank prepared on the basis
of the answers received from workers in the three enterprises. In the order of rank individual opinions were
given in the form of the so-called standard 'z' data. (The
'z' data are such transformed values the expected distribution value of which is 0 in the mean and standard deviation is 1. Interpretation of 'z' data is the following:
'0' value indicates the average; shift toward the positive
direction signifies marked presence of the variable while
the shift towards negative direction a less frequent
occurrence. Transformation into 'z' data was carried out
in order to prepare global order of rank despite the differing comparison basis of the individual organizational
units and within them of the individual workers (subjective comparison scales)). The order of rank of the most
characteristic work content factors in the opinion of the
45 workers sampled are the following: the need for continuous acquisition of new knowledge; variety of work; importance of maintaining contacts within the enterprise; high-
level specific knowledge; creative way of thinking and
self-dependence in performing work. Less characteristic
factors are: healt-damaging effects; physical and sense
organs' overload; unambiguousity (clear-cut) of performance requirements.

We consider that the above order of the characteristic
factors of work content can be acceptable as valid only
for the period of introduction. Its sreason is that CAD/
CAM today is considered to be an elite field showing quick
development, providing good chances for creative,
autonomous, self-realising work.

At the same time it is also true, that these activities
being relatively isolated, causing concerns about adjustments in the course of design and production, and hinder-
ing integration, as well as the setting up of a system of
interests the factor of time-pressure is felt more inten-
sively by many workers.

Work activity of this kind can increase the autonomy of
the workers although with the standardization of intellectual work it can cut back the number of decision possibilities. At the same time computers can strengthen the
direction's control over the parameters of the work activity.

Table 1. Order of rank of work content factors in jobs
with CAD/CAM in Hungary.

Order of rank	Work content factor	'z' scores
1.	Need for continuous acquisition of new knowledge	0,95
2.	Variety of work	0,79
3.	Importance of maintaining contacts within the enterprise	0,76
4.	High-level special professional knowledge	0,72
5.	Creative way of thinking	0,67
6.	Self-dependence in performing work	0,60
7.	Time pressure, work overload	0,50
8.	Sophisticated tasks	0,46
9.	Performance depends on the work of the connected fields	0,23
10,5	Important contribution to the enterprise's objectives	0,14
10,5	High-level general professional knowledge	0,14
12.	Individual responsibility	-0,09
13.	Work at fixed place	-0,10
14.	Significant nervous (psychological) stress	-0,30
15,5	Relative autonomy of the given unit within the enterprise as a whole	-0,50
15,5	Significance of maintaining contacts outside the enterprise	-0,50
17.	Clear-cut performance requirements	-1,1
18.	Overload of physical and sense organs	-1,2
19.	Health-damaging effects	-2,0

However, with the differentation of the tasks (resulting from taylorization of intellectual work, with its
division into sections) loads brought about by hazardous
conditions can increase, with less compensating motivation
in the subjective interpretation of the work. This influences the workers even today and could turn the relative satisfaction of a positve or neutral evaluation experienced at present into a negative one in the future. It
concerns e.g. the relatively unanimous evaluation of the

lack of physical and sensory training and of health damag-
ing effects. Those questioned generally considered psychological stress not really characteristic, although here
the opinions differ more than with the above two factors.
At the organizational unit where introduction has just
started and the new technology has not yet been extended
to the project as a whole, only to some minor parts of the
technical calculation,s the following disadvantageous
effects of CAM can be felt: overtime work, closer contacts
and parallel work deriving from the needs of cooperation.
In places, however, where the routine of CAD/CAM application has already been acquired, work content does not have
the same specially characteristic, specific features.
Thus, it can be supposed that different judgements by
individual organizational units are due to the circum-
stance that introduction is in different stages and also
the extent of integration of the new systems into the main
production processes differs.

In the second part of the questionnaire the workers
qualified their jobs on the basis of four global aspects
by the help of a five-level verbal scale, namely:
a) content, intricacy and qualification demand of the work
   to be performed;
b) importance of the job and its contribution to production target and to the objectives of the enterprise;
c) extent of cooperation and of maintaining contacts;
d) autonomy offered by the job, possibility of independent
   work-organization.

On the basis of the data it can be stated that a relatively uniform high value was given to jobs in each factor
examined, nevertheless from the lowst average value of
'b)' and its standard deviations it can be concluded that
within the enterprise there has not yet developed the role
and interrelation-system of CAD/CAM that would correspond
to its weight.

In the introductory phase on the basis of the workers'
opinions and of the case studies the following picture can
be drawn about CAD/CAM jobs.

Computers relieve designers of many burdens when solving routine tasks but at the same time they require much
complex and wide-ranging vision that was not necessary
until today. The designers should have not only constructional knowledge but also an 'overview' upon the problems
of technology and production management. In the past these
three fields were connected with one another successively
but today it has becme a simultaneous or at least an iter-

ational process. This results in considerable time gain
when the problems are solved but also requires more complicated and closer cooperation with the specialists in
other fields of design. This situation has its conse-
guences also in the field of professional training:
instead of highly specialized engineers professional
training should concentrate on specialists with comprehensive knowledge in several fields. Unfortunately, there are
only a few people who represent the views of not only a
designer but also of an efficiency engineer. That is why
the constructors and production specialists have difficulties in making their ideas acceptable, in establishing and
maintaining working relations.

These jobs are not of key importance for an enterprise
as a whole and do not influence decisively as yet the
present or future profitability. Potential mistaken decisions or measures do not involve as yet serious consequences with respect to the enterprise as a whole in Hungary.

Because of the coexistence of traditional and modern
working methods, jobs offer only relative self-dependence
for the workers. There are still a lot of tasks the working method, rank and timing of which is not decided by the
worker himself. The proportion of such tasks, however, is
expected to decrease in the future.

DIFFICULTIES OF UNDERSTANDING THE CHANGES IN WORK CONTENT

The jobs connected with CAD/CAM have a relatively high
social prestige and as a result of this compensation the
explicit appearance of the problems or their causes is
hindered. (They can be e.g. a privileged group in the
division of labour in the organization; the challenge of
the new high technology; the stimulation of participation
in the process of innovation).

Developments are carried out based on different starting positions (abilities, motivations, organisational preliminaries, possibilities) of the individuals or the
organizations. This situation makes it difficult to determine and generalize the specific features of the different
work contents and also of the requirements based on them.

The strong motivations of the initiators of the introduction and also the exteremely changeable attitudes of
the participating specialists make it difficult to draw a
conclusion about the factors of work content and their
favourable or unfavourable effects, on the basis of personal opinions.

In the course of the division of labour, as a result of
polarization in the qualification requirements, jobs with
richer and poorer work content are divided relatively
early even in this field but their unfavourable influences
towards conflicts have not yet been seen.

We have not yet had a differential system of work evaluation that would perceive the essential specific features
of these kinds of work content and could shape assumptions
concerning the probable reactions to the strains and also
their results. We can consider that it is caused mainly by
the fact that in the period of research and development
those 'follow-up' researches dealing with human factors
and interdisciplinary problems are missing and also that
the analysis methodology for the examination of the more
and more dominant psychical strains is relatively under-
developed.

WORKPLACE CHARACTERISTICS

The evaluation of the set-up of workplaces was carried
out with the help of an expert checklist and with help of
a questionnaire through which we enquired the opinion of
workers in the workplaces (36 persons) concerned (Frieling
et al., 1986.)

None of the workplaces examined by our experts was satisfactory from an ergonomic point of view. The furniture,
especially the chairs, is not suitable. Storage space is
not sufficient and people are crowded in a small space.
Air-conditioners are out of order or quite often there are
none. A serious problem is caused by bad general and local
illumination.

Those working in CAD are always complaining of pain in
their eyes, their waist, back and shoulders, and also of a
general feeling of ill-health.

It is a general experience that the financial management of our companies underestimate the importance of
setting up suitable workplaces for those working in CAD.

In order to make the results of the expert checklist
comparable with those of the questionnaires filled out by
the workers we have always counted what percentage of the
maximum scores is srepresented by the reached scores
(i.e.when evaluating the experts in a given field - e.g.
'CAD' furniture' - what percentage of the maximum scores -
i.e. 18 scores for 'CAD' furniture' - is represented by
the reached scores; while in the case of the workers'
questionnaire we determine what percentage of the maximum
of 4 scales is represented by the scale-value of the given

question). The classification of the workers' and experts'
characteristic for the given company has been determinded
by our adding and averaging the values of percentages.
The result are shown in Table 2 as follows:

Table 2. The averages of percentages of the workers' and
experts' evaluation

Companies	Experts' evaluation	Workers' evaluation
A	36,0 %	43,6 %
B	38,2 %	32,3 %
C	49,8 %	31,1 %

On the basis of the results reached we can conclude
that there are divergences of various extent between the
opinions of experts and workers at the different companies. While looking for the reasons for these we have come
to the supposition that on the basis of the 'objective'
evaluation of the setting up of workplaces given by the
experts, it is similarly or even more difficult to conclude the extent of the workers' satisfaction with their
working conditions than under the former technical-techno-
logical conditions.

The absulute faith that the introduction of the new
technology would <u>certainly</u> create better working conditions is questioned by these result, although indirectly.
The same objective working condition is estimated differently now by the workers, depending on how it is changed
by other factors of work content deriving from organizational and management relations, being favourable or unfavourable to them personally. On the basis of our experiences the divergences of evaluations are increasedly
present in the period of introduction and switch-over, but
considering the specific features of the development of
the new technology it is questionable whether these divergences can be substantially cut back in the future.

SOME FINAL REMARKS

On the basis of the results shown in our work until now,
also with the intention to initiate discussions on this
topic we would like to summarize those experiences of ours
that may have consequences on the analysis of work content
as well.

In our opinion, from a methodological point of view the difficulties are caused by the fact that while earlier technical changes were characterized by a relatively static state changing to another relatively static position through a dynamic process, in the case of the new information technologies the starting static state turns into a permanent changing process where it is more and more difficult to foresee and 'catch' the coming phases.That is why methodologically the most important challenge for us is how we can apprehend and follow the permanent changes of work content (qualification, cooperation etc.) in the future and how we can face them with different objective and subjective preconditions.

Such a change of view is in harmony with the recognition that in the predominance of the required abilities-qualifications and the motivating potentials (namely in the evaluation of work content) the key-role is more and more played by the dynamic characteristics of the division of labour determinded by the organizational structure, instead of what was earlier determinant, namely the relatively static and direct man-machine relations.
The necessity of the above mentioned changes of view is reflected and required also by the shifting of accents experienced in the fields of professional qualification (the prominence of learning in the workplaces) and of organizational developments (the increase of the role of the informal organizational structures).

REFERENCES

Frieling E., 1986, Ergonomische Gestaltung von CAD-Arbeitsplätzen. Gesamthochschule Kassel.

Hatvany J. and Guedj, R.A., 1982, Man-machine Interaction in Computer-Aided Design Systems. In: Analysis, Design and Evaluation of Man-Machine Systems. IFAC (IFIP/IFORS) IEA Conference, Baden-Baden, preprints, 265-272.

Majchrzak, A., et al., 1987, Human Aspects of Computer-Aided Design. London: Taylor and Francis

WORK ANALYSIS AND LOAD COMPONENTS IN AN AUTOMOBILE PLANT AFTER THE IMPLEMENTATION OF NEW TECHNOLOGIES

F. Klimmer, H. Kylian, K.-H. Schmidt and J. Rutenfranz
University of Dortmund
Federal Republic of Germany

INTRODUCTION

In the automobile industry a substantial structural change has taken place and is always taking place. This results from the introduction of new technologies into industrial work. In particular the increased adoption of robot technology represents a changeover from single purpose automation to flexible automation or even to the "unmanned factory" (Spur, 1979; Martin, 1984; Bullinger and Warnecke, 1985). It is assumed, that this change in technology results in an essential change in strain of the worker (Rutenfranz, 1984; Schmidt et al., 1985; Kylian et al., 1988). Often it is stated that such a change leads mainly to a decrease in physical work, especially heavy physical work, and is mostly accompanied by a synchronous increase in mental and/or emotional stress. If production becomes increasingly automated, the nature of the tasks performed by production personnel shifts from predominantly manual labour to work with a high amount of monitoring and control duties.

Therefore the essential aims of this study were to find out
- whether and to what extent the expected shift from physical to psychical components of work really occurs
and
- to what extent new and even unexpected load components are added to the daily work by the introduction of new technologies.

MATERIAL AND DESCRIPTION OF WORK

Our investigation was held at the automobile plant
Wolfsburg of the Volkswagen AG. 43 operators voluntarily
took part in morning and afternoon shifts in work places
after the implementation of new technologies. Two different structures can be pointed out for the 3 types of work
places we have investigated:
- highly automated assembly lines for both the shell
  assembling and final car assembling
- flexible systems with automatic assembly cells
  integrated
  in a so called driverless transport system.

Even if the structure of the work places was very different, in all cases the work mainly consisted of operating and supervising tasks. Besides nearly continuous
supervision, the operator was responsible for immediate
manipulations if they were needed for service and maintenance of the assembly systems. In the same way the operator had to correct or adjust the machines if the quality
control rejected some parts as unsatisfactory. All these
manipulations had to be done in the shortest time to
minimize the standstill of the assembly system. Moreover,
the work must be done in some cases under lack of space
and bad environmental conditions, like low illumination,
high temperature, oil spray etc.

In addition to these manipulations the operators had to
fulfill some switching: firstly to ensure the normal operation of all machines belonging to this part of the
assembly line the operator had to supervise; secondly as a
reaction to visual and auditory signals, which indicated a
state of the assembly line leading to a standstill, if the
operator does not immediately respond to it in a correct
manner.

METHODS

A summarizing analysis of stress components was carried
out by means of the "Arbeitswissenschaftliches Erhebungsverfahren zur Tätigkeitsanalyse" (AET) from Rohmert and
Landau (1979). The AET can be used for universal analysis of work systems structured in three parts: tasks, conditions of carrying out these tasks and the resulting
demands upon the worker. Work system, tasks and demands at
the work places are split up by the AET into a series of
items. The analysis of a job is done in the form of an ob-

servation/interview carried out by specially trained analysts, which means that the necessary analytical data are
collected first by the observation of the job and working
environment, and secondly by interviewing the incumbent
and his supervisor. As a general principle it must be
observed that the evaluation as a part of a job analysis
is related only to job and work place; that means that
individual characteristics of the worker will not be taken
into consideration in the AET-analysis. A representation
of the scores in the form of profiles, obtained by the
groups of items and firstly statistically treated, is
suitable to give a graphic survey of the extent or the
duration of stress during execution of given activities
(Rohmert and Landau, 1983).

As day-time specific stress indicators we have registered the temporal variations of both the different components of the work load and also the physical activities
due to the given task. This was done by conventional time
and motion study techniques. During whole shifts an obser-
verwas following the worker, registering the sequence of
all the different time elements as follows:

essential operating time: working time with direct
    influence on work advance, e.g. operating, controlling,
    supervising
auxiliary progress time: work time with only indirect
    influence on work advance, e.g. service, maintenance
work dependent time drop: during this time the operator
    cannot work because of an interruption of the work
    flow, but this time cannot be regarded as a pause
individual pause: free selected pauses of the operator's
    choice for e.g. smoking, drinking
work stop: this interruption of work is part of official
    regulations in the firm at which the operator can
    leave his work place for food intake
rest pause: additional pause for recreation; they were
    spread over the shift and arranged between the firm
    and the trade union.

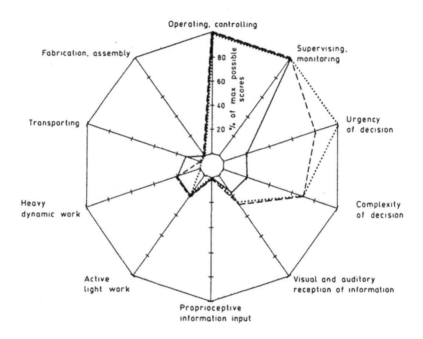

Figure 1: Frequency graph of some work demands for operators in the automatic car assembly with different work
structures

RESULTS

Because of only very small differences of the work
situation between the morning and the afternoon shift,
most of the results are presented without a differentiation between shifts.

In Figure 1 the frequency graph of some work demands is
presented comparatively for different operators in the
automatic car assembly. As expected, the item groups
"Operating, controlling" and "Supervising, monitoring"

showed the highest values in all types of work places. Concerning the item "Urgency of decision" there was a decline of the values with the highest scores for the shell assembly line and the lowest values for the final car assembly line. The scores of the "Complexity of decision " were identical for the shell assembly line and the driverless transport systems and substantially lower for the final car assembly line. Interesting are the demands of work indicated by the items "Active light work", "Heavy dynamic work" and "Transporting", which are not very pronounced but, nevertheless, are not to be neglected.

As a summarizing result of the time studies, Table 1 shows the time quotas of various working and non-working times during the whole shift for all operators in the shell assembly line, the driverless transport systems and the final car assembly line. The percentage of essential operating times was lowest for the shell assembly and showed significantly different values between the shell assembly line and the final car assembly line (p < 0.01). Regarding the percentage of auxiliary progress times an inverse tendency can be stated, but if summarizing essential operating times and auxiliary progress times to "working time", the differences between the different working conditions disappeared.

Table 1: Time quotas of various working and non working times for operators in the automatic ar assembly with different work structures. All figures are % of the total shift time.

Time element	Shell assembly (n = 15) Mean ± SD	Span	Driverless transport system (n = 12) Mean ± SD	Span	Final car assembly (n = 16) Mean ± SD	Span
1. Essential operating time	55.2 ± 7.7	41-67	57.8 ± 5.5	50-68	64.2 ± 6.2	49-72
2. Auxiliary progress time	19.3 ± 6.0	8-28	18.5 ± 5.2	11-28	11.7 ± 3.9	5-21
"Working time" (1. + 2.)	74.4 ± 7.3	64-85	76.3 ± 2.1	73-79	75.9 ± 5.1	60-83
3. Work dependent time drop	5.5 ± 5.7	0-15	0.4 ± 1.0	0- 3	2.2 ± 4.1	0-15
4. Individual pause	5.2 ± 2.9	1- 9	2.2 ± 2.1	0- 6	2.4 ± 2.3	0- 9
5. Work stop	6.2 ± 0.3	6- 7	6.4 ± 0.4	5- 7	5.8 ± 0.3	5- 6
6. Rest pause	8.7 ± 4.6	3-17	14.8 ± 1.0	13-17	13.7 ± 2.5	9-18

The percentage of work dependent time drops presented
for the shell assembly line a high mean and very high variation of the values for different operators and shifts.
The values were only half as much for the final car assembly and negligible for the driverless transport system.
The percentage of rest pauses was nearly constant concerning the final car assembly line and the driverless transport system, and was only half as much for the shell
assembly line along with a significantly higher variation
$(p < 0.01)$.

To enable an evaluation of the effect of the implementation of new technologies, in Table 2 the numerical data
of duration and frequency of manipulations and switchings,
done by the operator, are given. In the shell assembly
line and the driverless transport system each manipulation
took a longer time than in the final car assembly line.
Opposed to this, the total amounts of time for all manipulations during the whole shift were similar under all
working conditions. This resulted from the frequency of
manipulation which was double in the final car assembly
line compared with the other areas.

Table 2. Duration and frequency of manipulations and
switchings for operators at different types of work

	Manipulations during the shift					
	Duration				Frequency	
	in minutes		in % of shift time (without pauses)			
	Mean ± SD	Span	Mean ± SD	Span	Mean ± SD	Span
Shell assembly line (n = 15)	37,8 ±18,5	11,3 - 75,3	9,4 ±4,7	3,0 - 18,9	27,9 ±11,9	9 - 47
Final car assembly (n = 16)	38,7 ±18,8	13,7 - 92,7	9,5 ±4,6	3,1 - 22,2	50,1 ±22,4	21 - 91
Driverless transport system (n = 12)	32,4 ±15,8	11,6 - 65,3	8,9 ±4,5	3,1 - 18,1	22,8 ± 6,7	12 - 34
	Switchings during the shift					
Shell assembly line (n = 15)	4,0 ± 2,3	0,7 - 8,4	1,0 ±0,6	0,2 - 2,1	18,4 ±10,7	4 - 43
Final car assembly (n = 16)	26,6 ±13,4	4,4 - 53,8	6,6 ±3,4	1,0 - 13,0	44,1 ±19,1	11 - 80
Driverless transport system (n = 12)	17,5 ±10,9	4,7 - 40,1	4,7 ±2,9	1,3 - 10,4	55,1 ±34,6	10 - 105

The duration for each switching naturally was shorter than the duration for the manipulations. The total duration per shift came to 4 min, 18 min and 27 min for the shell assembly line, the driverless transport system and the final car assembly line, respectively. Concerning the frequency of switching the figures were 55, 44 and 18 switchings per shift for the driverless transport system, the final car assembly line and the shell assembly line, respectively.

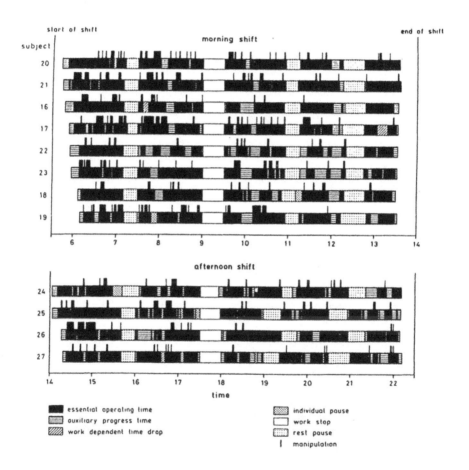

Figure 2: Temporal sequence of various working and non-working times for 12 operators in the driverless transport system during morning and afternoon shift

One further result of the time studies is presented in
Fig. 2 as an exemplary graph of all operators' work on the
driverless transport system. The graph shows both the
duration as well as the temporal sequence of different
working elements and the moment in which a manipulation
had to be done. It can be shown that the temporal location
of the work stop, caused by the official standstill of the
total line, was very homogeneous over all operators. A
rest pause at the same time and by all operators together
was made during the morning shift and the first part of
the afternoon shift, accompanied by a slight variation of
their duration.

During the second part of the afternoon shift the temporal location and the duration showed a great variation.
Regarding the other time elements there was a great
variation in
duration and sequence, such as e.g. the essential working
time with an uninterrupted duration of some minutes up to
nearly 1 hour, or the work dependent time drop which does
not occur regularly during all shifts (e.g. subjects 16 or
17). The results of the other working systems (see Kylian
et al., 1988) are very similar to those presented here.

DISCUSSION

Based on the results of the AET-analysis we could prove
that the implementation of new technologies leads to the
expected intense shift from physical to psychical work.
However, the remaining physical load was higher than
expected and therefore not negligible even if it was a
different height for the different working conditions
(Kylian et al., 1988). In the same way the AET-analysis
brought out great differences between the different types
of work concerning the items "Urgency and complexity of
decision" as well as the item "Visual and auditory reception of information". The question, if these results can
be taken either as characteristics for different work
structures or as indicators for different levels of automation, could not be answered completely by the AET-analysis. But the results of the time studies can give a more
detailed answer. While the "working times" were nearly
constant for all types of working conditions, the work
dependent time drops as well as the rest pauses showed a
great variation due to the different types of working conditions. It can be deduced that the work demand "Urgency
of decision" in combination with a considerable amount of
work dependent time drop, resulted in a reduced proportion

and great variation of rest pauses. Since the recreation time then might no longer be sufficient, the operator will compensate for this deficiency by taking more individual pauses.

Regarding additionally the duration and frequency of necessary manipulations, it can be stated that for all working types the desired and expected level of automation is not yet reached. The small portion of work dependent time drops at the driverless transport systems is not a result of a higher level of automation. Moreover, it is an advantage of the special work structure, which allowed maximisation of the operator's work.

The frequency and duration of the switchings contained two aspects. Firstly, it reflects to a certain extetd the level of automation reached, i.e. the more switchings are needed the lower is the level of automation. Secondly, it gives information about the operator's chance of developing special strategies with the of switching in good time and thereby to prevent prospective complications which perhaps could necessitate some manipulations, standstill of the line or work dependent time drops.

CONCLUSIONS

The expected shift from physical work to psychical work due to the implementation of new technologies has really taken place, but there remained a remarkable proportion of physical work, which is not to be neglected.

The desired level of automation is not yet reached in all types of work we have investigated. Maybe the amount of manipulation and switching can be reduced by checking the work structure and changing it.

Time studies, e.g. as presented before, are a prerequisite to discover the bottleneck on the total system, using different work structures for the car assembly.

REFERENCES

Bullinger, H.-J. and Warnecke, H.J. (eds.), 1985, Toward the factory of the future, (Berlin, New York: Springer)

Kylian, H., Klimmer, F., Schmidt, K.-H., Neidhart, B., Bubser, R., Brandenburg, U., Marschall, B., Daume, E. and Rutenfranz, J., 1988, Arbeitsphysiologische Feldstudien bei der Einführung neuer Technologien in der Automobilindustrie. In: Rohmert, W. and Rutenfranz, J. (Eds.), Die Bedeutung von Feldstudien für die Arbeitsphysiologie, pp. 168-186, (Köln: O. Schmidt)

Martin, T. (ed.), 1984, Design of work in automated manufacturing systems, (New York: Pergamon Press)

Rohmert, W. and Landau, K., 1979, Das Arbeitswissenschaftliche Erhebungsverfahren zur Tätigkeitsanalyse (AET),
(Bern: Huber)

Rohmert, W. and Landau, K., 1983, A New Technique for Job
Analysis, (London: Taylor & Francis)

Rutenfranz, J., 1984, Arbeitsmedizinische Probleme bei der
Einführung neuer Technologien. In: Der Innenminister
des Landes Nordrhein-Westfalen (ed.), Schöne neue Welt?
Über das Zusammenwirken neuer Technologien, pp. 145-
158, (Düsseldorf)

Schmidt, K.-H., Gutek, B.A. and Rutenfranz, J., 1985, Auswirkungen neuer Technologien auf die psychische Beanspruchung von Arbeitnehmern. Verh. Dt. Ges. Arbeitsmed.
25, 247-254

Spur, G., 1979, Produktionstechnik im Wandel, (München:
Hanser)

JOB ANALYSIS IN DESIGN WORK

Th. Müller, J. Springer and Th. Langner

University of Technology Berlin
Federal Republic of Germany

INTRODUCTION

At the University of Technology Berlin, a research-group "Non-technical Components of Design-Behaviour with Increasing Use of CAD" was established in March 1987, sponsored by the German Research Association (DFG), where different disciplines (philosophy, psychology, history, ergonomics, design-engineering, and production-engineering) investigate the effects the application of computers has on employees in the engineering and design field. In the division "Comparative Stress and Strain Analysis of Conventional and Computer Aided Design-Work" (Beitz/ Luczak) design-engineers and ergonomists together created a job-anAlysis-method which has already been tested in a laboratory study.

FORMER APPROACHES

Subjects of Job-Analysis in the Design Field

Job-analysis in the design field was done in the past following different issues and aims. E.g.:

- Finding potentials for increasing efficiency of work and preparation for computer-applications (e.g. Ehrlenspiel 1975, Eversheim 1978, Hildebrandt 1970, Kainz 1984, Saling 1978, Wiendahl and Grabowski 1972).
- Qualification requirements (e.g. Schiele 1978, American Institute for Design and Drafting 1983, cited by Majchrzak et al. 1987) and time budgets (Bullinger 1976, Hesser 1981).

- Surveys on the structure of the design-process (e.g.
  Müller 1988, Hales 1987) and the mental processes during
  problem solving in design tasks (Ballay 1987, Rutz 1985,
  Ullman et al. 1987).
- Changes in work situation due to the use of CAD (Bechmann et al. 1978, Derisavi-Fard et. al. 1988, Resch
  1987, Wingert et al. 1984, Zink 1983).

There seems to be a trend that studies dealing with
intensification of work ("same results in less time")
become less important, while there is an increasing number
of surveys asking for ways to improve the quality of
design and the most favourable properties of methodological and technological aids for the design-engineer. The
point of interest thereby shifted from the temporal structure of work to the mental processes in design-work. As
the latter are inaccessible to direct observation, there
is also a trend toward theories and methods influenced by
psychological research. There is also an increasing number
of laboratory studies. Besides that, there are surveys
aiming at the assessment of technology evolution, seeing
CAD-applications as an example for new technologies in the
field of skilled white collar work without being primarily
interested in the design process.

Methods used

Sometimes existing methods of job- and task-analysis
are used in their basic versions or in modified supplemented versions like work sampling (Bullinger 1976, van der
Heiden 1985, Kainz 1984), the TAI (Derisavi-Fard et al.
1988), or VERA-G (Resch 1987).

Other, non-standardized, methods are also used, like
non-covered participatory (Hales 1987) and non-participa-
tory observation (Müller 1988, Rutz 1987) as well as covered observation (Upmeyer et al. 1988), interview-tech-
niques (e.g. Bechmann et al. 1978, Eversheim 1978, Zink
1983), self-reporting (Hesser 1981, Derisavi-Fard 1988),
verbal-protocol-technique (Rutz 1987, Ullman et al. 1987),
eye-movement-recording (Krause 1979) and recording of key-
strokes at CAD-systems (Upmeyer et al. 1988). In addition
questionnaires to register the subjective expectations of
the job (Segner and Hesser 1982), the "mood" (Hales 1987),
and the perceived strain as well as psychophysiological
measurements (Derisavi-Fard et al. 1988) are also used.

The temporal resolution of these methods reaches from fractions of a second up to several days, the analysis duration from less than an hour up to years.

AIMS OF OUR STUDY

According to the stress-situation of the desig engineer or draftsman the application of CAD is characterized by two contradictory tendencies:

- Based on the principle of work-division, some (routine) tasks are transferred to the CAD-system. For the operator this is supposed to constitute a support, which gives him more freedom for creativity.
- On the other hand the use of CAD-systems requires additional knowledge concerning the structure and the syntax of commands, the structure of the data-base for description of the design-objects and the handling of the system devices. This is an extra stressor added to the proper design-process.

Which of these two tendencies is predominant constitutes the object of the study reported here, in which a conventional work place (drawing board) and a CAD-system are compared. Special regard was given to the type of task (detail or embodiment design).

The laboratory experiments in the first period of the project were worked out to clarify

- whether the results of work will change in quantity or quality by the use of CAD,
- whether CAD poses a support or a handicap in differing design tasks, and
- what effect the type of task will have on the work process and its results.

THEORETICAL CONCEPTS AND METHODS

In the abstract view machine design work consists of information processing. Accordingly, design work is a transformation process where a set of input information (design task, e.g. specification of product requirements) will be transformed to a set of output information (work results, e.g. technical drawing), which have a different structure and normally a larger extent than the input information. In this transformation process information will be selected, generated, and connected by using other

sources of information, such as the designers personal
knowledge or external knowledge bases e.g. handbooks,
catalogues or standards. It is in parts either a linear or
an iterative process, respectively.

According to this, a complete analysis of the design
activities includes three parts: Task analysis, analysis
of the activities during the design process, and analysis
of the design results. Corresponding to the general
questions in all of the three fields stress and strain
indicators are registered. Strain stands for all effects
of the work situation on the person and stress for the
factors of the situation itself (French et al. 1982,
Schönpflug 1987).

In the sense of the stress-strain-conception the design
task is a central factor of the strain for the designer.
For the laboratory experiments a selected set of design
tasks was classified in an expert rating (11 professors of
constructive engineering subjects) in 7 dimensions, which
could be reduced to three factors by a factor analysis.
These factors are 'function oriented design', 'production
oriented design' and 'graphic representation'. The selection of 8 design tasks of extreme factor-score combinations yielded a factorial experimental design of the 2*2*2
type with two levels in each dimension.

The participants of the experiments classified the
tasks after the experiment using the same scheme. This
yields a corresponding measure of strain to the stress-
scale classified by the experts.

The documentation of the activities during the working
session was based upon video technique. One camera shows
the progress of work on the screen of the CAD-system or on
the draftboard respectively, the second camera shows the
whole workplace. Both pictures were mixed and recorded on
one tape and afterwards coded with a list of items. On one
hand this analysis gives a profile of the actual stress
components, on the other hand it indicates resulting
strain, e.g. in identifying error-occurrences.

Parallel with the video documentation physiological
measures (heart rate, breath rate, elcetrodermal activity)
were recorded. In addition a questionnaire about the
experienced strain in a short form of BLV-questionnaire
(KÅnstler 1980) in accordance with Bronner and Karger
(1985) was used and reaction time and flicker fusion frequency were all measured, both before and after every work
session.

The work output in the form of a technical drawing was analysed under two major aspects: a quantity factor was set by counting geometric elements (lines, arcs etc.), text, hatchings and dimensions, which are necessary to represent the solution. This was a measure for the efforts in drawing. With a method based upon the use-value-analysis a quality factor was determined deciding whether the demands of the design task were performed or not. In addition the completeness of the drawing was estimated. Based upon these three measures and the time required some further descriptive variables were derived. These were firstly a theoretical demand of time for full completeness (working time/completeness), and secondly two measures for performance i.e. drafting performance (quantity/working time) and design performance (quality/working time). Thirdly the quotient of quality by quantity can be used as a measure for the efficiency of drawing.

RESULTS

Figure 1 shows the varying estimates of the design tasks by students (participants in experiment) and professors (experts). Task A is just an easy drafting task. The estimates of both groups are nearly identical and do not show significant differences. All of the dimensions were rated low and just some minor difficulties were seen with graphic representation and the required stamina for solving the task. At task F a cooler has to be designed for a defined part of a pipe-system. The students rated the difficulty higher than the experts and existing degrees of freedom were not recognized. Accordingly a lack of imagination was found among the results of task F.

For all of the 8 tasks Figure 1 also shows that the subjects had ranged the problems of function oriented and production oriented design and requirements of experience and creativity significantly higher than the experts.

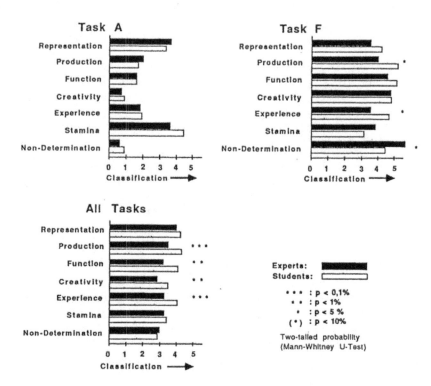

Figure 1: Ratings of design-tasks by experts and students

Figure 2 shows results from the coded videorecordings. From a qualitative point of view different activities can be differentiated. According to design methods, these are the design phases 'task clarification', 'embodiment design', 'detail design', and 'drawing' as well as activities of definition of functional or drawing aspects. In addition activities of information-retrieval from handbooks, standards etc. and visualizing the drawing information (especially the change between overall and detail view) are registered.

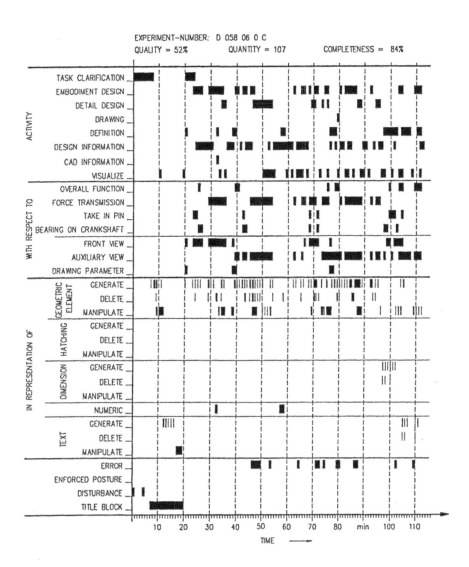

Figure 2: Example for coding of a videotape of a work-session

The activities are related to functional (e.g. sub-function) or drawing (e.g. views) aspects and are represented in different ways. Further the frequency of generation, manipulation and deletion of geometric elements, dimensions, and hatchings, as well as numerical specifications or text is recorded. In addition other detectable and important actions are coded like errors, enforced postures or disturbances.

Figure 3 shows the quality of working results depending on the applied tool and the three dimensions of task-difficulty. The working results elaborated with the CAD-system are significantly poorer. Looking at the dimensions of difficulty, only 'function oriented design' influences the quality of the result significantly. This influence is stronger than the influence of the applied tool.

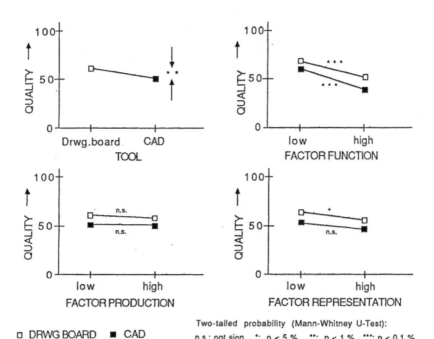

Figure 3: Quality of design-results depending on tool and dimension of difficulty

The method reported makes it possible to identify differences depending on the design task, the individual and the applied tool (CAD-system or drawing board). E.g., some subjects are working step by step in one view in contrast to a more functionally oriented way of working on one subfunction in different views at the same time. Moreover, it can be demonstrated, that there are sequences of actions showing how subjects are forced on a special way of work by the software of the CAD-system.

REFERENCES

Ballay, J. M.1987, An Experimental View of the Design Process. In: Rouse, W. B.; Boff, K. R. (Eds.): System Design - Behavioral Perspectives on Designers, Tools, and Organisations. New York, Amsterdam, London: North-Holland 1987.

Bechmann, G. et al.1987, Auswirkungen des Einsatzes informationsverarbeitender Technologien, untersucht am Beispiel von Verfahren des rechnerunterstützten Konstruierens und Fertigens (CAD/CAM). (Forschungsbericht KfK-CAD 114). Karlsruhe 1978.

Bronner, R.; Karger, J.1985 Beanspruchungsmessung in Problemlöse-Prozessen. Psychologie und Praxis, 29, 173-184.

Bullinger, H. J.1976, Ablaufplanung in der Konstruktion. Mainz: Krausskopf-Verlag 1976.

Derisavi-Fard, F.; Hilbig, I.and Frieling, E.1988, Belastung und Beanspruchung beim computerunterstützten Konstruieren. In: Frieling, E.; Klein, H. (Hrsg.): Rechnerunterstützte Konstruktion. (Bern: Huber).

Ehrlenspiel, K.1975, Leistungssteigerung in der Konstruktion. Konstruktion, 27, 365-373.

Eversheim, W.1978, Wie erkennt man Problemschwerpunkte im Konstruktionsbereich? In: VDI-Berichte Nr. 311. (Düsseldorf: VDI-Verlag).

French, J.R.P.; Caplan, R.D.and van Harrison, R.1982, The Mechanisms of Job Stress and Strain. (Chichester: John Wiley & Sons).

Hales, C.1987, Analysis of the Engineering Design Process in an Industrial Context. Dissertation University of Cambridge. (Eastleigh (Hampshire): Gants Hill Publications).

van der Heiden, G.H.1985, Ergonomoische Anforderungen an Arbeitsplätzen für Computer Aided Design (CAD). Dissertation ETH Zürich 1985.

Hesser, W. 1981, Untersuchungen zum Beziehungsfeld zwischen Konstruktion und Normung. (Berlin: Beuth-Verlag).

Hildebrandt, F. 1970, Arbeitsstudien im Konstruktionsbüro. Arbeit und Leistung, 24, 7/8, 126-129.

Kainz, R. 1984, Tätigkeitsanalysen im Entwicklungs- und Konstruktionsbereich. Zeitschrift für wirtschaftliche Fertigung, 79, 7, 349-351.

Krause, W. 1979, Augenbewegungsmessung zur Identifikation interner Repräsentationen bei Entwurfsprozessen. In: Klix, F.; Timpe, K. P. (Hrsg.): Arbeits- und Ingenieurpsychologie und Intensivierung. (Berlin (DDR): VEB Deutscher Verlag der Wissenschaften).

Künstler, B. 1980, Psychische Belastung durch die Arbeitstätigkeit. Probleme und Ergebnisse der Psychologie, 74, 45-67.

Majchrzak, A. 1987, Chang, T.-C.; Barfield, W.; Eberts, R and Salvendy, G.: Human Aspects of Computer-Aided Design. (London: Taylor & Francis).

Müller, J.1989, Möglichkeiten und Ergebnisse der analytischen Darstellung konstruktiver Entwurfsprozesse im aktivitäts- und ereignisorientierten Graph. Konstruktion (in press).

Resch, M. 1987, Die Handlungsregulation geistiger Arbeit. Dissertation TU Berlin.

Rutz, A. 1985, Konstruieren als gedanklicher Prozeß. Dissertation TU München.

Saling, K. H. 1978, Welcher Wandel hat sich im Konstruktionsbereich vollzogen? In: VDI-Berichte Nr. 311. Düsseldorf: (VDI-Verlag)

Schiele, O. H. 1978, Personelle Strukturen. In: VDI-Berichte Nr. 311. (Düsseldorf: VDI-Verlag).

Schönpflug, W. 1987, Beanspruchung und Belastung bei der Arbeit. In: Graumann C.F. u.a. (Hrsg): Enzyklopädie der Psychologie (D-III-1). (Göttingen: Hogrefe).

Segner, M.and Hesser, W. 1982, Vor lauter Störungen keine Zeit zum Arbeiten. REFA-Nachrichten, 3, 129-131.

Ullman, D. G.; Stauffer, L. A. and Dietterich, T. G.1987, Toward Expert CAD. Computers in Mechanical Engineering, 6, 56-70.

Upmeyer, A. et al.1987, Computerunterstützte Diagnosesysteme für die Bewertung von CAD-Software. In: Forschergruppe Konstruktionshandeln - Forschungsbericht 1987-1988. Technische Universität Berlin.

Wiendahl, H.-P. and Grabowski, H. 1972, Systematische Erfassung von Konstruktionstätigkeiten. Konstruktion, 24, 175-180.

Wingert, B.; Duus, W.; Rader, M. and Riehm, U.1983, CAD im Maschinenbau. (Berlin: Springer-Verlag)

Zink, J. K. 1983, Arbeitswissenschaftliche Aspekte bei der Einführung neuer Technologien. Zeitschrift für Arbeitswissenschaft, 37, 3, 134-137.